Transactions of the
American Philosophical Society
Held at Philadelphia
For Promoting Useful Knowledge
Volume 86, Pt. 4

——···•⋛•···——

# VITA
# VIRI CLARISSIMI ET FAMOSISSIMI
# KYRIACI ANCONITANI

by
## FRANCESCO SCALAMONTI

——···•⋛•···——

*Edited and translated by*

CHARLES MITCHELL
and
EDWARD W. BODNAR, S.J.

Library of Congress Catalog Card No.: 94-78512
ISBN: 0-87169-864-1
US ISSN: 0065-9746

# CONTENTS

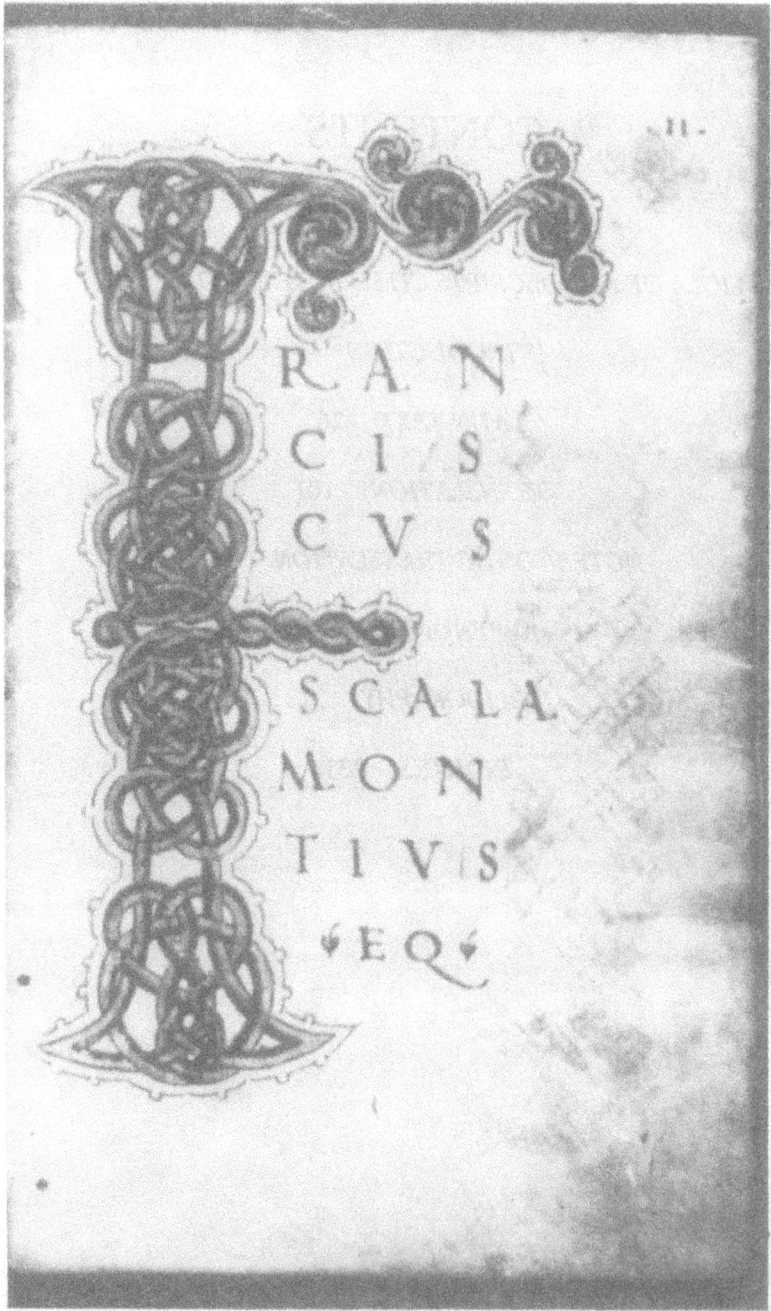

Fol. 11r. Authors first name and title. Treviso, Biblioteca Capitolare, MS 2, A/1 (olim I.138).

# ACKNOWLEDGEMENTS

We owe a particular debt of gratitude to the late Augusto Campana, who many years ago contemplated an edition of Scalamonti's *Vita Kyriaci*. When he learned of our interest in the life, he graciously agreed that we should take over the project. In addition, we are most grateful to Cecil Grayson for editing the Italian poems that occur in the *Vita*, and to Nelia Saxby, for translating them.

Our work on Ciriaco over the years has been supported by the following grants: C.M. received an American Council of Learned Studies Fellowship in 1965–1966; a John Simon Guggenheim Memorial Fellowship in 1970–1971; and a Ford Foundation summer research grant from Bryn Mawr College in 1972. He is especially grateful to the Warburg Institute of the University of London for its support over many years, and to the American Academy in Rome. E.B. received a grant from the Penrose Fund of the American Philosophical Society, 1960 (cf. the Society's *Year Book* for 1962, pp. 485–486); the Gennadeion Fellowship at the American School of Classical Studies in Athens, 1963–1964; a Senior Visiting Fellowship at the Dumbarton Oaks Center for Byzantine Studies, 1974–1975; a grant from the Translations Program of the National Endowment for the Humanities, 1979–1980; and travel grants from the American Council of Learned Societies in 1971 and 1983. In addition, he is grateful for the hospitality of the Institute for Advanced Study in Princeton during thirteen summers spent there between 1958 and 1976 under the auspices of Antony E. Raubitschek, the late Benjamin Dean Meritt, and Homer Thompson; and to the Maryland Province of the Society of Jesus and the Jesuit communities at the Novitiate of St. Isaac Jogues and at Georgetown University for their continued financial and moral support.

We wish to express our gratitude to the librarians and keepers of manuscripts past and present of the Biblioteca Capitolare in Treviso, the Gennadeion Library at the American School of Classical Studies, and the Biblioteca Apostolica Vaticana, as well as the other libraries whose manuscripts are cited in this work (see list of sigla, below).

Our warm thanks for special help and information go to a number of colleagues who have been most generous in sharing their time and expertise, especially Bernard Ashmole, Marshall Clagett, Paul Oskar Kristeller, Phyllis W. Lehmann, the late Robert van Nice, Nicolas Oikonomides, the late Erwin Panofsky, David Pingree, the late C.H. Roberts, the late Kenneth Setton, Francis Walton, and other friends and colleagues, too numerous to mention, whose help and advice have contributed to this work.

Charles Mitchell, good friend and indispensable collaborator for thirty-five years, did not live to see this volume in print. He died on 23 October 1995, when it was still in page-proofs. The project to edit the *Vita Kyriaci* was his from the beginning and could not have been completed without his encyclopedic knowledge of the *Quattrocentro* in general and of Felice Feliciano in particular. He is the primary author of the translation, where his 'fist,' as he would put it, is everywhere to be seen; the introduction is mostly his; and he was actively involved in our joint production of the Latin text and the notes. He is greatly missed, not only by his family, but by his many professional associates and former students.—E.B.

# SIGLA OF MANUSCRIPTS CITED IN THIS WORK[1]

| | |
|---|---|
| B1 | Berlin, Deutsche Staatsbibliothek, Hamilton 254 |
| B4 | Berlin, Staatsbibliothek, Preussischer Kulturbesitz, Berol. gr. qu. 89 |
| B5 | Berlin, Staatsbibliothek, Preussischer Kulturbesitz, Berol. lat. qu. 432 (formerly Bibl. Manzoni, 92) |
| Bu | Budapest, University Library, MS 35 |
| FL8 | Florence, Biblioteca Laurenziana, Laur. Gaddian. lat. 90 sup. 55 |
| FL11 | Florence, Biblioteca Laurenziana, MS Ashb. 133 |
| Fn8 | Florence, Biblioteca Nazionale, Targioni 49 |
| Fr4 | Florence, Biblioteca Riccardiana, 2732 |
| Lc | Lucca, Biblioteca Capitolare, MS 555 |
| Ma3 | Milan, Biblioteca Ambrosiana, R21 sup. |
| Maom | Milan, Archivio dell'Ospedale Maggiore, MS Miscell. n. 44 |
| Me | Modena, Biblioteca Estense lat. 992 (α.L.5.15) |
| M1 | Munich, Bayerische Staatsbibliothek, CLM 716 |
| N5 | Naples, Bibliotheca Nazionale 'Vittorio Emanuele III' V.E.64 |
| O2 | Oxford, Bodleian Library, Canon. Misc. 280 (Bodl. west 19756) |
| P | Parma, Biblioteca Palatina, Parm. 1191 |
| Rc | Rome, Biblioteca Casanatense, 3636 |
| T | Treviso, Biblioteca Capitolare, 2, A/1 (formerly I.138) |
| To | Turin, Biblioteca Nazionale J III 13 |
| Vb2 | Biblioteca Vaticana, Vat. Barb. lat. 4424 |
| VL9 | Biblioteca Vaticana, Vat. lat. 8750 |
| VL10 | Biblioteca Vaticana, Vat. lat. 10518 |
| VL11 | Biblioteca Vaticana, Vat. lat. 10672 |
| VL12 | Biblioteca Vaticana, Vat. lat. 13497 |
| Vo1 | Biblioteca Vaticana, Vat. Ottob. lat. 1353. |
| Vo4 | Biblioteca Vaticana, Vat. Ottob. Lat. 2967 |
| Vu2 | Biblioteca Vaticana, Vat. Urb. lat. 1435 |
| V11 | Venice, Biblioteca Marciana, lat. 14.221 (4632) |
| V12 | Venice, Biblioteca Marciana, lat. 12 (4002) |

---

[1]The designations for the MSS cited in this book are drawn from a master list of sigla assigned by Mitchell and Bodnar to all MSS known to contain Ciriacan material, not merely those that pertain to this particular study. Note that the second letter of a two-letter siglum is printed in lower case except when it is an 'L' (which could be confused with the number '1'). Thus 'FL' is used for 'Florence, Biblioteca Laurenziana,' whereas 'Fn' means 'Florence, Biblioteca Nazionale' and 'VL' means 'Vatican City, Biblioteca Apostolica Vaticana, *Codex Vaticanus Latinus*.' Total consistency, however, was considered impossible without the multiplication of symbols. The complete list will be published elsewhere.

# SIGLA OF MANUSCRIPTS CITED IN THIS WORK

# INTRODUCTION[*]

Ciriaco di Filippo de' Pizzicolli was born *ca.* 1391 in Ancona[1] and died some years before 1457, perhaps in Cremona.[2] He was the most enterprising and prolific recorder of Greek and Roman antiquities, particularly inscriptions,[3] in the fifteenth century, and the general accuracy of his records entitles him to be called the founding father of modern classical archaeology. The evidence of his activities comes from numerous and often fragmentary manuscripts, many still unpublished, of his travel-journals or *commentaria* (as he himself termed them), and from his copious correspondence, his literary *opuscula* and vernacular poems, and his memoranda and common-place books. A fair number of these survive in his own characteristic autograph,[4] but the majority of them survive in the form of copies or extracts by later hands. Any attempt exactly to reconstruct the original order and contents of Ciriaco's lost *commentaria* is a task, as Mommsen once wrote, as vain as that of trying to reassemble the scattered leaves of the Sibylline books.[5] The welcome with which Ciriaco's discoveries were received by such early humanistic scholars as Niccolò Niccoli, Leonardo Bruni Aretino, and Francesco Filelfo accorded him, despite Poggio Bracciolini's distaste for his abominable amateur Latin,[6] an important place in the history of Italian Renaissance humanism. And the probability that, under cover of his trade as an import and export merchant operating in the eastern Mediterranean and the Levant at a time when Christendom was under threat from the Turks, he was the trusted political informant of his patron, Pope Eugenius IV, gives him a not insignificant place in the history of mid-fifteenth century diplomacy.[7]

Of Ciriaco's early life and travels our knowledge rests uniquely—apart from a few early letters[8] and his long retrospective epistle, familiarly known as the *'Itinerarium'*,[9] addressed to Eugenius IV—on the materials for a *Vita* put together by his friend and fellow-citizen Francesco Scalamonti, which largely reproduces Ciriaco's own records and carries his biography down to late 1434 or early 1435. This *Vita*, as we shall call it, although it claims to be no more than materials for a biography, survives in a single manuscript now in Treviso,[10] which was published with certain omissions and emendations in 1792.[11] Our purpose now is to re-edit Scalamonti's *Vita* from the original manuscript with a translation and brief commentary. This introduction deals with the text and its previous publication, its authorship, its sources, and its likely date of composition. It concludes with a chronology of the events narrated in the *Vita*.

\* \* \* \* \*

---

[*]Throughout this edition authors will be referred to by name, year of publication, and volume- and page-numbers. For full references see Bibliography.

1

The *Vita* occurs on numbered fols. 22r–108r of the Treviso manuscript. The codex measures 218 x 117 mm.; its damaged and probably original fifteenth-century leather binding is decorated on front and back with a tooled arch-like motif; and (except for inscriptions added by another hand on the last two folios, 220v and 221r) it was written and illuminated and assembled throughout by Ciriaco's enthusiastic disciple, the Veronese antiquary and scribe Felice Feliciano (1433-*ca*. 1479)[12] at the behest of Samuele da Tradate, a Milanese-born *littérateur* and courtier of the Gonzaga in Mantua. It is written in Felice's brilliant formal book-hand, eighteen lines to a full minuscule page, and it is consistent all through, which indicates that the manuscript was transcribed at a run. The volume, whose binding is also by Felice,[13] originally comprised 221 folios, numbered (except for fols. 220 and 221) by Felice himself, together with an unnumbered blank gathering at the front. Today, however, it is incomplete, fols. 2, 21, 104, 122, 123, 149, 168, 170, half of 173, 174, 190 and 196, all of which undoubtedly displayed drawings by Felice, having been torn out by a vandal hand before 1775.[14] The book is written on a mixture of paper and vellum, which Felice utilized, as regards the numbered folios, in such a way that in every gathering the enclosing sheet is of vellum, while the inner sheets are of paper.[15]

To indicate the character of the book and the context in which Scalamonti's *Vita* appears, it will suffice summarily to run through its main components. The preliminary matter (fols. 1r–10r) consists of (a) a poem (fol. 1r) by Felice about not lending the book to others (inc: *Sempre se dice che un fa male a cento*), where he speaks either for Samuele da Tradate or perhaps for himself; (b) a title-page (fol. 3r) inscribed in black ink capitals in purple circles: *Itinerarius* [sic] *Kiriaci*, with reference, presumably, to the *Vita*; (c) a table of the contents of the whole book (fols. 3v–6v); (d) a two-page spread (fols. 7v–8r) in pale red capitals sprinkled with colored epigraphic leaves to the effect that Felice transcribed the book in the name and at the request of Samuele da Tradate;[16] (e) a second title-page (fol. 9r) with blue and green circles surrounding the title, in black ink capitals, *Repertorium veterum monumenta* [sic] *ex Felici Feliciano*, suggesting that the contents of the whole book were drawn from Felice's own collections; and (f) short texts (fols. 9v and 10r) on the founders of the four monarchies of the world, Ninus, Alexander, Tola and Romulus—an unexpected insertion that is explained, perhaps, by the fact that Lauro Quirini, for whose use Scalamonti put together the materials on Ciriaco's early life, bore the same name as the deified Romulus (Quirinus).

*****

After these preliminaries, the first main section of the book, comprising nearly half of it (fols.10v–108r), is Scalamonti's *Vita*, prefixed by a dedicatory letter of his to Quirini (*ca*. 1420–1480/1), a Venetian patrician and humanist,[17] explaining why and how he had compiled it. Quirini was proposing to write a life of Ciriaco, and had asked Ciriaco for a detailed account of his career. But

Ciriaco had been slow in providing this, so Scalamonti supplied it himself, having known Ciriaco as a close friend from Ciriaco's youth. The folios (fols.10v–21v) on which Felice wrote the title of the *Vita* and transcribed Scalamonti's dedication to Quirini are particularly splendid and characteristic of his highly individual verve as a draughtsman and illuminator. The title-page (fol. 10v) consists of a squat composite column whose crisply drawn and boldly fantastic capital and base are parti-colored in yellow and brown, while the shaft is inscribed, epigraphic fashion, in red capitals: *Vita clarissimi et famosiss. viri Kyriaci Anconitani feliciter incipit* with decorative leafed branch-work below. The first page of the letter to Quirini (fol. 11r) has a large initial F, which enframes the whole page along the top and left side and is composed of an elaborate curly interlace (derived perhaps from Romanesque ornament) whose knotted tendrils are colored yellow on one side and brown on the other to create a three-dimensional effect; and the whole page is filled out by the rest of the incipit in large black-ink capital letters: *(F)ranciscus Scala-montius eq(ues).*[18] All the remaining pages of the letter (fols. 11v–20v) are written in blocks of black-ink capitals enframed on all four sides by broad borders of angular interlaced pseudo-Romanesque strap-work, which is again parti-colored in either purple and brown or brown and yellow, the color-combinations being disposed, opening after opening, in syncopated sequence: a-b/b-a/a-b/b-a, etc.

The second main section of the book (fols. 108v–198r) comprises a substantial, though chronologically disordered and sometimes fragmentary, miscellany of Ciriaco's writings—opuscula, extracts from his travel-journals, letters, vernacular poems, occasional pieces, extracts and translations from antique authors, ancient inscriptions, modern epitaphs, etc.—which span his career from 1435 to 1449, along with at least one posthumous eulogy of him.[19] It is noteworthy that the first item (fols. 108v–119v) in this second section, immediately following upon the *Vita*, is Ciriaco's *Naumachia Regia*,[20] describing the naval battle at Ponza on 5 August 1435, when the Genoese defeated King Alfonso of Naples; the dedication of this piece to Scalamonti suggests that it was perhaps appended to the *Vita* when the latter came into Felice's hands to transcribe. All but two of the eleven torn-out folios displaying drawings that once adorned the book come from this second section of it, and on one of them (fol. 173), of which only the upper part was diagonally ripped away, we have the precious remains of two of Felice's colored copies of drawings Ciriaco made of beasts he saw in Egypt, probably in 1436:[21] a giraffe on the recto and an elephant on the verso.[22] Felice also enhanced the splendor and variety of this section of the book by occasionally varying the color of his inks[23] and the size and disposition of his lettering, by the introduction of impressively colored monumental title-pages (fols. 108v and 120v),[24] by enframing titles and inscriptions in colored circles (fols. 128v, 133v, 134v, 156v and 159r), and in the case of one Greek heading (fol. 192v) by setting it in a kind of *tabula ansata* picked out in yellow.

The third main section of the book (fols. 198v–220r)—to which
somebody, not Felice, tacked on extraneous inscriptions from Mantua and
Brescia (fols. 220v, 221r)—is in effect a vivid testimony of Felice's devotion
to Ciriaco's memory and example. It opens (fols. 198v–201r) with a letter
about Ciriaco, dated 1457, from a certain Antonio di Leonardo that forms a
connecting link between the strictly Ciriacan and the Felicean matter in the
volume, and thus gives a unity to its whole tripartite structure. The letter, in
translation, reads as follows:[25]

**1.** Antonio di Leonardo sends greetings to his friend Felice Feliciano. It
was a great joy to read your letter to me, because I discovered from it that
you are a lover and renewer of forgotten antiquities in this degenerate age
of ours. Such men are so seldom met with and are so scarce among us
that hardly any are to be found among mortals. You are therefore
universally to be praised, since you are, as it were, the sole survivor of an
infinite company.

**2.** You write a good deal in your letter about our Ciriaco of Ancona.
Would that he were still alive! But Nature, some years ago, put an end to
his life. He may be considered as a man who, among the ancients, would
have been most ancient: a man well learned in sundry matters, especially
in Greek and Latin literature, as his opuscula that are now circulating
bear witness: a man, in short, who travelled over almost the whole world.
With his own eyes he inspected buildings, temples of the gods, marble
statues, inscriptions, and all manner of antiquities. Nor was he ever
daunted by the harshness of the way, the cruelty of the sea, or the
weariness of long journeying: everything was most easy, agreeable, and
pleasant to him on account of his courage and the antiquities to be
discovered.

**3.** Let me give you one example among many of this man's patient
endurance. After he had investigated a certain region in Greece, he put his
little pack on board a ship and they set sail. But when they had sailed
eighty miles he heard from a friend that he had seen a certain inscription
behind the walls of a city they had just left. Ciriaco was greatly upset by
this, and when they made landfall, he left the ship and returned to see and
note down the inscription. He had no fear, as I said, of the longer route.

**4.** He was also known and welcome in almost every country, and was
particularly esteemed among the Turks—so much so that the father [26] of
the recent destroyer of Byzantium gave him a document signed by his
own illustrious hand, enabling Ciriaco to travel safely through cities,
towns, localities and villages without vexation, taxation or any other
injury, as if he were one of the Sultan's own household.[27]

**5.** So it has been a pleasure to tell you these few things among the many
I could have mentioned, since I see that you admiringly follow in Ciriaco's

footsteps, which are to be commended and approved by everybody dedicated to virtue.

**6.** Praise, therefore, the achievements of our brilliant Ciriaco; enquire into them, value, love, and cherish them. For you will be emulating no mean or unknown person, but a man illustrious by birth who afterward became more illustrious by his manly worth.[28]

**7.** To conclude: if your eye falls on anything in my house that is worthy of your humane erudition, ask for it, my friend, and it shall immediately be yours. Farewell, lover of antiquities and their ornament. From Venice, 4 October 1457.

**8.** And since, as befits a man of learning, you are seized by a relish for antiquity, I am sending you these inscriptions found in Torcello and Murano and I look forward to your remarks on them.

There follow three Latin inscriptions labelled "At Torcello, near Venice," "In Venice," and "At Murano, near Venice."[29]

The manuscript contains finally (fols. 201v–220v) Felice's well-known account (the *Memoratu digna* and the *Jubilatio*),[30] couched in flowery Ciriacesque language,[31] of the trip he made, in company with his friends Andrea Mantegna, Samuele da Tradate, and Giovanni Marcanova[32] round the southern shores of Lake Garda on 24 and 25 September 1464, to which is appended a little sylloge of inscriptions from the Garda and Veronese regions. On this sunny autumnal note, the book ends.

* * * * *

The subsequent history of the manuscript is totally obscure until the end of 1774 or the beginning of 1775, when it came into the hands of Girolamo Tiraboschi, who incorporated a detailed *précis* of Scalamonti's *Vita* into his chapter on the fifteenth-century discovery of antiquity in his *Storia della letteratura italiana*.[33] There Tiraboschi says that he had borrowed the volume from Ludovico Burchelati of Treviso through the good offices of Count Rambaldo degli Azzoni Avogari, canon of Treviso, and that he hoped one day to publish it himself—a statement corroborated by a transcript of Tiraboschi's letter of thanks to Count Rambaldo, dated 7 February 1775, which is pasted into the first gathering of the Trevisan manuscript.[34] Lodovico Burchelati still apparently owned the manuscript in 1792;[35] and another note inserted into the first gathering—which looks to be of late eighteenth century or early nineteenth century date—records that the book was given to the Capitular Library in Treviso by Msgr. Agapito Burchelati, Canon Theologian. Tiraboschi also records, both in his *Storia*[36] and in his letter to Count Rambaldo, that some pages were missing from the manuscript when he received it.

Tiraboschi did not in fact publish the manuscript himself. It was published with omissions, emendations and a good deal of rearrangement towards the end, with a long introduction and notes, by Giuseppe Colucci in volume XV of his *Antichità Picene* (Fermo, 1792) from a copy, as he noted, supplied to him by Tiraboschi. Colucci never apparently saw the original codex, and he relied heavily on Tirasboschi in preparing his edition of it.

Further light is shed on this transaction by Gennadius MS 96 now in the American School of Classical Studies in Athens, which was kindly brought to our notice by Mr. Francis R. Walton, the former Gennadeion Librarian. The volume, (*ca.* 1775; paper; approximately 13 x 9 inches; 343 folios in modern pencil foliation, 312 in an older one, bound in boards covered with decorative colored paper with vellum corner-pieces and spine; MS title on spine: *Vita Kyriaci Anconitani*) comprises three codices, which we will call G1, G2 and G3.

G2 (fols. 184r–331v in the later foliation) is a selective transcript of our Trevisan manuscript (T) made by an unidentified amanuensis, whom we will call X, under the direction of Tirasboschi, who instructed him to omit a considerable number of items he judged to be otiose or repetitive. Thus X did not transcribe Scalamonti's prefatory letter to Quirini because, as Tiraboschi and Colucci[37] noted, it had already been printed by Giovanni degli Agostini,[38] the only previous scholar who may perhaps have utilized T. Similarly, X did not transcribe the early part of Ciriaco's letter to Eugenius IV (T. fols. 180r–184r, inc. *Postquam de rebus prophanos in barbaros peragendis*) because this part, as Tiraboschi indicated, had been printed from another manuscript by Mehus in his edition of Ciriaco's so-called *Itinerarium*.[39] Nor again did X transcribe Ciriaco's letter to Filippo Maria Visconti about his visit to Egypt (T fols. 171v–172v) because Olivieri had already published it, from another manuscript, in 1763.[40] For the rest, generally speaking, the kinds of material Tiraboschi instructed X not to transcribe in G2 were inscriptions, insignificant letters, minor vernacular poems and occasional pieces, and extracts from ancient authors. Three portions of T, which were in fact (as we shall see) transcribed in whole or part by X into G2, are now missing from G2: (1) fols. 228–251 of G2 now consist of blank foliated sheets of paper different in make from the rest; these replace X's transcript of T fols. 64r–67v (= para. 105 [inc. *MEMORIAE*] to 110 [expl. *EIVS*] of our text), consisting mostly of inscriptions from Modena, Reggio Emilia, and Brescia, which presumably went astray before the three components of the present book were bound up together; (2) the old pagination skips from 140 to 157—the missing pages 141–156, now lost, originally contained X's transcript of Veronese inscriptions from T fols. 88r–97r (=sections 167 [inc. *COLONIA*] to 189 [expl. *CONTVBERNAL*]), though these were evidently (as we shall see) deleted by Tiraboschi; (3) G2 now lacks X's transcript of the Felicean matter from T fols. 201v–220r, and concludes on fols. 330v–331v with Antonio di Leonardo's letter to Felice (T fols. 198v–201r).

The second stage in the production of G2 was the work of Tiraboschi alone. When X had made his working transcript of T under Tiraboschi's instructions, he handed it back to Tiraboschi who with his own hand edited it, striking through a good deal of what X had transcribed (e.g., the Veronese inscriptions), correcting scribal errors, making quite a number of verbal emendations, underlining words and phrases to go into italics, and adding a few explanatory notes.

Now we come to G1 (fols. 1r–183r). Written throughout on paper bearing the same watermark as that used for G2, this is simply X's fair copy of G2 as edited by Tiraboschi, and it significantly includes the three portions (1), (2), and (3) now missing from G2, as described two paragraphs above. Thus in G1 we have Tiraboschi's virtually finished edition of the text of T; and this is the text—and this apparently alone—that Colucci faithfully followed (including italicizations) in his *Antichità Picene*, except that he reprinted Scalamonti's letter to Quirini from degli Agostini, somewhat drastically rearranged the materials in the later part of his text, added his long introduction and his footnotes, and omitted the Felicean matter transcribed after Antonio di Leonardo's letter at the end of G2 because he was concerned with Picenum, not Verona. Colucci is careful in the course of his print to note where items are omitted, but it is important to recognize, we repeat, that he is here referring to Tiraboschi's edition of T, as transmitted to him by G1, not to T itself. In short, the introduction of Gennadius MS 96 into the story enables us for the first time to explain precisely why Colucci's printed text, with all its omissions and variations, differs so substantially from T.

G3 (fols. 333r–343r), which no doubt slightly predates G2 and G1, is in Tiraboschi's hand, and consists of extracts he took from T, and his notes upon it, which he utilized for his biography of Ciriaco in his *Storia*.[41]

Two concluding points on the Gennadius manuscript may be added. The title *Vita Kyriaci Anconitani* written in ink on the spine seems to be in X's hand, which would suggest that Tiraboschi himself had its three constituents bound into one volume, and that X was a hack scribe and binder. Second, we know that Tiraboschi donated the volume to Colucci,[42] because the bottom of fol. 1r bears a small wax seal with the words. *Bibl.ᶜᵃ Colucci Ascoli* written alongside it.

\* \* \* \* \*

Failing Ciriaco himself, Lauro Quirini could hardly have found a better informant to give him reliable materials for his proposed biography.[43] Knight, lawyer, and diplomat, Francesco Scalamonti was descended from a French family which migrated from Arles to Ancona in 1114. Guillaume de Chaumon, the founder of this branch of the family, married an Anconitan wife in 1124 and changed his name to Scalamonti,[44] which means that Francesco was the scion of a noble family that had been settled in Ancona for three centuries. The date of his birth is not known, but as he says in his dedicatory letter to the *Vita* that he had known Ciriaco from his earliest childhood we can safely presume that they were more or less of an age. The earliest documents attesting to their close association date from 1435: in that year, as we have seen, Ciriaco dedicated to Scalamonti his account of the battle of Ponza (5 August 1435);[45] and on 29 December 1435, Ciriaco wrote a letter from Arta in northwest Greece to *Franciscus eques*, presumably Scalamonti, and to Crassus, another Anconi-tan,[46] describing the first leg of his tour of Dalmatia and Greece from Zara (Zadar) to Arta. At the beginning of this letter Ciriaco mentions that he had previously sent from Zara two letters (now untraced) to Francesco. On 16 February 1436, Francesco is named as Count Francesco Sforza's *luogotenente* in Fabriano, a post he held for two years;[47] and when he left his position in Fabriano, Francesco Scalamonti was immediately sent as an ambassador of Ancona to Sforza, who was then besieging Tolentino and in need of the small force that Francesco brought along.[48] On 17 September 1438, from Ancona, Ciriaco wrote a very warm reply to two letters from Scalamonti urging him to write the history of Venice and of the Milanese duke (Filippo Maria Visconti, d.1447), and to put aside his taste for pagan literature (*gentilitate posthabita*) and read more of the sacred writings of the orthodox Catholic faith.[49] Ciriaco modestly refused the first charge on the grounds that he could not rival the great historians of antiquity, but he promised to do something about the second without, however, neglecting the *veneranda disciplina* and the *aucto-ritas optima* of the gentile pagans. In 1441 Scalamonti was *podestà* of Norcia,[50] as he informed Ciriaco in a letter of 30 December of that year, when he complained that Ciriaco had not been corresponding with him as he was wont to do.[51] In 1450 Scalamonti was sent by Ancona on a diplomatic mission to the pope, and on another to Venice in 1452, when he was characterized as *il nobile cavaliere . . . dottore di legge e soggetto di molte qualità*.[52] Among his humanist friends was Francesco Filelfo, friend also of Ciriaco's, who addressed five letters to Scalamonti that we know of.[53] Another of Filelfo's letters, dated 22 June 1468, informs a mutual friend that Scalamonti died that year of the plague in his native Ancona.[54]

\* \* \* \* \*

Lauro Quirini, though much younger than Scalamonti and unable to claim any such familiarity with Ciriaco and his family as Scalamonti enjoyed, was not unqualified, as a youthful admirer, to attempt Ciriaco's biography. Born probably in Crete around 1420,[55] Quirini sprang from one of the twenty-four most ancient patrician families of Venice, a city with which Ciriaco had close connections, not least through his powerful Venetian patron Gabriele Con-dulmer (Eugenius IV). He studied in Padua, where he won his doctorate in Arts on 26 April 1440 and in Civil Law on 16 March 1448. In the following year, having in 1445 been refused membership in the Paduan College of doctors *in artibus*, he returned to Venice, where, perhaps on his own account, he gave a course of public lectures on Aristotle's *Ethics*. In 1451 and 1452 he was a *lector* in rhetoric and moral philosophy at Padua University, but he resigned his post in the latter year, and at the end of it returned to Crete, where he seems to have spent the rest of his life. He died in 1480 or 1481.

While still a student at Padua Quirini made contacts, friendly and other-wise, with many humanists, and embarked on a literary career.[56] In 1441, when Eugenius IV, driven from Rome, held court in Florence, Quirini lodged there in the house of Cardinal Bessarion, and in that year he wrote a lost Latin commentary on the vernacular sonnet on Friendship (the theme of the poetic competition) which Ciriaco contributed to the *Certame Coronario* organized in Florence by Alberti.[57] As we shall suggest below, it was very likely this encounter with Ciriaco that prompted Quirini to undertake his biography. The fact that Quirini was a Greek scholar himself—he translated the anonymous Greek tractate *De Sacerdotio Christi* transmitted in the *Suda,* and also a speech of Caesar's from Dio Cassius—no doubt played its part in fostering his desire to record the doings of so passionate a rediscoverer of antique Hellas. As for his other original compositions, Quirini wrote a *De Politia* in two books; on the occasion of the abortive second *Certame Coronario* (on the theme of Envy) he wrote a Lucianic *Dialogus de Gymnasiis Florentinis* in 1442;[58] between about 1446 and 1450 he composed three recently published pieces on nobility—a letter addressed jointly with Niccolò Barbo and Francesco Contarini to Pietro Tomasini, a polemical tractate, and a legal *consilium*—opposing the argument of Poggio's *De Nobilitate* of 1440;[59] in 1447 he wrote another Lucianic dialogue, *De Pace Italiae*; while a number of occasional eulogies and letters also survive from his pen.

*\* \* \* \* \**

It remains to consider the materials from which Scalamonti compiled his *Vita.*

Scalamonti explicitly says in his dedicatory letter to Quirini that he drew his information from Ciriaco's mother and relatives, and from Ciriaco's own mouth and numerous writings.[60] We have no means of distinguishing precisely what Scalamonti received orally, but the *Vita* again and again gives the impression of repeating or paraphrasing Ciriaco's own records, and Scalamonti tells us more than once in his text that he had original *commentaria* of Ciriaco's before him.[61] Unfortunately, however, none of these basic notebooks, relating to the years covered by the *Vita* (down to 1434 or early 1435), has come down to us, though it is clear, apart from Scalamonti's testimony, that such *commentaria* did once exist, at least for the later period dealt with in the *Vita,* because Sarayna, writing in the sixteenth century, gives an account of the amphitheater in Verona, inspected by Ciriaco in 1433–1434, which clearly is taken almost word for word from Ciriaco's travel-journal:[62] A comparison of Scalamonti's text (para. 165–166) with Sarayna's quotation illustrates how closely the author of the *Vita* followed the text of Ciriaco's *commentaria* at least on this occasion:

**Scalamonti:**
*Et denique Veronam*
*feracissimam et antiquam*
*civitatem ... venit,*
*ubi non exigua veterum*
*monumenta comperit,*

**Sarayna:**
*Et denique Veronam*
*feracissimam et antiquam*
*civitatem venit,*
*ubi non exigua monumenta*
*comperit,*

*praesertim* in hac urbe Ligurica
vidit Kyriacus,
ut in commentariis suis reposuit,
*labyrinthum* qui *harena nunc*
*dicitur,*
*et habetur quod constructum*
*fuerit*
*anno Octaviani* Augusti *XXXIX*

*ante* ortum *Christi tertio,*
*cuius pars exterior terrae motibus*
 *corruit,*
*nunc* extat *locus rotundus harenae*
*per totum magnis saxis*
*undique constructus*
et *perfilatus*
cum *cubalis intus*
et multis *antris multiformiter*
*redimitus.*
*In huius autem rotunditate*
narrat Kyriacus ipse quod
*extant scalae magnis lapidibus*
*appositae,*
*quae, quanto magis in* altitudine
    protendebant,
*tanto* plus *in* rotunditate
*videbantur ampliari;*
*et* secundum quod refertur,
*quinquaginta cubitis in* altitudine
    *extenditur,*
*in cuius summitate quidam locus*
*magnus et nobilis multiformis*
laboratus *marmoreo* de *lapide*
circumquaque *redimitus erat.*

*praesertim*


*Labyrinthum* quod *Arena nunc*
*dicitur,*
*et habetur quod constructum*
*fuerit*
*anno* imperii *Octaviani*
*trigesimo nono*
*ante* natalem *Christi* diem *tertio*
*cuius pars exterior terraemotibus*
 *corruit*
et *nunc* conspicitur *locus rotundus*
*Arenae per totum magnis saxis*
*undique constructus* est,
ut ita dicam, *perfilatus*
quum *intus cubalis*
vel *antris multiformiter redimitus*
sit.
*In huius autem rotunditate*


*extant scalae magnis lapidibus*
*appositae,*
*quae, quanto magis in* amplitudine
    protenduntur,
*tanto* magis *in* rotunditatem
*videbantur ampliari*
*et,* sicut nonnulli referunt,
*quinquaginta cubitis in* altitudinem
    *extenditur,*
*in cuius summitate quidam locus*
*magnus et nobilis multiformis*
elaboratur *marmoreo lapide*
circumcirca *redimitus erat.*

Further verbal correspondences, moreover, exist between passages in Scalamonti's *Vita* and two of Ciriaco's surviving set-pieces, namely his *Anconitana Illyriacaque laus et Anconitorum Raguseorumque foedus* about the trade-treaty concluded between Ancona and Ragusa in June 1440,[63] and the so-called *Itinerarium* addressed to Eugenius IV, which refers to the *Certame Coronario* that took place in Florence on October 22, 1441 and therefore was written after that date.[64]

Of the two last-named pieces only the so-called *Itinerarium* merits serious consideration as a source for the *Vita*, since it covers some of the same ground as the *Vita* and exhibits remarkable verbal similarities to numerous corresponding passages of that work (see Appendix V). It has, in fact, been argued that verbal coincidences between passages in the *Vita* and corresponding passages in the *Laus et Foedus* and the '*Itinerarium*' prove a dependence of the *Vita* on these later documents;[65] but it is preferable, granted Ciriaco's habit of mining his own notebooks for passages usable in letters, to assume that *both* the *Vita* and the '*Itinerarium*' and *Laus et Foedus* are dependent on the lost notebooks, and that therefore the *Vita* is not necessarily dependent on either the '*Itinerarium*' or the *Laus et Foedus*.

It is appropriate to discuss here another problem raised by the '*Itinerarium*' relative to the *Vita*: they sometimes seem to differ in presenting the chronological sequence of events. This problem has been solved, classically, by discounting the 'chronology' of the '*Itinerarium*' as unreliable and to prefer that of the *Vita*.[66]

This problem disappears, however, when one considers the differing natures of the two documents. The *Vita* is indeed a biographical record arranged in what the author considers to be the correct chronological order of events (though there is some confusion here as well).[67] The so-called *Itinerarium*, on the other hand, despite the title given it by its editor, is in actual fact primarily a rhetorical piece whose primary purpose, then, is not information, but persuasion. Written in the form of a letter from Ciriaco to Pope Eugenius IV, it argues in support of his request for a diplomatic assignment to the king of Ethiopia (*Presbyter Joannes*) to obtain that monarch's signature to the union of churches agreed upon at the Council of Florence in 1439 and subsequently signed by representatives of other churches in schism with Rome, an assignment which would also have given Ciriaco the opportunity to explore Egypt again, particularly the upper Nile, which he had not yet visited, and the North African coast as far as the Atlas Mountains. Because of the dual purpose of this requested mission, Ciriaco recounts his antiquarian travels in such a way as to impress the pope with the connections he has made with important persons in the politically strategic places of the Mediterranean world. To the careful reader it becomes apparent that Ciriaco was much more interested in advertising his first-hand knowledge of these places and his easy access to their local rulers than he was in giving an exact chronological account of his antiquarian travels; and that the groupings within the structure of the document are logical and rhetorical in character, according to persons and places, rather than according to strict order of occurrence.[68] Thus the 'confused' chronology and topography of the '*Itinerarium*,' so frequently noted, comes from misconceiving the nature of the document, as though it were intended primarily as a chronological account of his travels.

Another possible source of the *Vita* may have been one of the many manuscript editions of Cristoforo Buondelmonti's *Liber Insularum Archipelagi*.[69] In one instance (*Vita*, para. 73) it is evident that Buondelmonti's description of the island of Rhodes has crept into the text in an almost unintelligible form, for the *Vita* reads: *Viderat ibi praeterea **loci** eiusdem* *amoena pleraque et dulcissima visui prata virentia ac fructiferos regios paradiseos cedros et florentissimos hortos, dignum quarti climatis in orbe specimen et oecumenicae,* which is in part clearly a misunderstanding of Buondelmonti's *Deinde Rhodum appropinquamus, ubi tanta est viriditas arborum atque amoenitas locorum, quod est mirabile ad videndum et praesertim Paradisum a Florentinis factum,*[70] a reference to a country retreat built by the Italians (Florentines) in Rhodes. Scalamonti may have misread the text of Buondelmonti itself, which he introduced here into his otherwise Ciriacan source; or, more likely, he may have bungled an attempt to incorporate into the narrative a *testimonium* from Buondelmonti that Ciriaco had included in his notebook at this point, a not uncommon practice of Ciriaco's.[71] This opens up for the editor of Ciriaco's writings a mare's nest of possibilities, since Buondelmonti's book, which exists in a great number of MSS and in a variety of redactions, has not yet been satisfactorily edited, and we have no idea which of the extant copies, if any, Ciriaco possessed.[72]

When did Quirini conceive his idea of writing Ciriaco's biography? On this question our only internal evidence is the beginning of Scalamonti's dedicatory letter to Quirini where he says that he had recently, in Ancona, read a letter, written by Quirini in Padua to Ciriaco in Florence, about the projected life. Quirini's initial proposal, which Ciriaco had evidently welcomed, must have been made quite a time previously, because the later part of Scalamonti's letter makes it clear that Ciriaco had been dilatory in supplying the materials Quirini had asked for, so that Scalamonti felt obliged to compile them himself. What, then, were the likely order and dates of events? It has been suggested by Morici, on the basis of a letter he published, dated 4 November 1438, and addressed from Florence by Ciriaco to an unnamed correspondent, that Quirini resolved to write Ciriaco's biography before that date.[73] The letter includes the phrase *ex omnibus viribus tuis rem meam ad lucem deducere, quam sponte tua et humanitate pollicitus es mihi*; and Morici took the words *rem meam* to refer to the biography, hence identifying the unnamed addressee with Quirini himself. This theory, however, is highly conjectural, and Babinger reasonably rejected it,[74] for *rem meam* could mean anything and 1438, when Quirini was only about eighteen, is rather early a date, perhaps, at which to fix the beginning of his original literary career.

Thus all we know for certain is that Quirini made his request some time before the death of Ciriaco. Any effort to pin it down to a particular year will meet with failure unless some new evidence is uncovered.

When did Scalamonti actually compile this material and write it down? There is no way of knowing, for although the narrative ends in late 1434 or early 1435, it contains some apparent anachronisms that point to a date later than 1435. These passages will be pointed out and discussed in the notes to the translation as they occur in the *Vita*.

## Chronology of the *Vita*

Finally, we present the following chronology of events recorded in the *Vita*, constructed on the basis of internal evidence in the narrative itself and verified, wherever possible, by reference to fixed dates known from other sources. The text of the *Vita* is cited by paragraph numbers. External evidence is presented in the notes to the corresponding paragraphs of the translation.[75]

### 1391

Born after 14 April (*Vita*, para. 12).

### 1401

13 April, he visits Venice with his grandfather (para. 5–6) and Padua (para. 7).

### 1401-1403

In Ancona, he receives some schooling (para. 8)

### 1403-1404

Early in **1403** (*antequam duodecimum aetatis suae annum exactum vidisset*), his grandfather takes him to the Kingdom of Naples. Passing through Apulia, Samnium, Lucania, and Campania and stopping at Teano and Sessa Arunca, they reach Naples, then travel on to Salerno, Amalfi, Paestum, Tropea, Laconia, and Maida (para. 8–11). For a year (*per annum moram traxere*), he studies the rudiments of grammar at Maida (para. 11–12), after which they return to Naples at the time of an Anconitan ship's arrival to take Pope Boniface IX to the baths (**early in 1404,** para. 12). They return to Ancona by way of Sessa (para. 13).

### 1404

He begins an apprenticeship in Ancona (*iam decimum quartum aetatis annum agentem*, para. 14).

### 1406

Is put in charge of Pietro di Jacopo's business (*vixdum exacto biennio*, para. 14).

### 1411

Elected to the board of six *anziani* and becomes a senator (*anteaquam servicii tempus explicuisset*, para. 15).

### 1412

Early **1412**, finishes apprenticeship (para. 15). Before April, voyage to Egypt; sees antiquities of Alexandria (para. 17). On return voyage, visits Rhodes and Chios (where he is promoted to senior clerk); Miletus—passing

Samos and Icaria along the way—(para. 18); the Cypriote cities of Kirini, Paphos, Famagusta, and Nicosia and nearby Beirut; and Reggio in Calabria (para. 19), Messina, Gaeta, and Castellamare (para. 20).

## 1413

Returns with a new cargo to Alexandria after being blown off course by a storm that drove them past Ustica to refuge in the Sicilian port of Trapani (26 February 1413, para. 21). He is back in Ancona before September 1413 (*tribus semestribus exactis*, para. 22), rich enough to augment his sister's dowry. On 7 October 1413 takes part in repelling an assault on Ancona by Galleazzo Malatesta, afterward writing his first literary composition, an account in Italian of the event (para. 23).

## 1413–1415

Spends nearly two years in Ancona (*binos fere annos*, para. 31), partly in private life, partly as an *anziano*. Reads Dante, Petrarch, and Boccaccio. Engages in poetic correspondence with humanist friends (para. 23–30).

## 1415

Embarks on a journey to Sicily, stopping at Scilla in Calabria; sees the antiquities of Taormina; then via Messina to Palermo; inspects the antiquities of Palermo and the surrounding country, including Monreale (para. 31–34).

## 1417

On return voyage to Venice, visits Zara in Croatia (para. 35), where he hears of the election of Martin V (after 11 November 1417, para. 35). Disposing of his merchandise in Venice, he is back in Ancona by the end of the year (para. 36–37).

## 1418

Embarks early in September on a merchant ship headed for Constantinople, stopping along the way at Suasna in Epirus (13 September), Delos, and Sestos near Gallipoli, arriving at Constantinople 7 October (para. 37). The antiquities of the city are described (para. 38–42). He visits the Genoese colony of Galata/Pera (para. 43).

## 1419

Returns to Ancona, where he stays for some time (*per aliquot tempus moratus fuerat*), after which he visits Pola, inspecting its antiquities (para. 44). After a few days in Ancona, he returns to Chios, Gallipoli, Constantinople, stopping at Albuneo in Dalmatia on the way (para. 45). Back in Ancona, he engages in various business, including a commission to balance the books of a local merchant, which he does successfully (para. 46).

## 1420

Cardinal Gabriele Condulmer is appointed legate of the Marches on 7 February 1420 (para. 47). June–July, Ciriaco serves as *podestà* in Varano during plague in Ancona (note to para. 46).

## 1421 to 1423

Financial officer in the project to repair the harbor of Ancona (*fere biennio*, para. 47). The year is derived from the '*Itinerarium*,' dated 1441, which says this occurred *bis denos ante annos*. During this time Ciriaco begins to study Latin (*eodem legati tempore*, para. 53) and his interest in antiquities is sparked by close inspection of the Arch of Trajan at the harbor of Ancona (para. 54). In March 1423 he journeys from Ancona to Venice via Fano and Rimini (Appendix I, letter from Rimini, 15 March 1423). 6 August 1423, he resigns his financial post when Condulmer leaves for assignment in Bologna (para. 48). Exchange of poems between Ciriaco and Serafino of Urbino (para. 49–52).

## 1424

3 December (*Martino quinto pontifice, eiusdem pontificis anno octavo et ad III Nonarum Decembrium diem*), Ciriaco goes to Rome, where he stays for forty days as a guest of Cardinal Condulmer inspecting and recording the antiquities (para. 55); realizes their importance as historical evidence (para. 56), and laments their ruinous state (para. 56–57). Composes poem in praise of Pope Martin's nephew, Antonio (para. 58). Remains in Rome through Christmas and New Year's Day (*natalicia humanati Iovis solemnia ... et faustum recentis anni principium ab anno salubri milleno quatricenteno quinto atque bis denos eiusdem humanati dei et theogoni Iesu indulgentissimo nomine antiquatae legis ritu circuncisi et antiquis a Latinis bicipitis Iani nomine cultum, Kalendarum Ianuariarum*, para. 59).

## 1425

1 January leaves Rome for Ancona, stopping at Sutri, Viterbo, and Orvieto (para. 60).

## ?1426 ?1427

Elected *anziano* of Ancona (para. 61).

## 1427

13 May ?Ancona, finishes copying Ovid's *Fasti* (note on para. 76, *ad fin.*). 21 December, letter from Filelfo in Venice to Ciriaco in ?Ancona (note to para. 68).

## 1428

He sets out from Ancona, *illico exacto magistratu*, as commercial representative of Zaccaria Contarini in Cyprus (para. 61); after stops at Monopoli, Bari, and ancient Anterium in Apulia, he arrives in Constantinople, where he picks up the rudiments of Greek (para. 62); sailing on to Chios, he meets Andreolo Giustiniani-Bancha for the first time and buys a Greek New Testament (para. 63); thence by way of Rhodes to Beirut and Damascus (para. 64–66); then from Beirut to Famagusta in Cyprus, where he serves as vicar for the *podestà*, making decisions based on Roman law (para. 67).

## 1428–1429

He reaches Nicosia later in 1428 (note to para. 75), where he is received by the majestic King Janus Lusignan, who takes him on a hunt; Ciriaco completes Zaccaria's business within a year (*nondum expleto anno*) and purchases manuscripts of the *Iliad, Odyssey*, Euripides, and Theodosius (para. 68–71).

## 1429

(*[E]xactis rebus*), he leaves Nicosia after composing an inscription honoring King Janus (para. 72) and sails from Famagusta to Rhodes, where he inspects the antiquities, purchasing three recently excavated fragments of sculpture (para. 73). Making for Thrace by way of Chios, he translates a Life of Euripides while awaiting favorable winds at Kardhamyla (para. 74); then, by way of Tenedos to Gallipoli, where he unloads Zaccaria's goods and brings them by camel to Adrianople, the Turkish European capital (para. 75).

## 1429–1430

He winters (*per hyemem*) in Adrianople, selling his merchandise and listening to Greek lectures on Homer and Hesiod (para. 75). After 29 March 1430 (the date of the fall of Salonica), he buys Greek manuscripts (Ptolemy's *Geography*) and an Epirote slave-girl from the Turkish plunder of that city, and plans a journey to Persia (para. 75). At Gallipoli he ships goods (hides, carpets, and slave-girl) on to Ancona, then travels overland to Philippi to see its antiquities (para. 76); then on to Salonica, where he views its pagan and Christian monuments and buys more manuscripts (para. 77).

## 1431

Returning to Gallipoli some time after 3 March, he hears news of Condulmer's election on that date to the papacy as Eugenius IV (para. 78). Cancelling plans for travel to Persia, he sends off letters to influential friends in Italy and Dalmatia expressing his pleasure, and sets out to collect intelligence to support his projects for union with the Greek church and a crusade against the Turks (para. 78–79) with the aid of Memnon, a seasoned miltary advisor, in the principal Turkish-held cities and centers of Asia Minor.

Their first stop is Bursa, the Ottoman capital in Asia, where he pleads with the governor Canuza Bey to put a stop to the gradual spoliation of the temple at Cyzicus (para. 80–81). After revisiting Cyzicus (para. 82-83), he makes for Constantinople by land, stopping to inspect the antiquities of Nicaea (para. 84) before crossing the Bosporus at Scutari, which he takes to be ancient Chalcedon (para. 85).

In Constantinople, learning that the next ship for Ancona would not be leaving for a month (para. 85), he uses the intervening time to continue reconnoitering locations in Turkish-held Anatolia that are of strategic as well as antiquarian interest, sailing first to Lesbos, where he inspects the cities of Mytilene, Pyrrha, and Methymna (para. 86), then crosses to the mainland to see Pergamum (para. 87), then the ruins of ancient Cyme and Smyrna (para. 88), before proceeding on to Old and New Foglia on the mainland, and thence over to Chios to await his ship (para. 89–90) for Ancona (para. 91). Between 31 October and 6 November (note to para. 91), leaves Chios for Ancona.

After a few days at home Ciriaco hastens to Rome to see the new pope, whom he urges to call a council of union with the Greek Church and to proclaim a crusade against the Turks (para. 92).

## 1432

During this visit to Rome, he inspects the antiquities of Tivoli and Ostia (para. 93–96). He returns to Rome to see the pope (para. 204);[76] then, when he hears of rebel Anconitans practicing piracy, he hurries to Gaeta to advise a friend, the captain of an Anconitan ship sent to join the fleet charged with the mission to bring them to justice (para. 204–205); when this ship leaves Gaeta for Naples, Ciriaco, planning to meet it there, travels by land, keeping an eye out for antiquities, from Gaeta by way of Terracina, Minturno, Sessa, Capua, and Aversa (para. 206–209). He returns to Naples, whence he visits the Virgilian landmarks in Pozzuoli, Lake Averno, Cumae, Baiae and Cape Miseno (para. 209–210); after an excursion through Naples to Benevento (para. 211–214), he returns to the port city, where he boards his friend's ship, which first conveys to Messina emissaries sent by the pope to King Alfonso (para. 215), then sails to the Gulf of Taranto to join the Anconitan fleet; there, unable to attack the pirate ship because it is protected by Queen Maria d'Enghien, the fleet returns to Ancona with Ciriaco aboard (para. 215-216).

Some time between 8 July 1432 (note to para. 97) and April 1433 he goes to Siena with two papal ambassadors to meet emperor-elect Sigismund, whom he presents with a gold coin of Trajan as a model of a good emperor, and is received into his court (para. 97).

## 1433

Before 25 April 1433 (note to para. 97) he returns to Rome, presumably in the entourage of the emperor-elect. After Sigismund's coronation in Rome (31 May 1433) he again lobbies the emperor to press the pope for a council of union and a crusade against the Turks (para. 98). While touring the city's ruins with Sigismund he deplores the practice of burning up into lime the ancient sculptures, architectural pieces and inscriptions (para. 99). Leaving Rome for points north he first visits Pisa (para. 100); then Florence (before September 1433: note to para. 101). Brunelleschi conducts him around his dome, then in construction; he sees the baptistery and the public buildings, not omitting the ancient walls and theater of Fiesole (para. 104); and he meets the political and intellectual leaders of Florence as well as its leading artists (para. 101–103). A northern journey brings him to Bologna and Modena (para. 105–110), Parma (para. 111), Piacenza, and Pavia (para. 112, note).

## 1433–1434

Arriving in Milan, he inspects its monuments and copies inscriptions in the city and its surrounding area, including the castle and monastery of Pavia (para. 113–151), then on to Brescia (para. 152–164) and Verona (para. 165–189). After returning to Milan, where he spends several days with the duke (para. 190), he goes on to Mantua (para. 191–197) and Genoa (para. 198–204).

## NOTES TO THE INTRODUCTION

1. The date of Ciriaco's birth may be calculated in the following manner. Although our first *fixed* date is 1404, when Ciriaco was aged thirteen (see *Vita*, note to para. 12, and chronology, below), the *Vita* (para. 6) says that Ciriaco, aged about nine years, was in Venice on 13 April, when Michele Steno was doge. Since Steno did not become doge until 1 December 1400 (cf. Morozzo della Rocca and Tiepolo, 185), Ciriaco's visit to Venice occurred on 13 April *1401*, when he was still nine years old. We conclude, then, that he was born some time after 14 April in the year 1391.

2. Regarding the date of Ciriaco's death, the only documentary evidence we have is a statement on fol. 41 of the Trotti MS 373 in the Ambrosian Library in Milan, which says that he died in 1452 (*Kiriacus Anconitanus Cremone moritur anno domini McCCCCL secundo, mense **** die ****:* Sabbadini, 1910, 193, who says the scribe, Botta, first wrote *LXII*, then erased the *XII* and substituted *secundo*; Bodnar, 1960, 68, note 4). Cremona as the place of Ciriaco's death is corroborated by a verse eulogy in T (fol. 177r, ed. Colucci, 151, Bodnar, 1960, 68):

> O Kiriace, virum veterum monumenta requirens,
> Ethiopes, Indos, Arabes Theucrosque petisti.
> *Ossa Cremona tenet*, animus tamen astra petivit.
> Gloria Picentum, Piceni (*cod.* picenni) carminem habebis.

Attempts to find a record of his death in Cremona have so far proved unsuccessful.

We must now reject Jacobs' hypothesis (1929–30), summarized in Bodnar (1960, 67–68) that he was with Mehmed II as the sultan's tutor just before the fall of Constantinople (according to a Venetian 'chronicle' by Languschi), that he entered the city with the Conqueror, and made a drawing of the equestrian statue of Justinian after it was lowered to the ground from the top of its pillar in the Augusteion, and is referred to under the name *Kurizis* by Filelfo in a letter written to the sultan after the conquest. P.W. Lehmann, 1959, was the first to attack part of this hypothesis, arguing that the drawing, which is in a Budapest MS that found its way to the Seraglio and was later returned, was modelled on a medallion of Theodosius rather than on the statue. Babinger at first accepted the identification of *Kurizis* with Ciriaco (1954, 136), then gradually moved away from Jacobs' position, asserting that the MS in the Seraglio was probably never owned by Mehmed II (1962, 322–324), that it was not brought to Byzantium from Buda until 1526 by Suleiman the Magnificent (1966, 442), and suggesting that the drawing was indeed copied from a medallion, or perhaps a mosaic, but not in Constantinople, possibly rather in Crete, either in Candia (1962, 322–324) or in Gortyna (1964, 66–67), an island that Ciriaco visited several times, including 1435, 1445, and 1446 (1961, 76). Babinger also argued that the 'chronicle' of Languschi was a misnomer, since Languschi could not have been in Constantinople in 1453 and the text in fact parallels closely, and may even be based on, the account written by Nicholaos Sagundinos in that year. Patrinelis, 1968, accepted the arguments of Lehmann and Babinger and proved in addition that the Κυρίζις of Filelfo's letter was not Ciriaco, but a Greek named Dimitrios Apokafkos Kyritzis, secretary to the Sultan from 1446. Raby, 1981, put the final nail in the coffin of Jacobs' theory by showing that the Languschi text had been misread: the Italian tutor of Mehmed II was not *uno compagno d(etto) Chiriaco d Ancona* but *uno compagno d(i) Chiriaco d Ancona!*

We must also reject the suggestion by Harlfinger, 1990, 225–236, that MS Vindobonensis Hist, gr. 1, a copy of Ptolemy's *Geography* end-dated 31 October 1454, is the product of a collaboration between Ciriaco and the calligrapher, Skutariotes, from which he concludes that autumn 1454, is the *terminus post quem* for Ciriaco's death. This argument rests on Harlfinger's identification of the Greek notations on the maps as "unmistakably" in the hand of Ciriaco, a position convincingly rejected on palaeographical grounds by S. Gentile, 1992. 295n. We are grateful to Dott. Elisabetta Barile and Professors Nigel Wilson and Anna Pontani for the reference to Gentile.

3. Cf. Mommsen, *CIL* III, passim; De Rossi, 1888, II, 356–387; Ziebarth, 1902; MacKendrick, 1952; Ashmole, 1959; Bodnar, 1960.

4. Fava, 1944, identified a number of Ciriacan autographs and traced the evolution of Ciriaco's hand; for individual autographs see Mommsen, *Jahrbuch*, 1883; Sabbadini, 1910; Maas, 1915; Ashmole, 1959; Campana, 1959; and Mitchell, 1974.

5. *CIL* V, 1, p. 322 (preface to the *Veronensia*).

6. ... *Greca plurima latinis mixta, verba inepta, latinitas mala, constructio inconcinna, sensus nullus, ut vera responsa Phebi suboscura, aut dicta Spinge esse videantur, que preter Sibillam intelligat nemo.* ... In a letter to Leonardo Bruni, from Ferrara, 31 March 1438, ed. H. Harth, II, 1984, pp. 298–301, no. 13; *Opera Omnia*, ed. de Tonellis, II, 1859, pp. 161–164. See also Maas, 1915, 13–14; Bodnar, 1960, 20–21.

7. See Pall, 1937; Dabrowski, 1951; and Bodnar, 1988.

8. Ciriaco to Pietro de' Bonarellis, 15 March 1423 (text and bibliography in Appendix I); Ciriaco to Leonardo Bruni, 13 December ?1433, with Bruni's reply (texts and bibliography in Appendix II).

9. Edited by Lorenzo Mehus, 1742, from MS Vat. Ottob. lat. 2967, fols. 1–23. The nature of this document and its chronological 'unreliability' are discussed later in this introduction.

10. Treviso, Bibl. Capitolare, MS 2 A/1 (formerly I 138). We shall refer to it as 'T.'

11. Ed. G. Colucci, 1792, XV, 50–100.

12. For Felice see Mitchell, 1961, with bibliography, and Mardersteig, 1960.

13. A. Hobson, 1989, p. 73, fig. 59 (photograph of the binding) and Appendix 2, p. 255, no. 2: "Binding attributed to Felice Feliciano. . . ." See also figures 56 and 58 (pictures of fols. 10r and 120v). We owe to Hobson's book the new shelf number and the dimensions of the MS.

14. The year it was copied for Tiraboschi.

15. As in the autograph MS published by Maas, 1915 (B4).

16. T, fols. 7v–8r: *Felix Felicianus Veronensis hunc transcripsit libellum nomine ac rogatu clari et optumi Samuelis fil. Iacobini Tridatensis ex agro Mediolanensi viri magnanimitate ac ingenio atq. omni virtute decorati qui ad illustrissimam dicatus est Gunzagiam regiam vir quidem solertissimus antiquis reb. facetus ex ore cuius et gestu plurimus lepor emergit qui amicos ingenti munificentia semper complexus est opera cuius auctoritate pollent maxima quas ob res manus eas quib. hunc ipsum tractare ac percurrere contigerit oratas velim non in fide sed in reddendo citae fiant.*

17. For Lauro Quirini see now Branca, 1977; also, Babinger, 1961, 52–56, 104; and idem, 1964, 67 ff.

18. Fols. 10v and 11r are reproduced by Mitchell, 1961, pl. 32a.

19. See above, note 2.

20. For the latest and best edition of this opusculum see Sabia, 1977–1978.

21. For the date see Lehmann, 1977, 29, note 66.

22. Cf. Bertalot and Campana, 1939; van Essen, 1958 (with reproductions of the torn drawings on fol. 173); Bodnar, 1960, 22, note 7; Mitchell, 1962, 285–286 and notes; and Lehmann, 1977, fig. 30.

23. See Mardersteig, 1960, who gives recipes for various colored inks in the back of the book.

24. The drawing on fol. 120v is reproduced by Mitchell, 1961, pl.38c.

25. For the Latin text see Appendix IV. The paragraphs of both the Latin text and the translation have been numbered by the editors for ease of reference and to facilitate comparison. This same system has been employed with the text and translation of the *Vita*.

26. Leonardi rightly attributes the *laisser-passer* to Mehmed II's father, Murad II, rather than to the Conqueror himself. See next note.

27. This reads as if it might be a direct quote, in translation, from the sultan's *firman* itself. On 8 April 1446, in a letter from Foglia Nuova to Andreolo Giustiniani of Chios, Ciriaco announced his intention of going on the morrow with Francesco Draperio to Manisa, where Murad II, who in 1444 had abdicated (temporarily, it turned out) in favor of his twelve-year-old son, Mehmed II, was holding court, to obtain the cherished safe-conduct. Draperio, a powerful Genoese merchant in the Levant and a favorite of Murad, was undoubtedly Ciriaco's intercessor. The letter, which occurs in MS Targ. 49 of the Bibl. Nazionale in Florence (Fn8), fols. 21r–22r, was published only in part by Targioni Tozzetti, 1773, V, 450. See also Babinger, 1950, 255–259; 1978, 29, 41–45; and Bodnar, 1988, 264.

28. Ciriaco's family, though not well off (his father seems to have died when he was young and he had to earn his sister's dowry by service in the merchant marine), was apparently patrician, for he was elected to the Anconitan senate at an age earlier than the prescribed minimum (*Vita*, para. 15) and served several times as a magistrate of the city (*Vita*, passim).

29. For the texts of these three inscriptions see Appendix IV.

30. See Paul Kristeller, 1901, 472–473; Ziebarth, 1903, 480–481, with critical text of the *Memoratu digna* and the *Jubilatio* on 491–493; Mitchell, 1960, 476–478. For a recent discussion of these texts see Lightbown, 1986, 40, 94–96, and 258 (notes 48–52).

31. For an example of this language see Mitchell, 1960, 469, 476. For an interpretation of the nature of the *Jubilatio* based on Felice's use of Ciriacesque language see M. Billanovich, 1989.

32. For Marcanova see Dennis, 1927; Huelsen, 1907; Lawrence, 1927; and Mitchell, 1960, 475, 479.

33. Tiraboschi, 1783, 156–177; 1807, 177–201.

34. Ibid., 1783, 157.

35. Colucci, 1792, 4.

36. Tiraboschi, 1783, 157.

37. Colucci, 50, note 1; Tiraboschi, 1783, 157.

38. Degli Agostini, I, 227.

39. Mehus, 1742, 1 ff.

40. Olivieri, 1763, 55–56.

41. Tiraboschi, 1783, 156–177; 1807, 177–201.

42. Colucci, iv.

43. Spadolini, 1901, 70–72, who obtained the family history from a manuscript book lent him by a Count Scalamonti of Camerata Picena (70, note 3).

44. Spadolini, 1901, 70.

45. Originally published by Mehus, 1742, 58–65; see Bodnar, 1960, 27, note 2. Definitive edition by Liliana Monti Sabia, 1977–1978, unaffected by the later discovery of two new MSS (cf. Bibliography, 'Recent Work on Ciriaco,' s.v. Sabia).

46. Published by Mehus, 1742, 58–65; cf. Bodnar, 1960, 27, note 2.

47. Spadolini, 1901, 70b and note 1.

48. Spadolini, 1901, 71.

49. Moroni, 1650, 41–42; Mehus, 1742, 73–76.

50. Spadolini, 1901, 71. This notice occurs in Norcia, Archivio comunale, Riformanze, vol. 4, fol. 86v: *In die nomine anno domini MCCCCXLI ... die vero primo mensis decembr. nobilis et praestantissimus miles dominus Franciscus de Scalamontibus de Ancona honorem potestatis terrae Nursiae eiusque territorii et districtus pro sex mensibus proxime venturis hodie inchoatis ....*

51. Florence, Bibl. Naz. II, IX, 15, pp. 258–259; Volterra, Bibl. Guarnacci, MS 5031, fols. 32v–33r. Cited in part (from the Volterra MS) by Spadolini, 1901, 71b, and by De Rossi, 1888, II, 361a, note 3 (from the Florence MS).

52. Spadolini, 1901, 71.

53. Filelfo, *Epistolarum familiarium*, 1502, fol. 34r–34v (29 September 1444); 36v (31 October 1444); 71v (5 September 1452); fol. 190r (31 January 1467); and fol. 191v (27 June 1467). All are addressed to *Francisco Scalamonti equiti aurato*. Spadolini, 1901, 71, employs quotations from the first three of these to illustrate the relationship between Filelfo and Scalamonti.

54. Babinger, 1964, 67.

55. The following summary of Lauro Quirini's life is from P.O. Kristeller's introduction to Branca et al., 1977, 27. For a more detailed chronology of Quirini's life and writings see the 'Cronologia' by Seno and Ravegnani in the same volume, 11–18. They differ from Kristeller in placing Lauro's death between 1475 and 1479. See also Babinger, 1961, 53, and 1964, 68.

56. The following summary of Quirini's literary career is also from P.O. Kristeller, ibid., 29–31. See also Seno-Ravegnani's 'Cronologia,' in the same volume, passim, and Babinger, 1964, 69–71.

57. Ciriaco, in a letter to Pope Eugenius IV, the so-called 'Itinerarium' (ed. Mehus, 1742, 13–14): *Quin et hac utique in urbe* [i.e., Florence] *novissime quidem novimus Laurum Quirinum, Venetum patricium certe nobilem et latine graeceque perdoctum, qui quum nuperrime eo in carmine, quod in florentina scaena XI. Kal. Novembris* [= 22 October 1441] *de praeclarissima rerum amicitia materno quidem eloquio brevissimum habuimus, commentarium latine ornateque scripsisset, me quoque prima in parte antiquarum rerum curiosissimum repertorem vocitare maluerat.*

See also the letter of Iacopo Zeno to Ciriaco (Bertalot and Campana, 1939, 369). For Ciriaco's and Quirini's participation in the *Certame Coronorio* see G. Mancini, 1911, 202, who says that Ciriaco did not compete for the prize (a silver crown), but recited a sonnet *in persona, più attamente che certi altri, perchè è di singolare ed elevato ingegno.* He adds that Quirini wrote for the occasion of the *Certame* a *Tractatus perlepidus in gymnasiis florentinis*, now lost. Ciriaco's sonnet is preserved in MS II.V.160 of the Biblioteca Nazionale in Florence, fol. 33. See also Gorni, 1972, and Ponte, 1975, 133–136.

58. Published by L. Bertalot (with A. Wilmanns), 1923, 478–509 (text on pp. 483–493).

59. Branca et al. give editions of all three treatises.

60. ... *calamum cepi, et Kyriaci Anconitani nostri originem vitamque et peregrinationis cursum, et horum quaeque memoratu digna visa sunt, et quae carae parentis ab ore suorumve relatu, et ab eo ipso et suis plerisque litteris intelligere, noscere atque videre et percipere potui* (*Vita*, para. 3).

61. The word *commentaria* occurs six times in the *Vita* (para. 55, 76, 105, 113, 166, 191). We have treated it, not as the title of a book, but as a common noun meaning 'notes,' or 'notebook,' 'journal.'

62. Sarayna, 1540 II, xiii: *De Amphitheatro etiam legitur in quibusdam chronicis Amphitheatrum, quam arenam vulgo appellant, anno XLII Imperii Augusti extructum fuisse, et Cyriacus Anconitanus in quodam itinerario sic scriptum reliquit* (emphasis ours).

63. Published, along with the archival text of the treaty itself, by Praga, 1932–1933, 270–278. For the verbal correspondences see Campana, 1959, 494–498.

64. For the *Certame Coronario* see above, note 57. The texts of the relevant passages of the '*Itinerarium*' are gathered together in Appendix V.

65. Campana, 1959, 485–489, 492.

66. Tiraboschi, 1783, 165; Colucci, 1792, 32–36; De Rossi, 1888, II, 361.

67. See the 'Chronology' at the end of this Introduction.

68. That such linking expressions as *deinde, exinde* and *demum* need not be construed in a temporal sense is clear even from their classical usage (see the *Oxford Latin Dictionary*, s.vv.). Moreover, Ciriaco's relative disdain for exact chronology is evident even in the fragments of his *commentaria* that have come down to us: in almost every case there is a confusion in the order of presentation that is not always explicable on codicological grounds, leaving one with a strong suspicion that he kept his notebooks in rather a helter-skelter fashion. That Ciriaco was an inveterate name-dropper will be clear from even a cursory look at the Index at the end of this volume. For Byzantine names in this Palaeologan period see *Prosopographisches Lexikon der Palaiologen-zeit (PLP)*.

69. For Buondelmonti see Weiss, 1972, 198–200, with the accompanying bibliography, and Luttrell, 1986, 189–194 and 210–211.

70. Buondelmonti, *Liber insularum*, ed. de Sinner, 1824, 73, and Luttrell, 1986, 211, note 64.

71. See, for instance, Maas, 1915, regarding an autograph notebook of *parerga* kept by Ciriaco during his journey through the mainland of Greece (now MS Berol. graec. qu. 89 [B4]).

72. Cf. Mitchell, 1962, who argues that Bodley MS Canonici Misc. 280, a miscellany which contains (fols. 1–64) a copy of Buondelmonti's *Liber Insularum*, is entirely composed of Ciriacana. Although this is not an autograph of Ciriaco's, it strengthens the hypothesis that the traveler carried with him a copy of Buondelmonti just as he is known to have carried a Strabo (Bodnar, 1960, 54 and 118–119, with bibliography). See now also Luttrell, 1986, 211, note 64.

73. Morici, 1896, 8–12.

74. Babinger, 1964, 67, note 3.

75. For a recent attempt to construct a chronology of Ciriaco's entire life and career, including the years covered by the *Vita*, see Patitucci, 1991. The *Table Chronologique des principaux voyages de Cyriaque* in Colin, 1981, 561–599, begins only with the year 1435.

76. For the chronological anomalies occurring in this section of the *Vita* see the notes to para. 215–217 of the translation.

# A NOTE ON THE LATIN TEXT

For the convenience of the reader we have punctuated the text and divided it into paragraphs according to sense, not according to the rather arbitrary punctuation and paragraphing of the manuscript, and we have expanded most of the abbreviations. Numerals above one hundred are written as in the MS. Those below a hundred are spelled out. To facilitate comparison between the text and our translation, we have numbered the paragraphs in both.

Anyone experienced in Ciriaco's stylistic mannerisms can see them in Scalamonti's prose, which often seems nothing more than the transcription of passages from Ciriaco's diaries, changed from the first person to the third. In matters of orthography, therefore, in determining whether the misspelling of a Latin word is Felice's or Scalamonti's (and/or Ciriaco's) we have been guided by the surviving autographs of Ciriaco's writings. For instance, it was Ciriaco's habitual practice to write the diphthong 'ae' in full, whereas Felice tends to write simply 'e.' Again, the habit of doubling consonants in the interior of Latin words seems to be an idiosyncrasy of Felice's, not Ciriaco's. Regarding faulty syntax, where we have considered it necessary to correct Felice's evident mistakes, the actual readings of the manuscript are recorded in the *apparatus criticus*. If the error seems to be Scalamonti's (and/or Ciriaco's), we have tried to leave it unchanged unless an obvious correction is needed to clarify the intended meaning. Finally, regarding the inscriptions reported in the *Vita*, since it is impossible to recover Ciriaco's copies exactly as he wrote them down in his notebooks, or even as Scalamonti recopied them, we have reproduced them as they appear in Felice's capricious text, line for line and error for error. Proper editions of each of them can be found in the *C.I.L.*

## VITA CLARISSIMI ET FAMOSISSIMI VIRI KYRIACI ANCONITANI FELICITER INCIPIT

**1.**   Franciscus Scalamontius eques Anconitanus Lauro Quirino Veneto patricio viro claro salutem dicit.

**2.**   Cum hisce diebus nuper apud Anconem patriam elegantem illam epistolam tuam quam exacto tempore e Patavina urbe Florentiam Kyriaco Anconitano nostro destinasti[a] vidissem, clarissime Laure, tui ex ea nobilitatem animi existimare[b] coepi. Quom te tam rarissimi hominis vitam cursumque describere deligisse perceperam, rem certe bene merentem et honorificam sui et tuae dignam facundiae duco, nec te hac ipsa in re Italos inter doctissimos homines dormitante[c] quippe ingenio consideravi. Nam quis clariorem sibi nostro aevo materiem politiorem[d] iucundioremve in scribendo deligere posset quam[e] singularis viri vitam peregrinationemque[f] memoriae litterisve mandare? Qui solus in orbe post insignem illum geographum Claudium Ptolemoeum Alexandrinum ab Hadriani Caesaris tempore per tria atque decem annorum centena[g] orbem totum percurrere, regionum provintiarumque[h] situs et qualitates, montes, nemora, fontes fluviosque, maria et lacus atque nobilissimas urbes et oppida per Graeciam, Asiam et Aegyptum perque Ionicas insulas et Aegaeas visere indagareque sui quadam animi magnitudine et generositate ausus est. Et quicquid in his dignum nobilia inter venerandae veternitatis monumenta comperuit, Latine Graeceve honeste non in vulgaribus quidem litteris emendavit, et denique, ut saepe suo audivimus ore, quicquid in orbe reliquum est ad extrema oceani[i] promontoria et ad Thylem usque insulam et abmotas quascunque alias mundi partes videre scrutarique indefesso nempe

---

[a] cod. destinatas. Unless otherwise indicated, subsequent readings given in this *apparatus criticus* are those of the Treviso manuscript (T) that the editors have corrected in the text.

[b] extimare

[c] dormitanti

[d] policiorem

[e] quantam

[f] peregrinatione quem

[g] centona

[h] provintiasque

[i] occeani

26

animo proposuerat, suis quibusque incommodis, laboribus atque vigiliis omnibus expertis posthabitisque.

**3.**     Equidem, vir clare et vere Musarum decus virentissime Laure, ipsum te verum hac in parte Quirinum et Quirini nominis dignissimum possessorem exornatoremque cognosco, dum te tam dignam et honorificam provinciam cepisse conspicio, tam diligentem scilicet[a] Latini nominis exornatorem ornare atque insignia sua quaeque ornamenta insigniter perennia facere te primum omnes inter Italos[b] providentissime decrevisse. Igitur honeste ut late magis et integre opus perficere posses, ab eo ea ipsa in epistola vitae suae cursum omnem a natali die certo ordine tibi certius describere flagitabas. Qua in re cum eum tardiorem vidissem (nam in alienis potius quam propriis in rebus laudibusve solertem esse cognovi) et me sibi in primis ab ineunte aetate et a teneris, ut aiunt, unguiculis[c] amicicia, consuetudine et domestica omni familiaritate iunctum plane cognovissem, id mihi honestum et honorabile munus honos ipse atque honestas iniungere videbatur;[d] quod equidem abnuere nefarium duxi. Pro igitur munere suscepto calamum cepi,[e] et Kiriaci Anconitani nostri originem vitamque et peregrinationis cursum, et horum quaeque memoratu digna visa sunt, et quae carae parentis ab ore suorumve relatu, et ab eo ipso et sui plerisque litteris intelligere, noscere[f] atque videre et percipere potui, hisce benivolentiae dignissimae tuae brevissimo ordine describendum atque hisce transmittendum curavi.

**4.**     Vale et Kiriacum ipsum lege.

**5.**     . . . *[About 220 words are missing: cf. Note 5 of Translation.]* cavit. Ac eos bonis moribus litterisque erudire quoad licuit operam dedit. Interea Kiriacus, puer iam fere novennis,[g] ingenti et innata visendi orbis cupiditate, fatali quadam sorte et divino quodam afflante numine, Kiriacum Silvaticum tum forte[h] per Adriacum Venetias rei suae causa petentem invita parente avum quidem avide sequitur.

---

[a] silicet

[b] Italas

[c] unguinculis

[d] videbantur

[e] coepi

[f] nosce

[g] novenis

[h] fortem

**6.**       Nam tam celebris amplissimae civitatis fama iam tenerum pueri atque fatalem animum excitarat. Quam demum Idibus Aprilis Michaele Stenno duce splendidissimam[a] vidit et admiratus est mirificentissimam urbem. Et quemadmodum fata dederant inclytam hanc et insignem Italiae civitatem tantae sibi indagationis principium fore praedignum, ita eam ipsam avidius diligere amareque semper et ingenti laude attollere exornareque conatus est.

**7.**       Exinde puer ipse Kiriacus Kiriaco avo ipso ducente Patavinam adivit antiquam Enetum et egregiam urbem, quam, Francisco Carario principe,[b] magnam et triplici circundatam muro viderat et pleno undique flumine ablutam. Inde nobilem eiusdem civitatis arcem et ornatissimam principis aulam vidit, in qua primum in claustris vivos deambulare leones conspexisse memorabat.

**8.**       Exinde vero patriam suosque revisit et dilectissimam genetricem, quae summo studio puerum Francisco Zampeta paedagogo docente litteris erudire curaverat. Sed anteaquam duodecimum aetatis suae annum puer exactum vidisset, et Kiriacum avum ad Ladislaum regem maturare certis indiciis[c] percepisset, expretis omnibus et charae parentis precibus, avum sequi terra marique constituit.

**9.**       Et sic ex Piceno[d] per Mauricinos, Brucios et Salentinos campos perque Apuleos,[e] Sannitas, Lucanos atque Campanos Neapolitanum omne nobilissimum regnum percurrit, plerisque egregiis urbibus oppidisque visis, in quis pleraque vetustatum monumenta conspectare iam coeperat,[f] inter quae apud antiquam Thetidis urbem Achilei capitis simulachrum vetusto de marmore vidit. Sed primum ipso in regno apud Theanum oppidum per dies consedere eiusdem optimo cum principe, Geophedra Aliphi comite et magno totius regni camerario; exinde in Suessa apud ipsum Suesanum ducem Scyllaceique in Calabris comitem, grandaevum et regni maritimarum rerum omnigenum praefectum, ambo praeclara Martiana de domo fratres, quibus inclytis principibus Kiriacus avus antiqua familiaritate notus et carissimus erat, et cum his in Pannonia ab Karoli regis tempore versatus.

---

[a] *wrongly corrected to* splendidissimum

[b] principem

[c] iudiciis

[d] picenno

[e] apoleos

[f] ceperat

**10.** Exinde vero regiam Neapolitanam nobilissimam Campaniae civitatem venere, ubi Ladislaum ipsum regem, inclytum atque perstrenuum armis principem, inter parandam fabrifaciundamve classem in ipso urbis navistacio conspexere. Sed inde paucos post dies, insignibus tantae civitatis inspectis, Calabres petentes oneraria nave devecti, apud Salernum civitatem serenissimum ipsum regem secus mare hastiludium hippodromaleve spectaculum celebrantem florentissima stipatum militia respexere.

**11.** Exinde, urbe conspecta, per cymbam Lucania littora radentes et floridos laetosque Melphetanos Paestinosve Lucaniae colles desuper inspectantes, tandem exoptatis Calabrum oris incolumes applicuere, in quis Turpiam, Laconiam Maydemque oppida devenere. Et cum in Mayde Kiriacus avus consisteret, ex ea puerum nempe ad perdiscendas litteras Palphi Scyllacaei civis amici sui tutelae[a] commisit, ubi puer primum grammateis in ludis primos primae artis canones coeperat intelligere.

**12.** Sed ibi posteaquam per annum moram traxere, avus suus ex Mayde rebus exactis (nam et eo in loco divinam omnem historiam materni eloquii carminibus peregregie traduxerat), patriam denique remeare constituens, Neapolim iterum Tyrreno remenso[b] aequore revisit, ubi Anconitanam triremrem, ut Bonifacium pontificem ad balnea duceret, ab Anconitanis Marcone Torelliano[c] praefecto missam invenere.

**13.** Sed ubi exacta re inde concesserant, Suessam repetentes, aliquot per dies apud Suessanum ducem degere. Cuius in regia Kiriacus ipse puer puero inclyti ducis filio Ioanni Antonio tanta se consuetudine et familiari benivolentia iunxerat,[d] ut nullo inter se discrimine apud patriam maiestatem haberi se videbantur. Nam una eadem pueros adoleverat aetas parumper sed moribus doctrina dispares. Ast enim vero avus interea talibus posthabitis honoribus, ut fidem potissimum filiae servaret, Kiriacus puerum ad patriam charamque parentem exoptatum reduxit.

**14.** Reversi quidem in patriam civitatem, cum plerosque per dies avus puerum a suis multum deplausum blandiciis cognovisset, puerique mentem inertem consistere nolle plane scivisset, ac civitatem totam non liberalibus studiis sed mercemoniis potissimum maritimisque exercitationibus deditam

---

[a] tutelam

[b] Tyrrenno ve menso

[c] torelliane

[d]*corrected from* vinxerat

intellexisset, ac his artibus cives quamplures ditiores[a] ope auctos sane novisset, et puerum ipsum ex paupere ditiorem[b] evadere cupiens, de consensu matris quoidam ex affinibus suis diviti negociatori, viro quidem in civitate praestanti et patricio nobili, Petro magistri Iacobi physici clari[c] filio, puerum ipsum Kiriacum iam decimum quartum aetatis annum agentem septenale per tempus in negociariae rei servitium dederat. Qui posteaquam puer hisdem se deditum exerciciis cognoverat, non arithmeticae modo praecipuam artem, quin et geometricam et plenam denique negociariae rei disciplinam, nullo docente, se ingenii sui praestantia solertiaque fretus, brevi tempore, exemplaribus tantum inspectis, didicisse manifestum ostendit; et tanta demum fide, integritate, diligentia, vigilantia[d] atque solertissima cura in eiusdem patroni sui negotiis die noctuque gesserat et domi forisque, assiduis laboribus vigiliisque omnibus expretis, ut vixdum exacto biennio Petrus iam Kiriacum ad omnem rem gerendam paratum idoneumque existimans, ut publicae rei negociis quibus frequens cum consulari potestate sevir,[e] tum regulatoria dictatoriave trevir electus, inter patricios cives liberius habiliusque vacari posset, omnem sibi puero suae rei curam non modo domi mercisque omnigenae, quin et agrariae utique rei administrationem reliquit. Et sic puer ipse rem quodammodo magnam virili quodam animo suscipiens, ita per quinquennium mercaturam omnifariam exercuerat, ut divo et catholico genio suo ea utique in parte favitante Mercurio, non modice patroni sui opes augendo concreverat; et ita in his se aeque gessit, ut non suis modo <a> civibus, sed ab extraneis plerisque, qui tum forte saepius Anconitanis negociabantur, Perusinis, Florentinis, Venetisque laudatus est.

**15.**     Adolescens praeterea, anteaquam servicii tempus explicuisset, patrono potissimum curante optumo, nondum aetate idoneus primum ad consularem seviratus dignitatem, mox ad senatorium extra comitiorum ordinem ascendit, in quis se semper pace belloque egregie eximia cum laude gessit. Exacto sed

---

[a] dictiores

[b] pauperem dictiorem

[c] CL.

[d] dilligentia, vigillantia

[e] sevirum

enim cum[a] patrono constituto tempore, etsi materna pietas adolescentem ad se paupere in casa reduxerat, nunquam se tum ab honesta patroni[b] optumi consuetudine et benivolentia separavit.[c]

16. Sed enim interea quamquam in civitate puer expertus et non mediocriter eruditus se publicis privatisque negotiis exercere[d] sua cum dignitate et utilitate potuisset, animus tamen nobilis, qui eum ad visendas mundi[e] oras impellebat, peregrinis maritimisque negotiis immisceri compulerat, et ita se primum Ciucio Picennicoleo consanguineo suo Alpheriae cuiusdam onerariae navis patrono se navigationis principio scribam minorem iunxit.

17. Qua cum bona navi fructuum onerata ex Ancone per hyemem Illyrico superato altum per Ionium, Creta magni Iovis insula procul inspecta, vasto denique demenso Libyco Aegyptiacove freto, Alexandriam insignem Aegypti civitatem venit. Ubi primum ingentia Phariae praecelsae olim turris vestigia, regias ex Numidico lapide portas, maximum Philadelphi regis obiliscum, et magnam ex Dinocrate architecto[f] Alexandri Macedonis columnam, quam[g] hodie vulgus Pompeianam appellat, inspexit, ac alia pleraque vetustatum insignia monumenta; et ibi primum kamelos, dromedarios, struthiocamelosque nec non mymones et novos gentium habitus vocesque admiratus est. Vidit exinde ibi Sultaneum[h] principem magna eunuchorum servorum omnigenum caterva stipatum advenientem ingenti splendore, pompa eximioque honore a suis et externis hominibus in urbe susceptum.

18. Sed navis ibidem, Stephano demum Quirino Veneto patricio nobili curante, rebus omnibus exactis, ex Alexandria Rhodum, ex Rhodo vero Chium venerat, ex qua quidem nobili et Aegaea[i] insula Kiriacus adolescens, scriba

---

[a] eum

[b] patronis

[c] seperavit

[d] exerceri

[e] mondi

[f] in margin: Dinocrates architectus

[g] quae

[h] Saltaneum

[i] aegeo

maior creatus, Samium Ichareamque vidit, egregias et fama celebres in Asia insulas. Et tandem ad Ioniam veniens[a] Milesiam vidit, olim nobilem et nunc dirruptam vetustate urbem. Sed eiusce maximi amphiteatri et pleraque alia suae maiestatis eximiae conspectantur vestigia, quae hodie Graeciae vulgus palatia vocitare solent.

**19.**      Exinde vero Kariae Ciliciaeque littora perlegentes,[b] Cyprum opulentissimam olim insulam venere, ubi Kiriacus e navi esiliens Cyrinum oppidum veterem, Paphum, Amacostem atque regiam Leucosiam mediterraneam civitatem vidit. Inde Syriam navigantes Berutum venit; ex qua demum Italiam repetens et Caietam urbem per Scyllaea Carybdaeaque perniciosa vada, Regium Iulii nobilem Calabrum et antiquissimam civitatem venit.

**20.**      Inde Messanam insignem Siciliae civitatem et praeclaram viderat ac pulcherrimam urbem. Exinde vero per Tirrenum navigantes, Caietam antiquam et memorabilem Campaniae civitatem venit, ubi exonerata repparataque navi Castrum ad Mare venerat.

**21.**      Et inde castaneis avellanisque oneratis, Alexandriam iterum repetentes, Tyrrenum inde transfretantes, per Aeolias insulas ingenti ad IIII Kalendas Martias acti procella, ad Drepani portum ex Ustica insula maris noctu perniciem evasere, quam et antiquissimam urbem ut memorabilem Dardanidis Anchisae sedem conspectare maluerat. Et tandem extra moram, ad Beatae Nuntiatae[c] Virginis aedem solutis nauticis de more votis concedentes, inde Vulcaneam inter insulam et sinistrum Sicaniae littus Scyllaea rursus formidanda per vada transmeantes Aegyptiacam iterum Alexandriam revisere.

**22.**      Ubi demum exactis Ioanne[d] cum Michaele Veneto rebus, Anconem patriam repetentes per Illyricum, Dalmatica Ragusio nobili urbe et antiqua pulcherrimaque Epidauri colonia visa, et tribus demum semestribus peractis, Anconitanum portum suosque et proprios lares rerum experientia doctior opulentiorque revisit, ubi paucos post dies Nocolosam, sororem iam maturam viro et a matre conubio pactam, Bartholomaeo Libori filio Brondello desponsatam, aucta de se dote, honorifice dederat, et ubi Kiriacus in urbe aliquod per tempus tum privatis tum et publicis rebus intentus versaretur.

---

[a] venientes

[b] phegentes

[c] nuptie

[d] Ioannem

**23.**    Interea patria, hostilibus armis[a] incaute Nonis Octobribus noctu moenibus iam furto[b] sublimiori in parte captis, oppressa,[c] una aliis cum civibus cumque[d] Petro suo optimo olim patrono ad expellendum hostem civitatemque liberam incolumemque[e] servandam non exigua quidem pars fuerat; quam vero rem ipse primum materno quidem eloquio litteris haud inepte mandarat. Nam et in his quandoque sub patrono media inter negotia ingenium exercuerat, cum saepe Dantis, Petrarchae, Boccaciique poemata per ocium lectitare maluisset.

**24.**    Quibus de facultatibus cum doctiores inter viros verba aliquando non vulgariter habuisset, civis quidam ex his nomine Crassus, facundus quidem vir et eruditus, Kiriaci adolescentis ingenium admirans, haec denique nostro idiomate carmina sibi media sua inter se vice[f] misit.

> Siegui il tuo stille e non guardar al folle
>> Vulgo insensato: siegui quel valore,
>> Kiriaco mio, di quegli el cui splendore
>> Sé eternando, el nome e'l tempo extolle.
> 5  Lassa la cura d'este cose molle,
>> Ov'è ville il dilecto et vano amore.
>> Natura siegui, el tuo divin auctore
>> Natura [è] che al cielo el capo tolle;
> e virtù quella che, honorato in fama
> 10  Fa salir l'hom per arme o per scïenza;
>> Poi di eterna dolzeza il ciel l'adombra.
> E te che al suo cantar le muse chiama,
>> Non parvipender la divin' semenza[g]
>> Per fructo trar di quel che poi tutto umbra.

---

[a] patriam hostibus annis

[b] furtu

[c] oppressam

[d] cunque

[e] incolumenque

[f] interstevicia

[g] divina emenza. Emendations of these Italian texts are by Cecil Grayson.

**25.**     Quoi deinde Kyriacus talia per verba eodem carminum ordine respondit:

> Non per seguir lo stil che a l'alto colle
> > Di Parnaso ce pingie,—il suo valore
> > Sempre hai seguito et hor ti rende honore
> > Sì come a quel che meritando il volle,—
>
> 5   Spargo l'inchiostro delle nostre ampolle,
> > Ma per seguir il mercatal labore:
> > Scrivendo e canzellando, el dibitore
> > Per poesia nei mei libri s'incolle.
>
> Hor la virtù che sol da te s'indrama,
> > 10   Movendo verso me per sua clemenza,
> > Me mostra usir di quel che tanti adombra.
>
> Ma perché più longo ordo e magior trama
> > M'è oppo a ringratiar Tua Reverenza,
> > De ciò narrar fia qui mia rima sgombra.

**26.**     Et talia pleraque eiusdem generis carmina, ternarios, cantilenas et sextinas variis quidem temporibus edidit, et diversis per Latium viris claris et peritissimis misit; quae quom primum nostra in provintia iuvenis facundissimus ille Albertus Fabrianensis intellexisset, haec illico sibi elegantissime scripsit:

> Hor serato si vede il fonte Arpino.
> > Mantua, Smyrne, Corduba e Sulmona,
> > Et tu Delpho, Parnaso et Helicona,
> > Posto hai silentio al tuo cantar divino,
>
> 5   Ché, conspirante el summo Seraphino,
> > Un tal tra noi dal ciel organo sona,
> > Che fa il lume Atheniese e quel d'Ancona
> > Favilla spinta sotto fin rubino.
>
> Dunque prehendi da Daphne l'alme fronde,
> > 10   E pon con tua corea, Apollo divo,
> > Sacro diadema in cossì digne come.
>
> E tu, mare Adrian, aquieta l'onde,
> > E mostra pace, e ben poi dir 'son vivo
> > E morte voi altre aque senza nome.'

**27.** Verum et quae sibi decentia eodem ordine dicta reddiderat omittam.[a] Sed quae deinde Leonardo Iustiniano Veneto patricio, nobili et eloquentissimo viro, scripserat, hac in parte praetereundum non censui.

> Quel che con summa providentia et arte
> >Volgie col moto più alto e festino
> >La sancta mola del ciel christallino,
> >Movendo gli altri ciel di parte in parte,

5
> Vole del suo splendor tale adornarte
> >Qual circonscripto in oro fin rubino,
> >Unde non poteria mai mio picolino
> >Stil, quanto converia, tanto exaltarte;
> Perché del fior del tutto el marin piano

10
> >Se stende fino al ciel con care piume
> >La fama del valor Justiniano,
> Che come chiaro spechio di costume
> >Cossì la vita del bel viver humano
> >Mostra, facendo a tutti gli altri lume.

**28.** Quibus talia statim Leonardus ipse eodem ordine respondit:

> Quelle ample lode mie che in brieve carte
> >Conchiude[b] in stille altiero e pellegrino,
> >In te sol si converte[c] ivi, e il divino
> >Inzegno tuo traluce in mille parte.

5
> E già gran tempo le tue laude sparte
> >Quanto si calcha il bel terren latino,
> >Con tutto il cuor mi fero a te vicino
> >E d'un caldo disio vago ad amarte.
> Se cierchi in me virtù, troppo luntano

10
> >Dal ver ti allonghi, ché'l celeste nume
> >Non, come scrivi, a me larga la mano.
> Ma se amor cierchi, un abondante fiume

---

[a] obmittam

[b] *conchiude*: see footnote to translation *ad loc.*

[c] *converte*: see footnote to translation *ad loc.*

Vi trovarai, dil tuo valor soprano:
Virtù honorando a sé virtù risume.[a]

**29.**      Et subinde haec eadem illico dicta subiecit:

Qual sparir suole matutin pianeta
     Al pander de le come aurate e bionde
     Del sol che a men nocturna faza asconde[b]
     Con l'alma lampa sua diurna e lieta,
5      Tal dal suave suo stil vinta si aquieta
     La sparsa fama tua, né già risponde
     A l'alte rime, unde si stilla e fonde
     Accenti di ogni digno e gran poeta.
Sì suave hermonia tua voce rende,
10      Che quasi Orpheo, Apollo et Amphione
     Le labra a più bel canto mai non sciolse.
Quanto donque mia prima oppinione
     Dal vero è vinta, tanto più si accende
     L'amor che già gran tempo ad te mi colse.

**30.**      Quibús et Kyriacus ipse statim haec de more respondit:

In fin che i fiumi al mar seguir lor meta
     Non resta,[c] o l'ombre render monti e fronde,
     E che[d] le vaghe stelle il ciel circonde,[e]
     Convien tua fama al mondo esser cometa;
5      Ché l'alma rima tua dolce e ripleta
     De l'alta symphonia che mi confonde,
     Move dal pegaseo sì suave unde
     Che di gustarle omai sempre mi asseta.[f]

---

[a] *risume*: see footnote to translation *ad loc.*

[b] *asconde = si nasconde*: see footnote to translation *ad loc.*

[c] *resta*: see footnote to translation, *ad loc.*

[d] *e che*: see footnote to translation *ad loc.*

[e] *circonde*: see footnote to the translation, *ad loc.*

[f] See footnote to the translation, *ad loc.*

Ma quando ad humiltà tanto discende
10     Che'l mio stil basso al summo Hyperïone
       Extolle tra i cantor che'l canto extolse,
Non me puote honorar, ma son corone
       Et vostre alme virtù che tanto splende
       Quanto largir tra noi Peana volse.[a]

**31.**     Sed posteaquam binos fere per annos in civitate tum privatus tum consulari potestate sevir diversis in rebus egregie se exercuerat, ad navigationem iterum intentus navim conscendit, suis nonnullis et Petri olim patroni sui mercemonialibus rebus advectis; et denique Lucinio Brunellio praefecto per Liburneam Tharsatica Seviaque visis Siciliam iterum revisit, nobilissimam insulam. Sed antea in Calabris Scyllaceum conscenderat celebre promuntorium.

**32.**     Exinde Aethnaeo praecelso et fumifero Sycaniae monte procul inspecto, Thauromenium venerat, arduum atque vetustissimum oppidum, ubi et ingentia plura vetustatum monumenta conspexit; et inde Scyllaea rursus immania per vada, porthmo iterum formidabili superato, Messanam praeclarissimam civitatem revisit; et Pellaeo deinde promuntorio remenso Panormum[b] venit, antiquam et insignem Sycilliae urbem, ubi exonerata abietibus[c] nave plerosque per dies versatus est. Et ipsa in amplissima urbe primarios inter et generosissimos viros Jacobo Pizinga, Rogerio Spatafora equiti et Ioanni de Vintimillia comiti honorifica se familiaritate coniunxit, quibus cum humanissimis viris nobiles scenas, quas Toccos dicunt, sacra et superis ornatissima templa et magnificentissimi Armirati Clari Montis insignia regia vidimus, et conspicuum in arce regiumque Sancti[d] Petri sacellum lapidum porphyritum et mirae artis musaycae perornatum.

**33.**     Sed extra civitatis moenia uberos inter et melifluos campos apud Montem Regalem conspicuam[e] et insignem viderat Beatae Virginis aedem, in qua ornatissimas ex aere portas et nobile de marmore claustrum vidit et preciosa optumi Guglielmi aliorumque regum monumenta. Praeterea Clarissima in Valle repositum Sancti Martini pontificis monasterium una optumo

---

[a] vv 12–14: see footnote to translation, *ad loc.*

[b] pavornium

[c] abiectibus

[d] sunt

[e] conspicuum

cum viro et amicissimo nostro Trintio Foroflaviniano vidit, et deinde secus praefatam urbem Alcimon, nobile Bernardi Emcaprarei et inexpugnabile oppidum, inspexit.

**34.** Et denique Panormum[a] remeantes, cum ibi navis illa aeris alieni causa venundata mansisset et per idem tempus in Panormitano[b] portu quattuor Venetum onerariae triremes, Nicolao Donato imperatoria potestate praefecto, ex Britannia Venetias repetentes applicuissent, Kiriacus a Panormo quam[c] celeriter expeditus, hisdem longis navibus, rebus suis impositis, triremem Iohanni Magnimperio patrono conscendens, Venetias petiere.[d]

**35.** Et ex itinere in Illyrico, cum Iaderam insignem Liburnorum urbem venissent, ibidem Sanctum Venerium equitem clarum et Petrum Loredanum insignem virum pro Venetis ea in civitate correctores convenimus, a quis perhumane et honore eximio suscepti, primum de Martini quinti pontificis maximi in synodo Constantiensi[e] creatione, ut laetum unionis nuntium, laete grateque perceperant.

**36.** Sed postea Venetiis cum applicuissent, Kiriacus exoneratis navibus expediri se quam primum operam dedit, et e mercibus aere exacto, Anconem[f] et ad suos incolumis remeavit, cum alii ex navigatione socii[g] per Neapolim terrestri itinere patriam per multa incommoda revisissent.

**37.** At enim vero postea quam per dies in patria[h] cum suis moratus est, desiderans denique Bizantium magnamque Constantinopolitanam civitatem <videre>, onerariam navim Pasqualino patrono et consanguineo suo scriba Kiriacus ipse conscendit et tandem, Illyrico superato, Liburneis Dalmateisque plerisque insulis visis, ad Illyrici sinus fauces Suasnam et Ceraunia Epyri promuntoria Idibus Septembribus advenere. Exinde Corcyram ad insulam

---

[a] pavormum

[b] pavormitano

[c] panormos quis

[d] construe as = petiit

[e] inconstantiam si

[f] ancone

[g] sotii

[h] patriam

coryphaeas *Phaeacum et aereas arces*[a] videre. Inde Cephalonicas Zacintheasque insulas et Leucatae formidabile promuntorium conspexere et demum per Ionicum Strophades, antiquas et memorabiles Arpiarum domos procul adnavigantes videre. Et Mallea[b] denique promuntoria superantes, Peloponesiaca montana Archadiae prope colles visa posthabitaque, Cythara procul inspecta, et sparsas per Aegaeum insulas transfretantes, sacram inter Cycladas et nobilissima Delon[c] vatidici Apollinis insulam invisere. Exinde Miconem inter et Tinem transeuntes, Lesbeam secus insulam transvecti, Tenedum[d] ad Hellesponti fauces conspexere, et angustum fretum die noctuque transmeantes, hinc Asiae Frigiaeque fines radebant, hinc pinguem prope conspexerant Europam. Et ibi primum ad dexterum Thraciae littus Hellesponticam, Caliepolim prope, dirruptam vetustate Sexton venere, ubi primum Kiriacus pileatos et longipedes Teucros inspexit; et demum, Lelio Freducio egregio negociatore curante, expeditis rebus concedentes, inde Propontiacum per aequor Proconesiam videre procul, marmoream insulam, et tandem Bizantium Threiciam et insignem ad Bosphorum civitatem incolumes[e] Nonis Octobribus applicuere.

**38.**    Ubi posteaquam insigni et[f] amplissimo in portu consederant, Kiriacus primum ea in urbe convenerat Philippum Alpherium, consanguineum suum et egregium ibi pro Anconitanis civibus consulem, quo duce quaeque civitatis insignia et imperatoriam Manuelis[g] Palaeologi maiestatem vidit.

**39.**    Et inde primum ea ex amplissima trigonia urbe viderat ingentia atque nobilia ex cocto latere moenia maritimum a duobus partibus littus alteramque circumdantia terciam et mediterraneam partem; vidit et insignem illam et regiam de marmore Portam Chryseam a divo Theodosio conditam duabus marmoreis turribus munitam; et a facie prima ab extra marmoreae primae parietes ornatae videntur antiquis ex Phidia operibus ibidem ab eo principe aliunde deductis. Ibidem vero arma a Vulcano Achilli Thetidis gratia edita[h] arte fabrefactoris eximia conspectantur, <quae> hinc inde columnis pulcherrimis exornata[i] viderat.

---

[a] Virgil, *Aeneid* 3.291

[b] E mallea

[c] dellon

[d] tenendo

[e] incolumas

[f] e

[g] Manuellis

[h] aedita

[i] exornate

**40.**　　Deinde in urbe primum sacra divis ornata atque ingentia delubra, et ante alia insigne illud et maximum a Iustiniano Caesare Divae Sophiae conditum et admirabile templum, ingenti testitudine marmoreisque crustatis[a] parietibus et pavimento conspicuo nec non porphyreis serpentineisque magnis et innumeris sublime columnis viderat; et ante ipsum venerabile templum alta columna Heracleam illam mirificam aeneam equestrem statuam, arduum quippe et conspicuum opus.

**41.**　　Sed non longe sublimiori[b] in parte vidit nobile illud hippodromale theatrum marmoreis a capite in convexu columnis epistyliisque perornatum, ac in medio lapideis obilyscis aeneisque draconibus et speculatoriis plerisque marmoreis insigne, sed in primis illum[c] ingentem[d] unico ex Numidico lapide obilyscum[e] Phoenicibus caractheribus omni ex parte insignitum, [f] quem ex Latinis Graecisque litteris Theodosium[g] principem Proculo architecto curante cognoverant erexisse.

**42.**　　Viderat et binas deinde per urbem Theodosinas cocleas et insignes de marmore columnas Taurinam Xerolophaeamque eximiae altitudinis et mira architectorum ope[h] conspicuas et alias plerasque per urbem inspexerat immanes marmoreas porphireasque columnas, nec non aeneas et plurigenum lapidum statuas, bases[i] et epigrammata, nymphaea, fontes et arduos cocto de latere aquae ductus; et denique ornatissima viderat diversa per sacra et pulcherrima monasteria bybliothecas plerasque Graecis sacris et gentilibus litteris auro imaginibusque insignes.

**43.**　　Exinde alia ex parte ad ulteriorem portus ripam viderat Galatheam illam Peram, nobilem pulcherrimamque in conspectu Constantinopolitanae

---

[a] crustratis

[b] sublimior

[c] ille

[d] ingens

[e] obilyscus

[f] insignitus

[g] Thedosium

[h] mira ... ope: see note to the translation *ad loc.*

[i] basses

urbis coloniam,[a] turritis moenibus, aedibus sacris negociatoriis scenis, praetoriis et altis undique civium palatiis perornatam. Cuiusce portus[b] et optimi emporii littus frequens cetearum[c] onerarium navium multitudo compleverat.

**44.** Deinde vero Kiriacus rebus exactis eadem[d] cum navi Anconem iterum patriam remenso aequore remeavit. Ubi posteaquam apud suos per aliquot tempus moratus fuerat, Polam antiquissimam in Histria secus Italiae fines civitatem visere cupiens, naviculum conscendit et Illyrico transfretato eam ipsam venerat Polensium civitatem, quam magna ex parte dirruptam vetustate conspexerat. Sed nobilia pleraque suae antiquitatis vestigia vidit. Et SALVIAE[e] Postumiae Sergi duoviri[f] aedilis clari filiae egregias portas et aedificia pleraque ingentia viderat, et nobile ac magnis editum lapidibus amphitheathum,[g] quod Polenses voti sui compotes Lucio Septimio Severo et Antonino divis et caesareis fratribus dicavere; viderat et innumera per urbem et extra ad mare usque lapidea sepulchra, quorum pleraque nobilia exceperat epigrammata, Andrea Contareno tum pro Venetis praetoria potestate comite curante favitanteque.

**45.** Exinde vero cum paucos post dies Anconem patriam revisisset, ex ea denique plerisque navigationibus Chion, Calliepolim, Bizantium revisit, Alboneo in Liburnea primo ad mare oppido conspecto.

**46.** At et cum in patria diversis intentus negotiis versaretur, et Petro optimo olim patrono suo defuncto, Ioannes Lucae Tollentineus aromatarius nostra in civitate primarius, mortuo Nicolao Cossi Florentino qui libros suae societatis mercemonales curabat, ad hos in finalem calculum[h] redegendos, cum et periti in mercemonalibus socii illos bene deducere nequivissent, Kyriacum adolescentem huiusce rei [peritiam] peritum conduxit; qui cum difficile quodammodo esset et laboriosum opus, nam ad quattuordecimum annum res actae et interminatae permanserant, omnes tum ingenii praestantia sui Kiriacus ad

---

[a] colloniam

[b] pontus

[c] ceterarum

[d] aedem

[e] SALVIE

[f] II vir

[g] amphitreathrum

[h] chalchulum

verum summumque rationis calculum[a] libros egregie terminatos redegit, et Ioanne mortuo heredibus dedit eiusdem.

**47.**      Interea Gabriel Condulmarius, reverendissimus cardinalis Senensis[b] pro Martino quinto pontifice legatus, in Piceni[c] provintia Anchonem venerat, correctoriam pontificiaque potestate provintiam curaturus, qui cum paucos post dies Anconitanum portum reparare[d] decrevisset, et ob id civitatis introitus exitusque et aerarii curatores in melius redigere[e] maluisset, cum plures in urbe aerarii constituti essent, unum ex omnibus universalem in civitate aerarium deligendum per senatus consultum[f] curavit. Itaque treviri,[g] quaestores patritios inter cives creati, ratiocinatores quaestorianos fidos et peritissimos cum tota ex urbe deligere decrevissent,[h] Paulo Iuliano generali aerario delecto, ratiocinatores Nicolaum Luctarelium virum praestantem et hisdem in rebus iam diu exercitatissimum Kiriacumque ipsum adolescentem designavere; quo in negotio ita se diligenter et provide gesserat adolescens, ut expleto[i] semestri tempore collega abdicato[j] solus ipse magna cum laude tam diu eo officio praestiterat, quam diu Gabriel ipse nostra in civitate et provintiae legatione permanserat, auxiliatoribus scribis quos ipse delegerat adiuvantibus; quo in tempore et fere biennio Kiriacus adolescens ipse publicos omnes eiusdem quaestaoriae rei generis libros ac plerosque eiusdem negotii[k] ordines meliorem in formam facilioremque redegit. Ac rem publicam ipsam, multis et inexplicandis diu gravatam foeneribus et absque[l] Aegidii cardinalis tempore, sua potissimum cura et industria, civibus plerisque optumis iuvantibus, potissima ex parte liberavit.

---

[a] calchulum

[b] senensi

[c] picenni

[d] repparare

[e] reddigere

[f] *pe*R. S.C.

[g] III vir

[h] decrevisset

[i] explecto

[j] abdicatus

[k] negotiis

[l] aliusque

**48.** Etenim cum Gabriel cardinalis Martino iubente pontifice Flamminiae provintiae legatus Bononiam concessisset, Kiriacus se statim nostro sexviratu coram sponte abdicavit officio, cum non hisdem vulgaribus torpescere et implicari[a] negotiis sed potius eum ad orbem omni ex parte visendum generosus animus concitabat. Atque cum, paulo anteaquam ex Ancone legatus Gabriel excessisset, et Seraphinus Urbinas[b] <et> Memmius Gazarius Senensis, iurisconsulti ac primarii apud legatum praestantioresque viri et summa cum Kiriaco benivolentia coniuncti, pleraque invicem materni eloquii carmina misissent, ad hanc ipsam orbis explorationem fatalem adolescentis animum excitarunt; quorum[c] potissima eum inter et Seraphinum missa hisce reponenda delegi, et haec quae primum Kiriacus Seraphino misit:

**49.**    Quel spirito gientil, che Amor conserva
      Nella presaga mente al suo camino,
      Me pinse al summo del colle apollino,
      L'orme seguendo d'una biancha cerva,
5     Dove Thersicor[d] con la sua caterva
      Scorsi d'intorno al fonte caballino[e]
      Condur in forma humana un seraphino
      Coperto da le fronde di Minerva.
     Indi veder uscir di tal fontana
10    Diana nuda in come a l'aura sparte[f]
      Mi parve, e sotto un lauro Daphne e Peana;
     Poi d'un boscheto uscir Venere e Marte
      E, vista di costui la fronte humana,
      Cingierla e coronarla di lor arte.

**50.**    Quibus peregregie deinde talia Seraphinus ipse respondit:

   Le rissonante rime in chui si serva[g]
      Omne habito suppremo et pellegrino

---

[a] implicare

[b] urbinam

[c] quarum

[d] Thersicore

[e] "Cf. Persius, Choliambi (V)." - C.G.

[f] "Cf. Petrarch, Sonnet 90 (V)." - C.G.

[g] "Cf. Petrarch, Sonnet 120 (V)." - C.G.

> Che me corona, e fra'l ceto divino
>      Con summa intelligentia me preserva,
> 5    Ricerchan miglior lyra e miglior nerva,
>      Simile a quelle di Dante o Petrarchino.
>      Ma quanto può mio ingiegno picolino,
>      Rengratio prima, et priego che proterva
> Fortuna e invidia te[a] ritrovi vana[b]
> 10    sì, che i posterior legan tue carte
>      E la tua fama resti integra e sana.
> Tanto duri il tuo nome in omne parte,
>      Quanto si moverà l'opra mondana
>      E vegia[c] nei dì nostri laurearte.

**51.**      Ad quae ilico mutato et invicem alternato versus ordine replicando respondit:

> Qual circuncinto in oro fin rubino,
>      In cui raggio di sol fulgente serva,
>      O qual diamante di magior conserva,
>      Perla, ballasso, smiraldo o zaphino,
> 5    Qual chiare stelle in color celestino,
>      Rose con zigli verdigianti in herva,
>      Più vaghe di mirar[d] con l'alma serva
>      Dal[e] primo senso human per color fino,
> Tal nel secondo fia quasi coharte
> 10    L'alme al sentir de la diva e soprana
>      Tua rima digna di perpetuarte.
> E benché da me volli[f] alta e luntana
>      Sua voce, pure al son compresi in parte
>      Esser via digna più che Mantuana.

---

[a] *te*: see note to the translation *ad loc.*

[b] "Cf. Petrarch, Sonnet 130." - C.G.

[c] *vegia*: see note to the translation *ad loc.*

[d] C.G. suggests emending *di mirar* to *si miran*. See footnote to translation *ad loc.*

[e] *Dal*: see note on the translation *ad loc.*

[f] *volli*: see note on the translation *ad loc.*

**52.**      Quibus et talia utique Seraphinus eodem carminis ordine dicta remisit:

> Bench'io comprehenda esser venuto al chino
>      Il viver nostro in cui virtù si enerva,
>      E veggia l'età nostra facta serva
>      De vicii e de ignorantia, pur oppino
> 5   Che'l celico motor, che è tutto pino[a]
>      Di voler iusto e sancto, a te risserva
>      Resuscitar le Muse e sua[b] catherva
>      [Per] decreto [di] spirital distino.[c]
> Dovunque l'acque Adriace ne fian sparte,
> 10      O circuisse anchor l'onda occeana,
>      Veggio celebre via per eternarte.
> Fuggi la turba inerte e tanto insana,
>      Che vol ne l'altre cure enlaquearte,
>      E fa' la mente tua da lor prophana.

Quae quidem vatisona amicissimi hominis dicta innatam sibi generosam animi cupiditatem perbellissime confirmarunt.[d]

**53.**      Verum eodem legati tempore Kiriacus suo ab amicissimo Marco Pistoriense, egregio Anconitanae rei scriba, persuasus Latinam intelligere facultatem operam dare coepit; nec, ut saepe novi clerici solent, a primis grammaticae partibus incoharat, sed magno quodam[e] et virili animo, ut et melius Dantis poema, de quo satis eruditus erat, intelligere posset, sextum Maronis librum a Thoma Camaerense grammatico insigni, quem et Senecam dicunt, audire ausus est. Is enim ea tempestate Thomas nostra in civitate paedagogus et bonarum litterarum praeceptor publice auditores docebat. Sed eo extra ordinem cum Kiriaco foedere pactus, ut praeceptor ipse discipulo Virgilium, discipulus vero praeceptori ipsi Dantem lectitare deberet.[f] Sed

---

[a] *pino=pieno.* "The reduction of the Italian diphthong or the passage of Latin -e- to -i- in this interconsonatic position is a common feature of this area." - N.S.

[b] *sua=loro:* see note on the translation *ad loc.*

[c] "This line [MS Decreto per spirital distino] lacks one syllable. It is incomprehensible as it stands." - C.G. For the emendation see note on the translation *ad loc.*

[d] confirmavit

[e] quoddam

[f] debere

anteaquam invicem rem pactam absoluissent, diverso separati[a] itinere hinc inde se[b] disiunxere. At enim vero Kiriacus, cum divinam illam Maronis facundiam ea qua in parte audierat degustasset, tanto ardore animi ingeniique praestantia Maronis Aeneam ab se omnem percurrere enixe conatus est, ut non modo Virgilii operis[c] elegantiam et facultatem intelligere et familiarem poetam habere coeperat, quin et ab eo latinitatem ipsum facile perdiscere, intelligere exercerique peregregie visus est. Et ut ad Maronis notitiam per Dantis poemata venerat, per Maronem ad Homeri magni poematis Graecaeque facundiae cupiditatem notitiae nobilem convertit animum.

**54.** Interea cum apud Anconitanum <portum> insignem illum marmoreum divi Traiani Caesaris arcum diligentius[d] inspexisset, mirificum opus admirans, cognovit a superiori parte deficere[e] et auream illam equestrem statuam, quam inclytus olim ille Senatus Populusque Romanus huic optumo principi, huiusce saluberrimi portus providentissimo conditori, conspicuas inter divae Marcianae sororis Plotinaeque coniugis imagines mira quidem architectorum ope dicarat; cuius vero splendentem iconis effigiem ipse deinde optumus imperator huic tam egregiae maritimas inter ad Adriacum civitati civibus omne per aevum honorabile signum gestare regia pro[f] sua liberalitate donavit. Quae hodie per egregia publicaque civitatis loca ac purpurea praetoriana vexilla saepe per Latium et Ausonicas urbes enitescere videntur conspicue. Sed ex eo denique mirifico arcu hoc ipsum epigramma conscriptum est:

> IMP.CAESARI
> DIVI NERVAE
> TRAIANO.OPT
> VMO.AUG.GE
> RMANICO.DA
> TICO.PONT.MAX
> TR.PON.XVIIII.

---

[a] seperati

[b] de

[c] opus

[d] dilligentius

[e] defficere

[f] quoque

PLOTINAE.AVG.          IMP.IXI.COS.VI.            DIVAE.MARTIANAE.AVG.
CONIVGI.AVG.           .P.P.PROVIDENT                 .SORORI.AVG.
                       ISSIMO.PRINCI
                       PI.SENAT.P.Q.R.
                       QVOD.ACCESSVM
                       ITALIAE HOC.ETIA
                       M.ADDITO.EX.PE
                       CVNIA.SVA.PORTV
                       TVTOREM.NAVIG
                       ANTIB.REDDIDERIT.
                                   [*CIL* IX, 5894]

Hoc ipsum tam ingens et mirabile architectorumque conspicuum opus, et
ipsum et tam grave Latinis insignibus litteris epigramma, generoso Kiriaci
adolescentis animo ad reliqua per orbem nobilia vetustatum monumenta
perquirenda scrutandaque, ut suo saepius ore percepimus, primum quoddam
idoneum atque praedignum seminarium fuerat.

**55.**    Et sic se statim Romam inclytam ad urbem, ut[a] ex ea primum maxima
rerum atque potissima nobilium in orbe monumenta videret, quam avidissime
contulit, Martino quinto pontifice, eiusdem pontificis anno octavo[b] et ad III
Nonarum Decembrium diem, ubi paulo antea Gabriel cardinalis ex Bononia
abdicatus legatione venerat. Ad illum[c] Kiriacus apud Sanctum Laurentium in
Damasco se contulerat, a quo tempore quam laete benigneque susceptus,
quater denos per dies apud eum in urbe moratus, quotidie magnam per urbem
niveo suo devectus equo, quicquid tantae civitatis reliquum[d] extaret
venerandae suae veternitatis, templa, theatra, ingentiaque palatia, thermas
mirificas, obyliscos et insignes arcus, aquae ductus, pontes, statuas, columnas,
bases,[e] et nobilia rerum epigrammata incredibili diligentia sua viderat,
exscrutarat[f] exceperatque et, ut postea ex his quandoque digna conficere
commentaria posset, fide quoque suis ordine litteris commendavit.

---

[a] *et* ut  T

[b] VII

[c] illico

[d] reliqum

[e] basses

[f] excrutarat

**56.**     At et cum maximas per urbem tam generosissimae gentis reliquias undique solo disiectas aspexisset, lapides et ipsi magnarum rerum gestarum maiorem longe quam ipsi libri fidem et notitiam spectantibus praebere videbantur. Quam ob rem et reliqua per orbem diffusa videre atque litteris mandare praeposuit, ut ea quae in dies longi temporis labe hominumve iniuria conlabuntur, et memoratu digna visa sunt, penitus[a] posteris abolita non sentiat.

**57.**     Sed enim vero interim cum adolescens ille Martini pontificis nepos, inclytus Antonius Salerni princeps, ad venationem quamdam una cum Aloysio Verme et aliis plerisque ex urbe nobilibus iuxta Salernum pontem ivisset, cardinalis vero humanissimus Kiriacum una cum Petro Baduario affine[b] suo ad eam ipsam[c] venationem inspectandam misit; quibus equitando contigerat ut una cum Agabito Columna viro quoque docto arcum ex Capitolio Severi et Antonini divorum fratrum suspicerent, quibus ultima[d] in parte inscriptum erat:

.OB.REM.PVBLICAM
RESTITVTAM
IMPERIVMQ.
POPVLI ROMANI
PROPAGATVM
INSIGNIBVS
VIRTVTIB
EORVM DOMI FO
RISQ.S.P.Q.R.

[*CIL* VI, 1033, last two lines]

Quibus perlectis cum Kiriacus ad Agabitum amice dixisset: poteratne aetas haec iners Romanum principem suscitare quempiam, cui digne talia inscribenda forent? Qui tum adolescentem inspiciens: hunc ipsum fata puerum nostrae collapsae[e] iam diu civitati praestare admodo possent, qui ex nobilitate Romana ortus Martinum pontificem patruum favitorem potissimum habet. Ex quo cum ex venatione domi eodem die revertissent, Kiriacus puero ipsi Antonio haec statim eundem per Agabitum carmina ab se hac ipsa de re condita MISIT:

---

[a] poenitus

[b] afine

[c] ipsum

[d] ultra

[e] colapsae

**58.**    Driza la testa omai, inclyta Roma.

        Mira el tuo Marte e suoi nati gemelli,

        Che fur primi martelli

        A fabricar el cerchio de' tuoi colli.

5         Orna e racolli la già inculta coma,

        Ché questi vol che in te si rinovelli

        Fabii, Scipii e Marcelli,

        Che tanto hai çerchi già con gli occhi molli,

        E vol che omai ritolli

10       Quel sceptro sotto el qual domasti el mondo,

        <Che' è> 'l don dil summo Iove a Citharea

        Promisso[a] per Aenea.

        Vol che omai torni col gran sexto al tondo

        Quando sotto ogni pondo

15       Di tua famiglia due colonne tonde

        Han sostenuto in te l'ultime sponde.

    L'una nel divin foro el summo reggie

        Ha stabillito perché al ministero,

        Che fu concesso a Piero,

20       Torni sua sposa al seggio laterano

        Per congregar[b] quella smarita gregie,

        Che, vedendola tanto in adultero

        Star senza sposo vero,

        Serà dispersa al fin del occeano.

25       Hor l'ha conducto in mano

        Di MARTIN quinto, al chui governo sancto

        Dil pescator la già submersa nave

        Con quelle summe chiave,

        Che concesse li fu sotto 'l gran manto

30       son già drizate intanto

        Che foecundarà sì la fè christiana

        Che al tutto fia submersa la prophana.

    L'altra nel temporal human govern

        Ha già directa il nepo suo gientile,

35       Che in età puerile[c]

        Monstra dil gran valor pregiati segni

        Inclyto, illustre prince di Salerno

        Creato; nel suo appetito signorile

        Se dicerne il virille

---

[a] promisse

[b] congregare

[c] puerille

40       Animo ad sugiugar magiori regni,
           Che non fu già più degni
           Cesare e gli altri chiari augusti divi
           Per valor, se fortuna al par s' estende.
           Chè s'el ciel destro intende
45       Ad exaltar costui tra nostri vivi,
           Convien che anchor si scrivi
           Qual di Severo e di Antonin pregiato:
           "Questo ha l'imperio Roman[a] propagato."
      Questo fu al mondo dal buono Iove dato,
50       Tanto benigno[b] e sì pien di clementia
           Quanto la summa essentia
           Mostrasse in criatura al tempo nostro.
           Prudente, iusto, forte e temperato:
           Da diece stelle che gli dà influentia,
55       Sotto la qual pollentia
           De tre che raggia Lui dal divin chiostro,
           Sotto il cui splendido ostro
           Risponde in lui cossì viva speranza,
           Ardente carità e pura fede,
60       Che d'aquistar mercede
           Più non ricercha la prima possanza,
           Perché quella billanza,
           Che aiusta quanto volgie l'universo,
           Non mai vedrà cambiar del biancho en perso.
65      Cantion, che speri anchor cantar perfecto
           Quel che preliba de l'alto mistero
           Del buon Romano Impero,
           Che per queste due aspeta el gran ristoro,
           Vatene lieta al prince jovaneto,
70       Nepote al summo successor di Piero,
           E con parlar intiero
           Aprigli dil tuo [?cor][c] ogni thesoro,
           E se del tuo lavoro
           Volesse pur saper il novo auctore,
75       Di' che un suo servitore
           A lui ti manda, che naque in Anchona,
           Amator del honor di sua corona.
                    FINIS[d]

---

[a] romano

[b] benigni

[c] "A syllable seems to be missing: [cor?]." - C.G.

[d] FINIS added by Felice?

**59.** Praeterea ubi natalicia humanati Iovis solemnia Martinum per pontificem celebrata conspexerat, et faustum recentis anni principium ab anno salubri milleno quatricenteno quinto atque bis deno eiusdem humanati dei et theogoni Iesu indulgentissimo nomine antiquatae legis ritu circuncisi et antiquis a Latinis bicipitis Iani nomine cultum, Kalendarum Ianuariarum praeclarum diem, Andrea Constantinopolitano, ex praedicatorum ordine theologo insigni et sacri palacii magistro, pontifice coram egregie perorante, dedicatum viderat, exoptatam ad patriam remeavit.

**60.** Ex itinere Sutrium antiquissimum oppidum, turritum[a] Viterbium eiusque mirificas thermarum aquas inspexit, et apud veterem Ervetum urbem Beatae Virginis aedem de marmore ornatissimam viderat, ex qua conspicuum arte frontespicium ligneumque[b] orchestralem illum insignem atque pulcherrimum chorum maluit conspectare, et aeneas ante portas almae Virginis et[c] angelorum imagines.

**61.** Sed postquam in patria consederat,[d] cum nova per comitia sevir creatus una cum Paliaresio Pisanello aliisque collegis civibus rem publicam de more curasset, ex Venetiis interea a Zacharia Contareno consanguineo suo litteras accepit, per quas eum in Picenno vel Apulea in mercemonalibus exerceri quaeritabat. Ipse vero quom non ad pecuniae quaestus, sed ad nobiliora semper desiderium habuisset, et ut graecas quandoque litteras perdiscere Homerumve poetam facilius intelligere potest, orientales Graecas vel quascumque ad partes se potius quam in Latio exerceri maluisset, illico exacto magistratu ad Zachariam se Venetiis terrestri itinere contulit, qui cognito iuvenis animo, cum apud Cyprum res plerasque suas et diversa iam diu negotia exerceri habuisset, quibus Petrus praeerat, repetito Venetiis fratre, fratri in insula successorem suis in omnibus peragendis rebus Kiriacum misit; qui eam ob rem potius grate magis ea in parte negotium Kiriacus suscepit, ut quem iam diu celebri fama cognoverat, Ianum inclytum regem Ciprium praesentia videre, et sua quandoque gratia regiaque benivolentia et consuetudine honeste quaesita potiri atque perfrui posset.

---

[a] turritam

[b] lingueumque

[c] ea

[d] conscederat

**62.**    Itaque a Zacharia litteris ad fratrem Petrum acceptis, cum Anconem illico remeasset, paratam navim Nicolao Corseducio patrono conscendit et per Apuleam Monopolium Bariumque et Anterium collapsum vetustate oppidum vidit. Inde vero Bizantium venit, ubi navigium ad Cyprum Syriamve navigaturum expectans, primum Graeca litterarum principia modico ex tempore cognovit.

**63.**    Sed enim interea quom Anconitanam quandam navim onerariam Benevenuto Scotigolo praefecto apud Chium insulam adventasse intelligeret, exinde Syriam petituram, Kiriacus ad eam se statim contulit; quem patronus ipse et negociatores in ea euntes[a] Franciscusque Ferretri, viri Anconitani nobiles, quam laeto vultu animoque susceperant, et eo ipso curante iuvene Francisco erudito, Kiriacus honesta secum Andreolo Iustiniano, viro Maonensium praestantiae doctoque et diligentissimo[b] vetustatum cultori, benivolentia et consuetudine iunxerat, quo cum optumo viro pleraque vetustatis vestigia epigrammataque nobilia Graeca Latinaque collegerat; et[c] ibidem eo potissimum intercedente, regium illum Graecum pulcherrimumque Novi Testamenti codicem viginti aureorum precio emit.

**64.**    Expedita sed enim interea navi, et Kiriacus Nicolao Alpherio consanguineo suo curante suis confectis rebus, Syriam inde petentes per Aegaeum crebras inter insulas, Rhodum nobilem olim in Asia insulam applicuere. Et ex ea deinde haud mora concedentes Zephyro sufflante secundo Birutum venere, ubi exoneratis rebus Kiriacus se statim Damascum nobilissimam contulit mediterraneam Syriae atque vetustissimam civitatem, ubi Hermolao Donato Veneto patricio claro et inibi eo tempore negociatorum omnium praestantissimo nec non eruditissimo viro curante favitanteque, omnia tam amplissimae urbis egregia vetera novaque viderat.

**65.**    Sed extra civitatis[d] moenia sunt apostoli Pauli monumenta nostri, vicumque rectum, et dirruptam Annaniae prophetae casam, Ioannisque Damasceni doctoris beatissimi templum insigne, praeterea nobilem et turritam praecelsis moenibus arcem; sed omnia fere vetusta inter moenia aedificia Athemir begh potentissimo Persarum rege collapsa et solo aequata videntur.

---

[a] euntes: contes

[b] dilligentissimo

[c] ex

[d] civitatem

Viderat utique deinde nonnullas antiqua ab arce Sydonum reliquias, et aenea pulchra auro argentoque permista vasa mira et expolita fabrefactorum arte conspicua, e quibus ab eo empta quaedam sua inter eiusdem generis supellectilia[a] vidimus. Vidit et ibi ingentem camelorum copiam advenisse, qui tum ex Arabica Felici Sabaeisque partibus et Gedrosiis multa plurigenum specierum aromata mercemonii causa Damascenum ad insigne emporium deferebant.[b]

**66.** Erat ea in civitate praeterea vir quidam dives opum et negociator primarius nomine Musalach, qui filios saepe mercaturae causa ad Aethiopas et Indos mittere solitus. Kiriaco illas quandoque partes adire desideranti binos a Sabaeis nuper remeantes ostendit. Et cum expeteret[c] ex his bonam sibi societatem dare, quam libere pollicitatus est.

**67.** Sed interea cum expeditus inde Byruthum remeasset navimque et socios revisisset, navis denique expedita Anconem repetit.[d] Kiriacus vero per Tripolim Genuensi nave subvectus, Cypriam Amocestem venit, ubi Evangelistem de Imola physicum doctum et Zachariae nostri amicissimum convenit. Ex quo cum intelligeret Petrum paulo ante rebus sine ordine relictis Venetias navigasse, ipso Evangelista suadente constituit ibidem manere dum a Zacharia litteras et suis in[e] rebus ordinem haberet. Et interim ne tempus omni[f] ex parte vacuum amitteret, praefecti urbis vicarius electus,[g] cum ibi magistratum praetoria potestate gessisset binos fere per menses, Romanas sibi leges et omnia iuris consultorum egregia dicta tum primum videre lectitareque non sine incremento peritiae et oblectatione contigerat. Nam eo tempore causas, solum origine legum inspecta, laudatissime dixit, nec non civibus concordiam[h] et quietem imponere operam solertissimam dedit.

---

[a] suppellectilia

[b] deferebantur

[c] expediret

[d] reppetit

[e] in suis in

[f] omne

[g] ellectus

[h] concordia

**68.**     Sed e Venetiis demum acceptis a Zacharia litteris, per quas rem suam
agere Kiriacum vehementer angebat, licentia ab eo magistratu[a] non sine
difficultate impetrata, Leucosiam regiam civitatem pergit. Ubi primum
serenissimam Iani regis maiestatem visere se contulit, quem posteaquam
inclytum principem viderat atque praeclare loquentem audierat, perbella[b]
praesentia[c] clarum suum et eximiae laudis nomen superatum cognovit. Qui
splendidissimus rex cum Kiriacum vidisset et eleganter[d] regiis suis de laudibus
casibusque perorantem audierat, eum primum quam laeto vultu animoque
perbenigne suscepit; et Bandino de Nores Hugoneque Soltaneo equitibus regiis
et primariis in aula suis adstantibus Kiriacum ipsum honorifice statim sua
regia familiaritate decoravit, ac optimatum suorum numero regio de more
socium aggregavit.

**69.**     Nec non Zachariae in rebus ex quibusque suis agendis regium omne
suum auxilium obtulerat; Kiriacus vero, maiestati suae gratiae actae datis
deinde ex Zacharia litteris, Lodovici Corarii Venetum vicebaioli auctoritate a
Petro Berardino Leonelloque actore rebus Zachariae Petrique[e] fratris omnibus
acceptis, ita res ipsas per civitatem et extra diligentia solertiaque sua
peregerat, ut nondum[f] expleto anno negotium omne suum expleverat, debitores
creditores in chalchulum et paucissimos numero redegit.

**70.**     Sed interim vero saepius inclyto cum rege ad venationes exercendas
totam fere insulam exploravit. Et quod ad tam clari principis cumulum
claritatis accedit, hoc loco praetereundum non duxi. Nam, ut e suis novimus
litteris, dum rex ipse suo stipatus nobili comitatu aequos[g] degens per campos
perque colles et *invia lustra* varias inter feras aliferas exercens pardos, adeo
se laetus in auro, arcu pharetrisque insignis gerebat, *qualis* olim pulcher

---

[a] magistratum

[b] perbelle

[c] praesentiam

[d] elleganter

[e] patrique

[f] nundum

[g] equos

*Apollo* per *hibernam Liciam*[a] *aut per iuga Cynthi* suos *exercere choros*[b] venabulis in armis splendidissimus conspectabatur.

**71.**    Sed enim vero insuper pro bona Kiriaci fortuna, cum ex quadam felici pardorum venatione onustus praeda ad villam quandam se rex inclytus recepisset, et nobilem quendam ex Dacia[c] iuvenem equestris ordinis insignibus decorasset, Kiriacus ad vetustum quoddam monasterium pergens, et libros de more perquirens, abiectos inter et longa squalentes vetustate codices antiquam Homeri Iliadem comperit, quam cum laetus cognovisset, non facile a monaco litterarum[d] ignaro tetravangelico intercedente volumine comparavit. Liber[e] enim ille primum et praedignum Kiriaco auxilium fuit Graecas non omnes litteras ignorare. Habuit et deinde alio a chalochiero in Leucosia Odissiam et Euripidis plerasque tragediasque ac Theodosii grammatici Alexandrini vetustatum codicem, quae omnia, dum aliquod[f] dabatur ociolum, percurrere intelligereque operam diligentissimam[g] dabat.

**72.**    Etenim cum exactis rebus ab insula discedere decrevisset, pro digno de se munere regi optimo hoc sibi ponendae dicandaeque statuae inscribendum epigramma reliquit:

.IANO.CLEMENTIS
SIMO.PRINCI
PI.OPTIMO
NOBILISSQ.HIER
VSALEM CYPRI
ARMENIAEQ.
.REGI.
POPVLVS.CYPRIUS
QVOD SVA INSVPE
RABILI.VIRTVTE
PERENNI CONS
TANTIA.ET.LON

---

[a] litiam

[b] Cf. Virgil, *Aen.* 1.498, 4.143–144, 151.

[c] datia

[d] litteris qui

[e] liberum enim illum

[f] aliquot

[g] diligentisimam

GANIMITATE RE
GNVM.PIENTISSI
MVM HOC PLVRI
FARIAM NEFAN
DORVM
IMMANITATE
INFESTISSIMISQ
COLLAPSVM
PRAELIIS
BARBARICA
DENIQ..
INCVRSIONE
SVBLATA
RESTI
TV
I
T
[ = Apianus and Amantius, p. 506]

**73.**     Postea vero concedens ab eo per Amacosten, navim quandam
Genuensium conscendens, suis Zachariaeque rebus abductis, Rhodum venit,
ubi posteaquam per dies consederat, invenit inter primos et digniores homines
Boetium Tollentinensem optimum heremitani ordinis theologum et metro-
politaneum Rhodianae ecclesiae pontificem, qui eum ut eadem ex provintia
virum pergrate vidit. Et eo duce Kiriachus[a] aliam ibi cognoverat et honorificam
benivolentiam vendicarat Fantini Quirini, Rhodiana religione equestris ordinis
venerandissimi fratris, quibus iuvantibus multa per civitatem et extra per
insulam vidit vetustatum nobilia monumenta antiqua, moenia, columnas,
statuas, bases[b] et Doricis litteris epigrammata, e quis[c] plebis sacerdotis marmoreum caput, Veneream statuam, et Liberi patris imaginem, quas a Graeco
calohiero tum forte defossas emerat et per Bartholomoeum sororium
Anconem[d] ad patriam misit, cum is navi quadam[e] Anconitana Bonifacio
patrono Hierosolima petens Rhodum applicuisset. Viderat ibi praeterea loci
eiusdem amoena pleraque et dulcissima visui prata virentia ac fructiferos

---

[a] Kiriachum

[b] basses

[c] aequis

[d] Anchonem

[e] quandam

regios paradiseos cedros et florentissimos hortos, dignum quarti climatis in orbe[a] specimen et oecumenicae[b] latitudinis medium.

**74.**     Kyriacus vero Thraciam petens exinde per Aegaeum Chium Andreolumque suum revisit, quocum suis compositis rebus, Calliepolim petens inde concessit, et non longe a portu Boreis obviantibus crebris ad Kardamilum eiusdem insulae se bona portum cum navi recepit, ubi cum per dies secundas auras expectantes consisterent, socii Genuenses nonnulli nobiles e navi ad terram desilientes, alii per arbores visco[c] pictas decipiunt aves, alii quidem escatis sub unda hamis varigenos laqueare pisces amabant. Kiriacus vero, ut non omnes diei[d] horas omni ex parte vacuas amitteret, dum Graecos <libros> quos e Cypro nuper adduxerat perlegeret, in Euripidis poetae vitam incidit, quae cum paucis litteris complecteretur Latinam fecit, et apud Chium Andreolo Iustiniano amico incomparabili misit.

**75.**     Postridie vero Austro secundante Cardamilum reliquit Tenedonque venit, et insulam olim nobilem suaeque antiquae civitatis vestigia conspectare placuerat; et inde angustum per Hellespontum ad Threiciam[e] in Cheroneso Calliepolim venit, ubi exoneratis rebus, Petro Simone Polidoro Anconitano negociatore curante, camelis rebus suis onustis, Kiriacus regiam Adrianupolim mediterraneam Thraciae civitatem petit, ubi Iohanne Rimatres Taraconesio negociatore regio intercedente, magni Theucri principis Murath Begh praesentiam regia sua in aula vidit, et magno apparatu saepe equitantem, et spectacula sagitaeque certamina, alto in malo phiala argentea in praemium posita, suos inter conspicuos hippotoxotas lato campo ingenti splendore celebrantem[f] conspexerat. Sed cum ibidem per hyemem ad negotia expedienda moram traxisset, dum aliquid dabatur ocii, Λίω Bolete Graeco grammatico Iliadem Homeri et Hesiodi in re agraria principium audivit, et eo curante ex Thessalonicea praeda Graecos nonnullos codices emit, et praecipue Claudium Ptholomaeum Alexandrinum, geographum insignem sibi accomodatissimum, comparavit. Praeterea Kiriacus ea in civitate cognoverat Nicolaum Ziba, Genuensem virum doctum et negociatorem praestantem, qui semper inter Persas Hircanosque et Parthos versatus in mercemonialibus erat, et cum eo illas quandoque partes visere composuit.

---

[a] orbeo

[b] oecumeniae

[c] viscos

[d] die

[e] trehiciam

[f] celebrante

**76.**     Sed inde cum exacta re concessisset, Calliepolim remeavit. Et cum ea forte tempestate Anconitanam navim Thoma Blasii patrono per Hellespontum velis[a] transeuntem vidisset, ad eam se statim peranterea scapha devectus contulerat, et in ea, coriis[b] tapetisque ad Zachariam transmittendis per Laelium oneratis, Claraque ancilla Chaonia, praeclarae indolis puera, quam ex Theucrorum praeda apud Adrianupolim emerat, eandem[c] per navim Massiellae matri Ciucio consobrino intercedente missa, Calliepolim iterum Nicolino nigro fidissimo liberto suo comitatus[d] revisit, quocum et Theucris comitantibus agogitis nobilissimas Macedoniae partes videre contendit, et per Ematheos Philippicosque campos ad Philipppos ipsam venit, civitatem praeclarissimam, ubi multa veternitatis eximiae monumenta conspexit et temporis labe collapsa[e] de marmore moenia theatrumque et ingentia innumeraque principum atque militum sepulchra, quae inter et ingens in via spectaculum videtur:

C.VIBI.COR.[nelii] MIL.[iti]
V.[quintae] LEG.[ionis] MACE
          DOCAE          [*CIL* III, 647 and 7337]

unico de lapide monumentum, quod hodie Alexandri Bucephali praesepium incertum Graeciae vulgus appellat, prope quod hinc inde pleraque epigrammata comperit et digne suis adiecerat commentariis; quae potissimum loca visere nobilem iuvenis animum incitasse cognovimus, quod apud Nasonem in Fastis de morte[f] divi Caesaris lectitarat:

testes estote Philippi
et quorum sparsis ossibus habet humus.[g]

**77.**     Exinde vero per seras se statim ad Thessalonicam[h] contulit, antiquam Macedoniae atque nobilissimam ad mare urbem, in qua primum egregia inter amplissimae civitatis monumenta vidit medio in foro Pauli Aemilii nostri

---

[a] vellis

[b] coris

[c] eundem

[d] commitatus

[e] colapsa

[f] more

[g] Ovid, *Fasti* 3.707–708

[h] Thesalonicam

mirificum arcum, et diruptum[a] Dianae templum, ex quo marmoreae[b] in epistiliis statuae deorum quam plurimae conspectantur; vidit et nostrae religionis sacras plerasque ornatissimas aedes, in quis potissimum inspectare placuerat nobilissimum Demetrii trophaeafori[c] martyris delubrum; viderat enim insuper antiqua ex Lysimaco turritaque cocto de latere moenia, eiusque et aliorum heroum poetarumque epigrammata; et in tripode Musarum apud Heliconem olim posito de Homeri Hesiodique tempore mentio non vulgaris habetur. Ibi etenim libros plerosque Graecos sacros[d] gentilesque emit, et per birremem apud Chium ad Andreolum suum transmisit.

**78.** Exinde per Adrianopolim se iterum ad Calliepolim contulit, ubi acceptis ex Ancone litteris novit, Martino quinto maximo pontifice defuncto, Eugenium quartum optumum sibi successorem V. Nonas Martias creatum esse, quem cardinalem Senensem Gabrielem Condulmerium Picenni provintiae legatum apud Anconem per biennium fuisse memoravimus, qua de tam digni viri optimi electione[e] laetum Kiriacum statim apud Adrianopolim[f] Nicolao Ziba, et in Liburnia Iaderae Georgio Begnae, in Italia vero Iordano cardinali Ursino, Leonardo Aretino, mihique et aliis amicis plerisque dignis, haec talia scripsisse suis epistolis cognovimus eadem haec fere per verba:

> Ego enim tam magni optumique principis mortem infelicem ecclesiae[g] ac Italis fere omnibus perniciosissimam fore putabam; nunc vero perbeatam magis atque quodammodo opportunam arbitror accessisse, dum tam pium, humanum, clementem, sapientemque et religioni deditissimum hominem sibi delectum successorem intelligo.

Et subiecit:

> Nam et si quando optumus ille *divum pater et hominum rex*[h] Italiam[i] religionemve nostram per sacerdotem quempiam

---

[a] dirruptum

[b] marmore

[c] tropheaphori

[d] sacris

[e] delectatione

[f] Adrianupolim

[g] eclesiae

[h] Virgil, *Aen.* 1.65; 2.648; 10.2, 743

[i] italam

restitutam fore annuerit, ego sub tam optimo pontifice auctam propagatamque videre putem,[a] cum et eum semper se maximis in rebus ecclesiae provide, constanter, aeque, pie magnanimiterque gessisse recolimus.

**79.** Dixit. Et deinde Kiriacus, relicta Persarum quam[b] cum Nicolao Ziba constituerat exploratione, expedire[c] se et Italiam ad patriam remeare ac ipsum ad pontificem sanctissimum maturare[d] decrevit, et sibi, de piissima Graecorum et totius orientalis ecclesiae[e] unione et digna in Theucros expeditione expertior factus, quae pro re digna visa sunt litteris et ore detegere.

**80.** Et ut plenius rem ageret, Memnonem, Karoli[f] olim Cephaloniae magnifici ducis filium, virum elegantem et perstrenuum armis, nuper ex[g] amplissima magni Theucri aula adventantem convenit, a quo pergrate susceptus, multa et praedigna hac[h] de re invicem conserendo, civitates et praecipua loca quae in Asia sub Theucri dictione manebant videre explorareque constituunt; et sic ex Calliepoli per Hellespontum ad Asiam transeuntes Prusam sub Olympo regiam Bythiniae civitatem venere, quam populosam et opulentissimam vidit vetustis novisque ornamentis conspicuam.

**81.** Sed ubi Babylano Palavisino Genuensi, viro nobili et negociatori egregio, curam mercemonalium rerum suarum dederat, ipse una cum Memnone ad Canuza Begh, pro Theucro in provintia satrapem ad Olympi montis diversoria praestolantem,[i] se contulerant; qui ad finem suum Memnonem Kiriacumque, postquam cognoverat, perhumane suscepit. Nam et ille natione Graecus Graeceque perdoctus erat, et multa sibi de antiquis et nobilibus in ea

---

[a] putetis

[b] qua

[c] expidiri

[d] maturae

[e] eclesiae

[f] Kroli

[g] et

[h] ac

[i] praestulantem

provintia rebus et de insigni Cyzicenorum[a] delubro egregie periteque com-
memorabat. Cui Kyriacus, cum ex eiusdem templi ruinis pleraque elaborata
marmorea apud Montaneam, maritimum Prusiae civitatis emporium, ad nova
in urbe aedificia instruenda deducta vidisset, ne tantae aedis vestigium posteris
penitus[b] aboleri videretur, persuasit ne deinceps permitteret ut aliquid ex
parietibus, columnis et epistiliis extantibus tanti nostram ad diem spectaculi
dirueretur,[c] cum ob venerandae antiquitatis pudorem[d] tum et sui magnique
Theucrorum principis honorem. Quae cum vir ille doctus intellexisset
dignissima verba, id se lubens facturum promisit.

**82.**     Et Kyriacus magno eiusdem visendi operis incensus amore, cum
exinde Prusam illico revisisset, agogite quodam ductore Theucro, Cyzicon
nobilissimam Asiae civitatem venit, quae, ut aiebat, ad promuntorium
Propontiaci littoris contra Praeconesiam insulam sita est, sed undique nobilia
magnis undique lapidibus moenia ingentiaque civitatis aedificia immensis
convulsa ruinis solo undique collapsa iacent.

**83.**     Sed extant <et> praecelsa videntur excellentissimi templi vestigia Iovis
altae de marmore parietes, in quis adhuc aurei fili signa conspectantur, quo de
opere[e] C. Plinius in suo de naturali historia libro inquit: Durat et Cyzici[f] delubrum
in quo filum aureum commissuris omnibus politi lapidis[g] subiecit artifex, et
reliqua. Stant et ornatissima in fronte aedis diversaque deorum simulachra, et
ex longo ordine columnarum amplissimae bases,[h] et quamvis maiori ex parte
columnae solo collapsae sint tres[i] et triginta numero adhuc suis cum
epistiliis erectae videntur, ubi tale Kyriacus Graecum exceperat epigramma:

.ΕΚ.ΔΑΠΕΔΟΥ.
ΜΩΡΘΩΣΕΝ.
ΟΛΛΗΣ.ΑΕΙΑΣ.
.ΑΦΘΟΗΙΗ.
ΧΕΙΡΩΝ.ΔΙΟΣ.
ΑΡΙΣΤΕΗΩΤΟΣ.

[Ashmole 1956, pp. 187–188]

---

[a] Cyricenorum

[b] poenitus

[c] dirrueretur

[d] podorem

[e] ope

[f] Cyrici

[g] lapidibus

[h] basses

[i] tris

Et alia hic inde per urbem epigrammata comperit, ac ingentes de marmore
portas amphiteatrique vestigia, et magnum terriquatientis[a] Neptuni simulachrum, atque omnia conspectanda eum perbelle excitasse ferebat. Haec
eadem quae apud Nasonem poetam elegantissima[b] lectitarat elegia:

Hinc et Propontiacis haerentem Cyzicon[c] oris
Cyzicon[d] Aemoniae nobile gentis opus.

**84.**    Exinde vero cum Prusam revisisset, relictis Babylano reliquiis,
Zachariae nomine rebus et compositis, cum Memnone pro expeditione in
Theucros agendis cum pontifice conditionibus Italiam per Bizantium remeare
constituens, ut Nicaeam nobilem Bythiniae civitatem videret, terrestri itinere
agogite Theucro ducente Constantinopolim petit; et cum ad ipsam paulo extra
iter[e] Nycaeam civitatem venisset, eam ad lacus Bythiniae ripas turritis cocto
de latere moenibus sitam invenit, et ad portam TI. CLAVDI GERMANICI, ad
turrim vero Traiani epigrammata Graeca comperuit, et talia per urbem egregia
veterum monumenta conspexit, et magnam oecumenicae[f] illius celeberrimae[g]
synodi basilicam.

**85.**    Exinde die noctuque iter adcelerans[h] per silvas et difficilia loca, ad
Calcedoniam Bythiniae deletam[i] vetustate maritimam urbem, vicinum Bizantii
emporium quod hodie Scutorion dicitur, venit, et illico scapha Galatheam
Peram magnamque Constantinopolim revisit, ubi Pascalinum Anconitanum
consanguineum suum sua cum navi post mensem Anchonem ad patriam
navigaturum invenit; et ne interim vacuum tempus amitteret,[j] et <ut> dignum
quid per Asiam indagaret, se apud Chium insulam transeuntem per Aegaeum
navim expectaturum composuit.

---

[a] terri quantis

[b] ellegantissima

[c] Cyricon

[d] Cyricon

[e] inter

[f] occamenici

[g] celleberrime

[h] adcellerans

[i] delectam

[j] ammiteret

**86.** Exinde Tarraconensi bireme devectus, Lesbeam Mitilennum, egregiam et olim potentissimam civitatem, adivit, ubi Georgio Gathalusio praeside favitante plurima civitatis insignia vidit: theatra, columnas, statuas, bases,[a] inscriptionesque Graecas atque Latinas et conspicuum de marmore arcum, quem Tetrastilon dicunt, olim per praesidem insularum

.FL.VALERIO
DIOCLITIANO
CONSTANTIO
ET
MAXIMIANO
NOBILIS
SIMO
DEDICATVM.                    [*CIL* III, 450]

**87.** Deinde vero acceptis a praeside ad Theucros in Asia correctores[b] litteris, visis et antea per insulam altis et antiquis de marmore aquarum ductibus et urbium Pyrriae Methymnaeque disiectis vetustate muris, exiguam per cymbam ad Asiathicum proximum littus venit, et inde Pergameam ad nobilem et olim metropolitanam[c] Asiae civitatem adscendit et indigena ducente Theucro amplam undique urbem perscrutavit et ingentes hinc inde vetustatum reliquias inspexit: immania templa, duo maxima amphiteatra, collosseaque nonnulla de marmore deorum heroumve simulachra, et egregia inter sepulchra ingens et magnis editum[d] lapidibus instar altissimi montis tumulum.[e] Quin et omnigenum denique nobilium antiquitatum vestigia vidit et egregia pleraque Graecis Latinisque litteris epigrammata.

**88.** Exinde se ad Aeoliam Cumem, antiquissimam Hesiodi patriam et longi temporis labe collapsam civitatem, adierat. Hodie et ab incolis Chrysopolim vocitatam audierat; et cum ibi[f] nil notatione dignum vidisset, Ioniam venit et Smyrnas antiquam eiusdem regionis urbem et Homeri praeclari nominis insignem vidit. Nam et ibi vetusto in lapide comperit epigramma quod illam Homeri patriam[g] fuisse significabat, ubi pleraque suae vetustatis vestigia, portum insignem, et cocleam altissimam columnam inspexit.

---

[a] basses

[b] correptores

[c] metrapolitanam

[d] aeditus

[e] tumulus

[f] ubi

[g] portam

**89.** Inde vero Phocaeas vetustam novamque venerat et ingentes inibi aluminum[a] mineras vidit, ubi Fredericum Iustinianum Andreoli sui socerum eiusdem loci patronum offendit, ac eo iuvante aurea Philippi, Alexandri Lysimachique numismata insignia comparavit.

**90.** Exinde vero ad littus quod[b] est in conspectu[c] Chii insulae venerat, ubi perenteream scapham conscendens Chium urbem Andreolumque suum revisit ac Nicolinum nigrum libertum, qui ex Calliepoli reliquis rebus suis scriniisque adductis eum praevenerat [et] patronum expectaturus. Et ibi[d] Kyriacus per dies apud ipsum Andreolum cum lectitando Graecos[e] quos ad eum e Thessalonica[f] libros miserat, aptando tum suas quascumque res expediendo, Pascalineam e Bizantio navim expectans, morabatur.

**91.** Interea cum magnam Venetum classem Chium hostiliter impetere crebra fama Aegaeum fere totum excitasset, Anconitana navis Paschalino quem supra memoravimus praefecto Chium applicuit. Cuiusce civitatis ordo, ne forte ab ea transeunte hostes de iis novi quid exploratum haberent, Pascalineam navim in portu firmari iussit. Sed cum quartum[g] post diem, Andreolo Kiriaci gratia intercurante, Maonenses eam libere navigare permisissent, eadem in navi Kiriacus ipse suis impositis rebus concessit, et apud Cassiopeum Corcirae insulae portum in Venetianam classem incidit. Sed Andreae Mucenigo praefecto oblatis Genuensium litteris, expedita navis per Illyricum tandem Anconitanum ad portum applicuit.

**92.** Ubi postquam suos incolumes Kiriacus revisit, suis expeditis rebus, paucos post dies una cum Astorgio Anconitano pontifice ad urbem maximum ad pontificem Eugenium se contulerat, quem ad magnam Petri basilicae aulam, Aloisio optumo cubiculario suo curante, vidit et sibi primum duo hydrochoa Indica porcellanea auro elaborata speciosissima vasa dono dederat; et multa deinde sibi de excolendissima Graecorum unione, ac dignissima in Theucros expeditione, Memnonisque optuma hac in re compensatione, ore litterisque perbellissime declaravit. Qui optumus et prudentissimus pater Kiriacum primo

---

[a] alaminum

[b] quidem

[c] spectu

[d] ubi

[e] graecosque

[f] thesalonica

[g] quantum

ut devotum filium perbenigne suscepit, et omnia ab se delata audierat et optima in mente reposita, ad ea se pro tempore diligentem operam daturum promisit.

**93.**    Interea Kiriacus, ut proximas extra urbem vetustates indagaret, Tybur antiquissimam civitatem petierat; et per celebrem Tyburtinam viam hinc inde multa veternitatis monumenta conspexit, et ad pontem Lucanum Marci Plauci insignia triumphalia ornamenta regiosque Hadriani Caesaris hortos,[a] quorum pleraque videntur ornatissima scenarum spectacula.

P.PLAVTIVS

PVLCHER.TRIVM

PHALIS.AVGVR

III.VIR.A.A.A.F.F.

Q.TI.CAESARIS

AVG.V.CONSVLIS

TR.PL.PR.AED.AE

RAR.COMES.DR

VSI.FILI.GERMA

NICI.AVVNCVLVS

DRVSI.TI.CLAVDI

CAESARIS.AVGVS

TI.FILI.ET.AB.EO

CENSORES.INTER

PATRITIOS.LAET

VS.CVRATOR.VI

ARVM.STERNEN

DARVM.A VICINIS

LAETVS.EX.AVCTO

RITATE.TI.CLAV

DI.CAESARIS.AVG

GERMANICI.PRO

COS.PROVINTIAE

SICILIAE

VIBIA.MARCI.FIL

LAELIA.NATA

PVLCHRA                        [*CIL* XIV, 3607]

**94.**    Et Tiburtinam ipsam denique civitatem altis in collibus eminentem viderat, et eximia vetustatum vestigia et sacram Saxono Herculi atque dirruptam aedem.

---

[a] ortos

HERCVLI
SAXONO SACRVM
SEX.SVLPITIVS
TROPHIMVS AEDEM
ZOTHECAM CVLLI
NAM PECVNIA SVA
A SOLO
RESTITVIT.IDEMQ.
DEDICAVIT.K.DECEMBR
L.TVRPILIO DEXTRO
M.MOETIO RVPHO
COS.T.VTHYCVS
PERAGENDVM CVRAVIT.     [*CIL* XIV, 3543]

**95.**     Tiburtinaeque Sybillae colosseum de marmore caput[a] vidit, et ingentes Germanici Caesaris aquarum ductus per quos clarus ille princeps caeruleos cursus[b] amoenosque fontes in urbem aere suo perducendos curavit. Viderat et Cymbricum pontem quem Salarium dicunt et nobilem unico ex lapide M. ANTONII ANTIL. PR. tumulum secus Tyberim ad quartum ab urbe lapidem situm, ac alia ex parte insignem illum quattuor e marmoribus integris turlum una cum Iordano Ursino venerandissimo cardinale prospexit, et Martini pontificis incuriam, qui opus egregium dirui[c] permiserat, accusavit.

**96.**     Et inde Hostiensem ad portum se contulit et insignia antiquitatis suae vestigia conspexit et ab eo non longe Traiani optumi principis amplissimum navistatium.

**97.**     At enim cum inde ad urbem remeasset, Sigismundum inclytum Pannoniae regem et designatum <imperatorem> [in] Romam petiturum Italiam Senasque venisse perceperat.[d] Cuius legati,[e] Gaspar regius secretarius et Comus pontifex, ad Eugenium pontificem maximum venere; et ubi de adventu imperatoris ad urbem Cardinale de Comitibus et Berardo de Camerino, non

---

[a] capud

[b] curtios

[c] dirrui

[d] percoeperat

[e] legata

absque Kiriaci persuasionibus, composuerat, Senis ad principem redeuntes Kiriacum comitem habentes[a] aditum sibi ad Caesarem praebuere; a quo perhumane susceptus, multa et praedigna sibi Kiriacus de rebus gestis maiestati, honori dignitatique suae congruentibus et dignis in barbaros expeditionibus applicavit. Et sibi utique peregregium[b] munus dederat aureum Traiani[c] Caesaris numisma, ut optumi principis imitandi[d] exemplar haberet, et Anconem potissime patriam eodem ab principe exornatam memoria quandoque recenseret. Qui munificus princeps, Brunoro della Scalla Veronensi[e] Baptistaque Cygala Genuensi[f] adstantibus, claris consiliariis suis, Kiriacum caesarea familiaritate donavit.

**98.**     Et cum postea inde ad urbem ab Eugenio maximo pontifice aureo diademate insignitus maximis intentus negociis versaretur, et ex Liburnia illustres[g] comites[h] Stephanus Bartholusque Phrygipenates, Seniae civitatis principes, Romam ad eundem Sigismundum visendum[i] venissent, cum his Kiriacus ad eum se iterum contulit; et cum sibi et comiti[j] Mathaeo[k] claro praefecto suo coeptis[l] de rebus recensendo multa saepius retulisset, ad ea se lubentissime optumo cum pontifice paratum respondit, sed antea ad perniciosam Basiliensium coniurationem dissolvendam operam dare oportere.

---

[a] habentibus

[b] pro egregium

[c] Traianum

[d] immitandi

[e] veronense

[f] genuense

[g] illustri

[h] comitaes

[i] viscendum

[j] comites

[k] Mathico

[l] caeptis

**99.**     Praeterea dum tanto cum principe Kiriacus ingentes vetustatum reliquias undique per urbem[a] disiectas[b] aspexisset, ut gravi lacessitus iniuria, talibus denique dictis, Latinorum afflatus numine,[c] principem excitarat:

> Equidem non parum putabam caesarei principis animum lacessere, quod qui nunc vitam agunt Romana inter moenia homines, marmorea ingentia atque ornatissima undique per urbem aedificia, statuas insignes, et columnas tantis olim sumptibus, tanta maiestate, tantaque fabrorum architectorumve arte conspicuas et nobilia in his magnarum epigrammata rerum, ita ignave, turpiter et obscene in dies ad albam tenuemque[d] convertunt[e] cinerem, ut eorum nullam brevi tempore speciem vestigiumve posteris apparebit. Proh scelus! et o, vos inclytae Romulae gentis manes, aspicite *haec meritumque malis advertite numen.*[f] Nam et ea praeclara sunt veterum monumenta, virorumque nobilis praesertim animos ad res maximas gerendas et ad gloriae et immortalitatis studium vehementer accendunt.[g]

Qui optimus princeps ignavam[h] hominum incuriam vituperans, nobilem iuvenis animum harum rerum curiosissimum laudavit.

**100.**     Kiriacus vero deinde cum ceteras[i] et praeclaras Italiae urbes videre indagareque maluisset, Pisas antiquam et olim insignem Tuscorum civitatem adivit, et eiusdem quaeque insignia vetusta novaque conspexit, et multa temporis labe hominumve incuria solo undique collapsa videntur; et quod magis adnotatione dignum considerasse aiebat, marmoream cathedralis ecclesiae domum et insigne illud et ornatissumum cimiterion, quod incolae Campum Sanctum appellant.

---

[a] orbem

[b] desiectas

[c] nummine

[d] tenuenque

[e] coruertunt

[f] Cf. Virgil, *Aen.* 4.611: accipite haec meritumque malis advertite numen

[g] accedunt

[h] ignaviam

[i] ceteris

**101.**    Exinde vero Florentiam venit, Fluentinam olim clarissimam Romanorum coloniam, nunc vero Tuscorum insignem[a] et omnium florentissimam Latinorum urbem, ubi praeclara multa et insignia rerum ornamenta vidit, et primum amplissima vivo de lapide moenia, portas deinde regias, et latissima strata viarum, sacra et superis ingentiaque delubra, quae inter ad coelum alta testudine attolentem vidit maximam illam et insignem[b] beatae Reparatae Virginis aedem, quod et mirificum opus Philippo ductante nobilissimo architecto omni ex parte perspexit, et marmoream ornatissimam Cienceriam turrim; sed in conspectu conspicuum illud et marmoreum divi olim Martis, nunc vero Baptistae Ioannis sanctissimi delubrum, tribus[c] aeneis ornatissimis[d] divinae historiae portis exornatum, partim eximium Nencii[e] nobilis fabrifactoris opus, et intus ab alto undique pendentibus aureis purpureisque civitatum vectigalium[f] donis completum; alta quoque magistratuum[g] praetoria et turritas arces, scenas publicas et privatas, civiumque palatia, et conspicuas undique per urbem aedes, et denique ad Arni fluvii ripas lapideos quattuor et amplissimos pontes, Rubacontem, Veterem, Sanctae Trinitatis, et Carrareum, ac ingentia in foro Leonum ferrea publicaeque libertati dedicata claustra.

**102.**    Etenim exoptabilius quoque viderat amplissimos inter cives Cosmam Medicem, Nicolaum Uzanum, Pallam Strocium, et inter clariores Leonardum Arretinum illum Latinorum doctissimum, Karolumque, et Philelphum Picenum[h] nostrum, quos inter avidius vidisse memorabat Nicolaum Nicolum, illum aetate nostra biblicultorem insignem et unicum Philadelphi illius studiosissimi Ptholomaei Alexandrini diligentissimum consectatorem,[i] quo cum curiosissimo viro multa de antiquis dignissimis in orbe rebus compertis per nobilissimas Asiae et Europae per orientem urbes, perque Ionicas insulas et Aegaeas, non absque iucunditate invicem conferebantur; et potissimum de mirifico Cyzicenorum[j] delubro vir diligens audire gaudebat. Et interim una

---

[a] insignem *inserted later, same hand*

[b] insigne

[c] tris

[d] ornatissimus

[e] *in margin, same hand*: Nencii

[f] victigalium

[g] magistratum

[h] picennum

[i] consectorem

[j] Cyricenorum

cum Karolo Aretino, visa eximia bibliotheca sua, nummis[a] imaginibusque antiquis, et insigni Pyrgotelis lupercalis[b] sacerdotis simulachri cavata ex nicolo gemma, et talarati aeneo[c] MERCVRII agalmate, videre simul et Kosmae viri opulentissimi preciosa multa eiusdem generis supellectilia.[d]

**103.** Et apud Donatellum[e] Nenciumque, statuarios nobiles, pleraque vetusta novaque ab <eis> edita ex aere marmoreve simulachra, et demum, Leonardo Arretino amicissimo suo curante, regio in civitatis praetorio apud amplissimum ordinem viderat antiqua illa e Pisis deducta legalia Pandectarum volumina, et denique extra moenia apud egregium Cartusiense monasterium viderat insignia sacrorum monumenta pleraque et Chrysostomi clarissimi doctoris caput et eximium Flavii Iosephi de Iudaica antiquitate librum.

**104.** Sed quod potissimum adnotari placuit, alto in colle adscendens viderat Fesulanae[f] antiquissimae civitatis moenia magnis undique lapidibus condita, et collapsi amplissimi amphitheatri vestigia.

**105.** Postea vero Mediolanum petens per Bononiam Mutinam venit, antiquam Togatae Galliae civitatem, ubi plerasque vetustatis suae reliquias comperit et epigrammata pleraque nobilia, quae Scipionis sui optimi pontificis gratia adnotanda et suis digne commentariis reponenda CVRAVIT.

MEMORIAE
.L.PEDVCEAE
.IVLIANAE.
MORIB.NATAL.AC
PVD.PRISCIS INLV
STRIBQ.FOEMI.IN
COMPARAND.QVAE
VIXIT.ANNOS
.XIII.
.D.XLVII.CVM MA
RITO FECIT.ME.
.V.D.XX.
L.NONIVS.VER.                    [*CIL* XI, 832]

---

[a] numis

[b] luparcalis

[c] talerati aenea

[d] suppellectilia

[e] *in margin, same hand*: donatellus

[f] Fessulanae

**106.** Ad marmoreum tumulum.

D.M
P.VETTIO
P.FIL.CAM.SABI
NO.EQ.P.IIII.VIR
AED.POT.ET MAG.
MVN.RAVEN.
CORNELIA MAX
IMINA.MARITO
INCOMPARAB.ET
SIBI.VIVA.POSVIT          [*CIL* XI, 863]

**107.** Alio in tumulo in foro posito.

V.F
CLODIA
PLAVTILLA SIBI
ET.QVERCONIO
AGATHONI
MARITO OPTIMO
ET LVCIFERAE
.LIB.
IN.FR.P.XX.IN.AGR.P.XX.
.H.M.H.N.S.          [*CIL* XI, 884]

**108.** Ad sepulchrum alterum marmoreum.

BRUTT.AVRELIANAE
C.FILIAE MVSOLANAI
PATRON.ET ASTERI
AE.C.F.NEPTI MAR
CELLINAE
.X.COMIT.ET.MARI
NAE.ET.GALLIGANI
.COSS.
ORDINARI.QVAE.VIX.
ANN.XXXVII.MENS.
.X.DIES.XVIIII.
OB MERITA HO
NESTATIS ET CON
CORDIAE CONIUGA
LIS.FL.VITALIS.V.C.
.PROTEG.
ET NOTARIVS VXORI
AMANTISSIMAE.ET.SIBI          [*CIL* XI, 830]

**109.**    In fundamentis campanilis[a]    cum quattuor figuris.
C.SALVIVS.C.L.                SALVIA.C.F.
AVCTVS APOLL                  PRIMA FECIT
.V.                           .V.
P.PLOTIVS.P.L.                SOSIA.ƆL.
VRBANVS APOLL.                AMARYLLIS

[*CIL* XI, 855]

*[drawing of two heads]*                *[drawing of two heads]*

**110.**    In episcopatu in ornatissimo lapide.
D.M
C.MATERNIO
QVINTIANO
VETERANO
EXPRAETOR
MATERNIA
BENIGNA
FILIA
.E.M.AVRELIVS
MAXIMVS
GENER
OB
MERITA EIVS                [*CIL* XI, 839]

**111.**    Inde vero per Regium Lepidi[b] Parmam venit, egregiam civitatem, et apud cathedralem Beatae Virginis aedem sacra Largi, Cyriaci et Smaragdi monumenta conspexit, et ante templi postes Macrobii nostri memorabile indigne neglecto epigrammate monumentum.

**112.**    Exinde itaque concedens, Placentia Ticinoque visis, et una cum Antonio Panormita Augustini sanctissimi episcopi, Severinique Boetii et paucis aliis vetustatum monumentis compertis, ad exoptatam denique Mediolanum nobilissimam Insubrium civitatem venit, quam amplissimis[c] munitam suburbiis, copiosam rerumque omnigenum opulentissimam vidit, vetustis tam et novis conspicuam ornamentis.

**113.**    Vidit praeterea Nicolaum Floro Flavianum, amicum antiquissimum suum et optumum ducalem ad aerarium quaestorem, qui postquam eum

---

[a] campanillis

[b] Laepidi

[c] amplissimus

perbenigne susceperat, cum eiusdem epistolares orationes ad inclytum Philippum ducem illico detulisset, Urbano Iacobo optimo suo intercurante secretario, Kiriaci annuente principe votis, nobilia multa vetustatum monumenta viderat, et insignia Latinis litteris epigrammata[a] suis adiecerat commentariis, et primum in quodam scalarum[b] gradu aulae ducalis celeberrimae:

.O.V.F.

MAG.STATIAE

MAG.VXORI.ET

C.RVFIONI PATRI

ET

CASSIAE MATRI

TRIBONIAE HILA

RAME ET GINIO

MODE                    [*CIL* V, 6099]

**114.**   Apud divae Theglae delubrum vetustissimum.[c]

.V.F. . D.M.

MAGIVS

PARDION

SIBI ET

OPPIAE VALERIANAE

CONIVGI.ET.Q.OPPIO

CONSTITVTO                    [*CIL* V, 6037]

**115.**   In aedium pariete Henrici Panigarolae.

PLVTIAE HERMIONI

ATILIA HERMIONE

ET

ATILIVS GALLICA

MATRI

DVLCISSIMAE                    [*CIL* V, 6069]

**116.**   Apud sanctum Marcum.

FVFIA  SYNORIS

CHRYSIPPO

CONIUGI

FEC

I

T                    [*CIL* V, 6008]

---

[a] epigramma

[b] scallarum

[c] delubro vetustissimo

117. In ripa fossae urbanae.

L.VALERIO VIRILLI
ONI.VI.VIR.IVN.FRA
TRI PIISSIMO VRAD
SARIO.SACCONIS.F.
PATRI
TERTIAE TREXAE MAT.
SEPTVMIAE SECVND.SEP
TVMIAE EXORATAE.FILIAB.
VALERIAE TERTVLLAE VA
LERIAI VRBANAI SORO
RIB.LAETILIO BLANDO
VALERIAE SPICVLAE
VEGETO.LIBERT.AL
FRIMVS.CENS.
.T.F.I.                          [*CIL* V, 5896]

118. In urbanarum muro fossarum.

D.M
MARIAE.FESTIVAE
QVAE VIXIT.ANN.XX
XIIII.M.II.DIES.V.
MARIVS
MONTANVS.DOMINAE
ET CONIVG KARISSIMAE
OB EXIMIAM ERGA SE
PVDICITIAM
ET MARIA FESTA
ET MARIVS HIPPOLYTVS
MATRI KARISSIMAE              [*CIL* V, 6039]

119. In fossae muro urbanae.

D.M
SEX TRVTTEDIO
SEX.F.POL.SABINO
INFANTI DVLCISSI
MO.SEX.TRVTTEDIVS
CLEMENS.PATER    [*CIL* IX, 5931, Ancona]

120. Ad sanctum seraphicum.

VALERIVS.QVI
VIXIT.IN.SECVLO
.ANN.XL.
.M.X.D.V.IANVARIVS

EXORCISTA
SIBI ET CONIVGI FECIT [*CIL* V, 6276]

**121.** In aula post divi Nazarii phanum in hostii parte.
C.ALLIVS.PVD.
SIBI ET
NOVELLIAE FVSCAE
VXORI
.C.ALLIO MAXIMO
.C.ALLIO FVSCIANO
.C.ALLIONI GELLIONI
ET.NOVELLIVS VERVS [*CIL* V, 5940]

**122.** In urbanarum muro fossarum.
M.IVNIO PATRONO.P.M.
PIENTISSIMO.ET
.P.VARIO.EVTYCHO
CONIVG.DVLCISS.LIBERTIS
LIBERTAB.IN.FR.P.XV.IN.AG.P.XV. [*CIL* V, 6024]

**123.** Alio in loco.
D.M
NOVELLIVS
AEQVALIS
SIBI ET EGNATIAE
L.F.PRIMIGENIAE
VXORI
CARISSIMAE
ET SECVNDO
MATVRO.MESSA
LAE SVCCESSORI
MODESTO
LIBERTIS SVIS
.T.F.I. [*CIL* V, 6051]

**124.** In urbanarum muro fossarum
MORTARIAE
P.F.PIISS.MASCEL
LIO FELIX.ET
LVTATIA.CHRI
STINA.FILIO
DVLCISSIMO
MEMORIAM
POSVERUNT

CONTRA
VOTVM                        [*CIL* V, 6045]

**125.** In aula divi Simpliciani.

M.VALERIVS
MAXIMVS
SACERDOS
D.S.I.M.STV.
ASTROLOGIAE
SIBI.ET
SEVERIAE APR
VXORI
.H.M.H.N.S.                  [*CIL* V, 5893]

**126.** In divi Nazari delubro.

FAVSTVS.VI.VIR
ET.AVGVST.QVI
INTER.PRIMOS
AVGVSTALES.A
DECVRIONIBVS
AVGVSTALIS FAC
TVS.EST.VIRIAE
MAXIMAE VXORI
CARISS.ET.VRSO
LVPVLLONI LIBERTIS
FVTVRIS                      [*CIL* V, 5859]

**127.** In palatii[a] fronte praetoriani.[b]

C.ATILIVS
C.F
SECVNDVS
SIBI.ET
VALERIAE
P.L.CROCIN.
VXORI
SVAE.ET.IVVENI
VERNAE.SVAE.VIX.
A.X                          [*CIL* V, 5959]

---

[a] palatio

[b] praetoriano

**128.** In vetustissima basi[a] sancti Dyonisi.

D.M
.I.O.M.IMMQ.
MAXIMI.ET.MAXIMAI
CALVINI MAXIMVS
MATRI
INCOMPARABILI              [*CIL* V, 6041]

**129.** Ad sanctum Petrum.

D.M
Q.VITELLI
SATVRNINI
VITELLII
VERANIVS
ET CONSTANS
VI.VIR
IVNIORES
PATRI.OPTIMO              [*CIL* V, 5905]

**130.** In aulae porticu[b] post sancti Amabilis[c] phanum.

.P.VRSIO
SEX.FIL
POLLIONI
PATRI VETTIAE
LEPIDAE  MATRI
P.VRSIO.P.F.PAVLO
VI VIR IVN.FRATR.
CVR.AER
P.VRSIO ELAINO
.F.PIISS.
VRSIA.P.F.PRISCA              [*CIL* V, 5906]

**131.** Iuxta sancti Marci templum.

C.SATTIVS
.C.L.FELIX
SIBI ET
C.SATTIO
.C.F.

---

[a] vetustissimo bassi

[b] porticum

[c] Amabili

.O.V.F.
PATRO
NO      [*CIL* V, 6083]

**132.** In sancti Georgii templo in basi quadam.
V.F
ATILIVS.MAC
RINVS.SECVNDVS
ATILIO.MACRINO
.PATRI.
ET.SVRAE.PVPAE
.MATRI.
ET.MACRINO
PRIMO.FRAT.
ET.MACRINAE
.SECVNDIN.      [*CIL* V, 5956]

**133.** In pariete sancti Stephani.
P.VALERIO
.P.LIBERTO
.PALAT.
TACITO
VI.VIRO.SENI
ORI.ET.AVGVSTALI      [*CIL* V, 5895]

**134.** Apud sanctae Mariae templum secretum in basi.
L.ARVLENVS
ANOPTES
APOLLINI      [*CIL* V, 5762]

**135.** In divi Victoris templo.
D.M
AMANTIO
DVLCISSIMO
POSVERVNT
PARENTES
VERNA
PATER
ET LVPVLA MATER
.FILIO.
INNOCENTISSI
MO      [*CIL* V, 5942]

**136.**   Apud sanctum Nazarium in basi.

DIIS.MAN

L.REYNO PHI

LETO AMATORI          [Not found]

**137.**   Ibi prope.

DIIS.MAN

L.GRAECINIO

POMPEIANO.ANIMVLAE

.IVCVNDISS.

QVI VIXIT ANNOS

XXIIII.MATER POSVIT

AEMILIA POMPEIA

SIBI          [*CIL* V, 6019]

**138.**   In basi quadam apud sancti Donini templum.

IOVI

IVNONI

MINERVAE

Q.VOCONIVS

EX

VOTO          [*CIL* V, 5771]

**139.**   Apud Brutianum rus agri Mediolanensis.

V.F

C.FABIVS

PLACENTINVS

SIBI.ET

COELIAE

OLYMPIADI

UXORI

AMANTISS.

ET.SVIS          [*CIL* V, 6006]

**140.**   In foribus sancti Bartholomoei templi.

.V.F.

M.SVLPICIVS

M.F.ACCEPTVS

SIBI.ET.M.SVLPICIO

.CASTO.

PATRONO

EROTI CENNAMO

CONLIBERTIS.PAT

RONI.ET.L.LVCILIO

FLORO AMICO          [*CIL* V, 6100]

**141.** In phani foribus sancti Bartholomoei.

V.F
Q.CAMPILIVS
Q.F
VIRILLIO VI.VIR
.IVN.SIBI.ET.
TATINIAE.M.F.
VERAE.UXORI
Q.CAMPILIO
PATRI
CASTRICIAE
CONDEXVAE
MATRI                    [*CIL* V, 5853]

**142.** In fossarum muro urbicarum.

CISALPINI
L.T
TRANSALPINI
.PATR.
COLL.NAVT.
COMENS
HERED.FAC.CVR.          [*CIL* V, 5911]

**143.** Ad sanctum Marcum.

I.O.M
C.CASSIVS.C.F.
T^HYRSVS.VI.VIR
V.S.L.M.                [*CIL* V, 5776]

**144.** Derthonae ante postes monacorum sancti Martiani.

C.ORISCVS
ECNATI.FRON
TONIS
ET.IVLIAE.EVTYCHI
LIBERTI.FILIVS
ANN.XVI.HIC
ADQVIESCIT             [*CIL* V, 7386]

**145.** In fossae muro urbanae.

D.M.
RAMMIAE
CALLITYCHE
FILIAE PIENTISS.       [Not found]

**146.** Apud Tradatem veterem Mediolanensem vicum.

VOTIS OMNIB.
CAELESTIB.CONSEN
TIENTIB.BENEVERTEN
TIBQ
L.PARIVS.HERMES [*CIL* V, 5634]

**147.** In silvis procul a Tradate litteris inscriptis videntur:

TREBVC.
CARPENTVM
BONA.NOCTE
VADE.DORMITVM [Not found]

**148.** Mediolani extra portam Comensem in aede sancti Simpliciani in ornatissimo tumulo.

.Q.VIRI SEVERINI.
ATTIA SEVERINA.ET.Q.VIRIVS
ONESAS PARENTES
Raptus ego superis patribusque ablatus inique
Cum frui debueram aetate florida luce
His requiesco locis vitam cui fata negarunt
Praecipitem memet superi mersere sub aulas
Ac tumulo mersere gravi usus et arsque
Mihi fuerat studioso corde reperta
Maxima quadripedum cura studia quoque plura
Fuerunt ingenio semper plenus probitate beatus
Et quandoque simul patribus finito limine vitae
Manibus his quieti pariter sociavimur una
Quisque legis doleas diu pes talia fata
QVI.VIXIT.ANNOS.XXVIIII
MENS.V.D.V
ET.ATTIO.EPICTETO.LIBERT. [*CIL* V, 6128]

**149.** In alio lapide.

V.F
AVE.ALCIME.BENE
TIBI.SIT
D.M.
C.IVLIO ALCIMO
RAVENNATI
COMPARATOR
MERCIS SVTORIAE
ET VIRIAE MARCELL
CONIVGI OPTIMAE

ET HERMIAE.LIB.ET
CAETERIS LIBERTIS
LIBERTABQ.MEIS
ET VIRIAE MARCELLAE
.H.M.H.N.S.                                    [*CIL* V, 5927]

**150.**      Derthonae in marmore ecclesiae maioris.[a]
QVART.COMINIVS
.C.F.SIBI ET
TERTIAE PETRONIAE
M.F.VXORI ET
L.COMINIO.C.F.ET
C.COMINIO C.F.
FRATRIBVS ET
TERTIAE COMINIAE
SORORI ET
AMPLIATO ET FELICI
.LIB.                                          [*CIL* V, 7385]

**151.**      Et extra utique Ticinianae arcis ab antiquae gentis origine gestarum rerum insignes machinarum reliquias, preciosamque supellectilem, hortosque regios, et ingentia ferarum claustra, nobile sui magnificentissimi parentis opus, inspexerat, et Claraevallis Cartusiensiumque nobilia monasteria.

**152.**      Deinde vero se Brixiam contulit, ubi plura veternitatis conspexit, videlicet:

L.CHAMVRIVS
L.L.PANDARVS
IIIIII.VIR.AVG
SIBI ET
ZENONI.LIBERTO                                 [*CIL* V, 4403]
*[no heading]:*
.L.
.C.M.I.
IN.FR.P XX                                     [*CIL* V, 4639]
IN AG P XX

**153.**      In lapide aquae sanctae in aede sanctae Iuliae.
D.M
L.CAELI.ARRIAN.
MEDICO LEGIONIS

---

[a] maiori

.II.ITALIC.QVI.VIX.
ANN.XXXXVIIII.MEN.
SIS[a].VII.SCRIBONIA
FAVSTINA
CONIVGI
KARISSIMO                    [*CIL* V, 4367]

**154.**   Alio in loco.

M.NONIO.M.F.
FAB.ARRIO PAVLINO
APROCI XV.VIR.SACR.
FAC.CVLTORES.LAVDVM
EIVS                         [*CIL* V, 4340]

**155.**   Alio in lapide.

CAECILIAE.L.F.
MACRINAE.P.
SENECIVS GARVLLVS
F.AB HEREDIBVS
TESTAMENT
F.I                          [*CIL* V, 4470]

*[no heading]:*

L.VALERIVS
MARCELLINVS
.L.D.NEPOS.D.D.              [*CIL* V, 4332]

**156.**   Alio in marmore.

P.CLODIO.P.F.
FAB.SVRAE
Q.FLAMINI DIVI
TRAIANI PONTIF
II VIR.QVINQ.TRIB.
LEG.II.ADIVTRIC.
PIAE.FID.CVRAT
REI.P.BERGOM.
DATO.AB.IMP.TRA
IANO.CVRAT.REI
.P.COMENS.DAT AB
IMP.HADRIANO
COLLEGIA FABROR
.ET.CENT.                    [*CIL* V, 4368]

---

[a] MEN/SISIS

**157.** In aede sancti Bartholomei in monte.

ACCEPTO CHIAE
SERVO LANARI
PECTINARI
SODALES.POSVER          [*CIL* V, 4501]

**158.** In aede sancti Sandri.

.B.M.IN PACE
FLANIGO SCVTA
RIVS SCOLA TER
TIA QVI VIXIT.ANN.
.L.M.XXV.ET
MILITAVIT.AN.VI.CO
GNATVS DVLCISSIMVS
SORORIO AMANTISS.          [*CIL* V, 4369]

**159.** Alio in marmore.

QVINTIA RESTITVTA
C.PETRONO FAB.FRON
TONI.VI.VIR AVG.BRIX.
OB MERITA VIRO PIEN
TISSIMO          [*CIL* V, 4463]

**160.** Prope turrim de la Palata in pariete domus privatae.

COLLEGIA.FABR.ET
CENT.L.CORNELIO
PROSODICO VI.VIR
AVG.BRIX.ET.VERON.
SACERD.COLLEG.IVVE
NVM BRIXIAN.PRI
MVM INSTITVTIS OB
MERITA EIVS HONORE
CONTENTVS IMPEN
DIVM REMIS.IN.TVT.
HS.N.D.          [*CIL* V, 4416]

**161.** In pariete hospitalis extra aedem sancti Francisci.

L.POBLICIVS HEBE
NVS SIBI.ET.OPTATE
MVLVIAE CONTVB.
ET VELLIAE FIRMAE
PISAINAE          [*CIL* V, 4676]

**162.**    In aede sanctae Agathae.

FL.LVPPIO EX
PRAEP.AVR.SEVE
RINAE MATR.DVL
CISS.QVAE.VIX.A.
LXXV.M.VII.VALE
MIHI MATER PIEN
TISS.                    [*CIL* V, 4370]

**163.**    In eodem loco.

VICTOR.ARTHE
MIO.FRATRI.BE
NEMERENT.QVI
VIXIT.ANNOS
QVINQVEGINTA
ET MENSES QVAT
TVOR.AETERNVM
.SALVE.
QVI LEGERIS              [*CIL* V, 4766]

**164.**    Extra aedem sanctae Agathae in pariete.

.C.QVINTIVS.C.F.
FAB.CATVLLVS
DECVR.BRIXIAE
SIBI.ET
CORNELIAE.M.F.
MAGNAE VXORI
ET.Q.QVINTIO
.C.F.FRATRI
C.QVINTIO SECVN
DO.PATRI.ANTONIAE.
CATVLLAE
MATRI
.T.F.I.                  [*CIL* V, 4460]

**165.**    Et denique Veronam feracissimam et antiquam civitatem olim a Gallis conditam venit, ubi non exigua veterum monumenta comperit. Hanc praeterea urbem praeterfluit fluvius Athesis nomine, secundum quod dicit Papias, licet aliqui eum Athacem vocent, dicentes illum esse de quo meminit Lucanus; alii dicunt Athacem esse Ticinum, sed Papias dicit quod Athax est fluvius inter Laudnum et Remos iuxta Renum: sed Veronae fluvius est.

**166.**    In hac urbe Ligurica vidit Kyriacus, ut in commentariis suis reposuit, laberinthum, qui harena nunc dicitur, et habetur quod constructum fuit anno

Octaviani Augusti XXXIX, ante ortum Christi tertio,[a] cuius pars exterior terrae motibus corruit, et nunc extat[b] locus rotundus Harenae per totum magnis saxis undique constructus et perfilatus cum cubalis intus et multis antris multiformiter redimitus <sit>.[c] In huius autem rotunditate narrat Kiriacus ipse quod extant[d] scalae magnis lapidibus appositae, quae quanto magis in altitudine protendebant, tanto plus in rotunditate videbantur ampliari; et secundum quod refertur, quinquaginta cubitis in altitudine extenditur, in cuius summitate quidam locus magnus et nobilis multiformis laboratus marmoreo de lapide circumquaque redimitus erat.

**167.**      Vidit praeterea portam geminam triumphalem Bursariorum vivo de lapide constructam, quae[e] duodecim numero exornata fenestris[f] conspectari videtur,[g] ubi tale Kiriacus Latinum exceperat epigramma.

COLONIA AVGVS
TA.VERONA.NO
VA GALLIENIANA
VALERIANO.II.
ET.LVCILLO.COSS.
MVRI VERONEN
SIVM FABRICATI
EX DIE. III.NON.A
PRILIVM
DEDICATI.PR.NON.
DECEMBR.IVBENTE
SANCTISSIMO
GALLIENO AVG.N.
INSISTENTE.AVR.
MARCELLINO.V.P.
.DVC . DVC.
CVRANTE.IVL.
MARCELLINO      [*CIL* V, 3329]

---

[a] tercio

[b] estat

[c] sit *supplied by edd. from Sarayna text* (*see Introduction* and note to the translation *ad loc.*)

[d] estant

[e] quem

[f] finestras

[g] conspectare videntur

**168.** Alio in loco ibi prope.

DEO.MAGNO
AETERN
L.STATIVS DIODO
RVS.QVOT.SE PRE
CIBVS COMPOTEM
.FECISSET.
.V.S.L.M.      [*CIL* V, 3221]

**169.** In civitacula.

CLAVDIAE.TI.F.
MARCELLINAE
BELLICI
SOLLERTIS
.CO.
M.ET.Q.HORTENSI
PAVLINVS.ET.FIRMVS      [*CIL* V, 3338]

**170.** Super flumen Athesis.

VETO RELIQVIAS.
PVPRONVS CALLISTVS
HOMO  OPTIM
HIC IACET      [*CIL* V, 3830]

**171.** In cimiterio sancti Nicolai.

LOCO PVBLIC.
DAT.D.D.[a]
PARCIS . AVG
.SACR.
L.CASSIVS.VERVICI
.F.NIGRINVS.VI.VIR
.AVG.
.V.S.L.M.      [*CIL* V, 3281]

**172.** In cimiterio sancti Firmi maioris.

P.GRAECINIO
.P.F.POB
LAGONI
ORNAMENTIS.CONSVLARIB.      [*CIL* V, 3340]

**173.** *[no heading]*

OCTAVIA. .L.
.HILARA.

---

[a] *Gloss in ?Felice's hand*: decreto decurionum

V.F.SIBI.ET
L.CAELIO.L.L.
STATVRAI. VIRO
SVO.ET.
L.CAELIO
L.F
FIRMO
FILIO
.H.M.H.N.S.                    [*CIL* V, 3689]

**174.**  In curia pauperum.

MAGISTRI
M.LICINIVS.M.F.PVSILLIO
SEX.VIPSANIVS.M.F.CLEMENS
Q.CASSIVS.C.F.NIGER
MINISTRI.
BLANDVS.C.AFINI.ASCLAE.SER.
MVRRANVS.P.CLODI TVRPIONIS.SER
AVCTVS.M.FABRICI HILARI.SER.
COMPITVM REFECERVNT
TECTVM
PARIETES.ALLEVARVNT
VALVAS LIMEN DE SVA
PECVNIA
LARIBUS DANT COSSO
CORNELIO LENTVLO
.L.PISONE AVGVRE COS.          [*CIL* V, 3257]

**175.**  In tumulo marmoreo sito in maiori ecclesia.

P.IVLIVS.APOLI
ONIVS.SIBI.ET
ATTIAE VALERI
AE.CONIVG.OB
SEQVENTISS.
VIVVS.PARAVIT
ET EIVSQ.
DEI.COR.IN.ARC.
CONDIDIT
ET
LOCVM SERVIO
DEDICAVIT                      [*CIL* V, 3643]

**176.**  In aede divi prothomartyris.

D.M
C.CALVENTI
FIRMINI

CVRATORES
INSTRVMENTI
VERONAES
EX NVMERO
COLLEG.FABR. [*CIL* V, 3387]

**177.** In alio loco cum figuris.
EX TESTAMENTO
P.SACIDI.Q.F.
POB.PATRIS
P.SACIDI.P.F.AN.VI.
M.SACIDI.P.F.AN.IIII. [*CIL* V, 3734]

**178.** Et alibi.
CN.SERVILIVS
CN.L.
SYRVS
V.F [*CIL* V, 3748]

**179.** In phano divi Proculi.
PHOTINO
VESTIARIO
NICEPHORVS.LIB.
PATRON.OPTIM.
ET.SIBI .V.F. [*CIL* V, 3460]

**180.** Ibi prope in hortulo.[a]
D.M
L.NOVELL.
R-IODAN.
.T.F.I. [*CIL* V, 3677]

**181.** In domo ecclesiae antedictae.
D.LIVIAE.M
VENVSTAE
M.LIVIVS FORTV
NATVS
LIBERTAE.ET VXORI
BENE MERENTI
ANN.XXIII.M.VII.D
XVII [*CIL* V, 3657]

---

[a] hortullo

**182.** In vetustissimo sepulchro.

C.GAVI.C.F.QVINTAN

ANN.XLIII.M.X.C.GAVIVS

MENODORVS.FILIO PIISSIMO

D       PATER.INFELIX       M

AEQVIVS.ENIM.FVERAT

VOS HOC MIHI

FECISSE

ET.SIBI       [*CIL* V, 3627]

**183.** In abbatia sancti Zenonis.

V.F

M.GAVIVS

SEVERVS SIBI ET

CORNELIAE

EPIMELIAE

CONIVGI OPTIMAE

BENE MERENTI.ET.

M.GAVIO SERENO

ET CORNELIAE RESTI

TUTAE

LIBERTIS       [*CIL* V, 3628]

**184.** In hortulo sancti Zenonis.

QVARTVA

HIC VIDVA VIXIT

ANN.LXXX

MARCELLINVS CARIS

SIMVS FRATER.CARIS

SIMAE SORORI ET

PIENTISSIMAE

MERITE

FECIT

QUEM OMNES ECLESIA

DILIGEBAT       [*CIL* V, 3419]

**185.** In pillo quadrato marmoreo.[a]

AVENIAE

BASSARIDIS

FILIAE.OPTIM.

M.GAVIVS

CORNELIVS

---

[a] = in pila quadrata marmorea?

AGATHE.MER<sup>ite</sup>
AVENIANVS
OMNI.INIVRIA
DEBILITATVS                    [*CIL* V, 3382]

**186.**  Ab alio latere

VIXIT.ANN.
XXV.MEN.IIII.
DIEB.XIIII.
OMNI SENSV
VITA PIETATE
PERFECTISSIM               [*CIL* V, 3382]

**187.**  A tertio latere

ΘEA
XAPIC
BACCAPIC                    [*CIL* V, 3382]

**188.**  Ab alia parte lapidis

MANV MISS.
ALVMNA
ANN.IIII.DIER.
XVII.AMAVENA
MACRO
SPLEND<sup>ido</sup> AEQ<sup>uiti</sup> R.<sup>romano</sup>
OMNI HONORE
FUNCTO                      [*CIL* V, 3382]

**189.**  In alio lapide

CN.<sup>a</sup>CORNELIVS
CVRVINI
.L.NERITVS
VI VIR
AVG.SIBI.ET
CLODIAE  TONNI
ANAE.L.CHRESTAE
CONTVBERNAL.           [*CIL* V, 3393]

**190.**  Exinde postquam diligenter omnia vetera perscruptasset, Mediolanum iterum reversus est, ubi per dies aliquot magno cum principe moratus est.

---

<sup>a</sup> *gloss in same hand*: gneus

**191.**     Deinde vero Mantuam petiit, civitatem[a] vetustissimam Italiae in provintia, quae quondam Venetia, quae et Gallia Cisalpina nuncupatur, prout egomet in suis commentariis repperi; mentionem dignissimam, ni fallor, hoc loco praestantiae tuae destinandam[b] curavi.

**192.**     Haec enim civitas sita fuit, secundum quod refert Isidorus et Paulus Longobardus, a Mantho: *<Manto>[c] Tiresiae filia post interitum Thebanorum in Italiam delata <Mantuam>[d] condidisse dicitur . . . et dicta Mantua quod manes tueatur,* ut scribit Isidorus: ab ipsa etiam Mantho dicta est Mantua civitas. Virgilius vero, qui ex hac urbe traxit originem, non minimum civitati decus, dicit quod filius eiusdem Manthos, Ogus nomine, eandem civitatem a matris nomine Mantuam appellavit. Ipsa autem dicta est Mantho sive Manthos quia denominatur[e] a manes et tueor, quia manes, id est deorum mortuorum, tueretur. Haec, alii ut dicunt, de quodam viro nomine Tibere filium habuit, qui dictus est Obius sive Obnus, et idem dictus est Bianor a bis fortis, scilicet corpore et animo. Unde Virgilius: *sepulchrum incipit apparere[f] Bianoris.* Hic, ut quidam volunt, condidit Mantuam, quam ex Manthois matris nomine Mantuani nominaverunt.[g] Fuit autem Tiresias huius Manthois genitor, magnus Thebanorum vates, de quo meminit Statius[h] in Thebanorum historia. Haec de exordio urbis huius patent[i] ex auctoribus memoratis.

**193.**     Tempus autem fundationis eius expressum inde habetur; antiquissimum enim opinari potest ex quo vel a Mantho Tiresiae vatis filia vel a filio ipsius Manthois constat conditam. Nam interitus Thebanorum, sive Thebarum expugnatio, facta per Graecos post diutinam obsidionem pro certamine regni

---

[a] civitas

[b] destinandum

[c] Manto *supplied by edd. from text of Isidore (see notes on translation ad loc.).*

[d] Mantuam *supplied by edd. from text of Isidore.*

[e] dñatrix

[f] parere

[g] nominavit

[h] Stacius

[i] patet

<inter> Ethioclem et Polinicem,[a] Edipi Thebanorum regis filios, Troianum praecessit excidium per annos circiter sexaginta hoc modo: Edipus enim tempore Abimelech iudicis Israel erat. Troia vero excisa fuit anno tertio Abdon iudicis Israel. Ab ultimo vero anno Abimelech usque ad tertium Abdon fuerunt anni sexaginta. Troiae vero excidium praecessit conditionem urbis Romae per annos CDXXXI secundum Hieronymum. Condita fuit autem Roma anno ante Christi adventum per annos DCCLII secundum Orosium; et sic, etiam non computatis annis qui praecesserunt ab interitu Thebanorum, post quem, ut dictum est, fuit Mantua aedeficata,[b] usque ad excidium Troianum, si recte calculabitur,[c] invenientur MCLXXXIII anni praeteriti a Mantua condita usque ad Salvatoris adventum. In cronicis autem Mileti sive Eusebii habetur quod condita fuit Mantua anno nativitatis Abraam DXXX, qui fiunt annis ante urbem conditam DCLXX. Nam Abraae nativitas praecessit urbem conditam, secundum Augustinum, circiter MCC annos, quod testatur libro XVIII de civitate Dei, de quibus si detrahantur anni DXXX, qui fuerunt a nativitate Abraam usque ad aedificationem[d] Mantuae, ut dictum est, restat fuisse ab aedificatione[e] Mantuae usque ad conditionem Romae annos[f] DCLXX, quibus si addantur anni DCCLII qui fuerunt ab urbe condita usque ad Christi adventum, recte calculando[g] anni MCCCCXXII.

**194.** Hanc civitatem praeterfluit amnis Mincius Padum influens, quam etiam munitissimam et inexpugnabilem reddit lacus[h] eam ambiens. In suburbano quoque pago super ripam ipsius lacus sito, qui et Pietolis dicitur, natus fuisse fertur Virgilius, urbis Mantuanae decus eximium, in quo enim loco Kiriacus ipse prudenter perscruptatus est si aliquid dignum invenisset veternitatis, praesertim de Marone Virgilio; qui[i] apud ripam fluvii Tartari hoc vetustissimum repperit epigramma:

M.VERGILIO.M.F.
ANTHIOCO.VNIGENITO
SIBI ET PAMPHILO.          [*CIL* V, 3827]

---

[a] polinitem

[b] hedificata

[c] calchulabitur

[d] hedificationem

[e] hedificatione

[f] ante

[g] calchulando

[h] locus

[i] quod

**195.**    Mantuae ad puteum in lapide.

L.ANNIO.L.L.DIPHILO
MAIORI
L.ANNIO.L.L.DIPHILO
MINORI
L.ANNIVS.DIOMEDES.
LIBERTEIS                        [*CIL* V, 4066]

**196.**    Alio in loco.

*[shown under an arch:]*
CASSIAE.L.F.
TERTIAI.MATRI                    [*CIL* V, 4072]

**197.**    In parietibus ecclesiae[a] sancti Silvestri.

V.F
FVRIA.SEX.F.PRIMA
SIBI.ET.M.ACILIO.LF
VIRO.ET.P.FVRIO
P.F.VIRO.ET.
.Q.CAESIO.M.F.
VIRO                             [*CIL* V, 4073]

**198.**    Et deinde vero se Januam contulit, insignem maritimarum Lygustiae civitatem, quae secundum Plinium <in> libro de naturali historia in provintia est Liguriae, quae nunc Longobardia dicitur. Scribit enim quod haec civitas protenditur a Vintimilio et fluvio Merula usque ad Sigestrum et flumen[b] Macrae, in qua provintia est Janua et fluvius Pulcivere. Paulus[c] vero Longo-bardorum scriptor historiae scribit quod est in quinta Italiae provintia, quae Alpes Cociae dicitur, et quod ipsa provintia a Liguria usque ad mare extensa ab occiduo Gallorum finibus copulatur; in qua Terdona, monasterium Bobii, Janua et Saona civitates habentur.

**199.**    Scribitur in cronicis quod Janus, quidam princeps Moisi contempo-raneus, de orientis partibus in Italiam veniens, ibi primus omnium regnavit, quamvis [ut] ab aliis historiis dicatur quod Abraae tempore regnaverit. Hic Januam civitatem construxit et de suo nomine Janiculam appellavit, et ibi ad hoc probandum adducuntur Solini verba dicentis: *Quis ignorat vel editam vel conditam a Jano Janiculam, a Saturno Saturniam?*

---

[a] eclesiae

[b] flumine

[c] palus

**200.** Alius Janus Troianus origine post Troiae excidium in Italiam venit. Dicit etiam quod cum idem Janus [dum] navigaret et ventum prosperum haberet loco qui Albarium dicitur, obscuritas[a] grandis in aere apparuit quae vulgo Albasia dicitur, apud alios Cigaria, quae [a] loco nomen dedit Albanum. Procedens vero loco, qui Galiganum dicitur, cum terrae situs illi placuisset vela[b] calavit; unde et locus sic dictus est. Loco vero, qui Serzanum dicitur, saltans in terram descendit, et ex illo saltu Serzanum vulgo, quasi saltus Jani, locus ille nomen accepit. Veniens autem ad ipsam civitatem Ianiculam, castrum ibi aedificavit[c] loco qui nunc Castellum vocatur,[d] fecitque turres et fortilicia ubi nunc est archiepiscopale palatium, et muris fortissimis communivit, et sic eam ampliavit Ianus secundus. Convenientibus etiam ibidem diversis habitatoribus, civitas magnificari coepit. Quod autem de Iano cive Troiae refert, dicit tantum se per famam publicam et antiquam novisse.

**201.** Subiungit quoque quod Ianua fuit aedificata[e] per annos CVII ante urbis Romae conditionem, et ante adventum Christi per annos MVᶜXLVI,[f] et in tertia mundi aetate. Hoc autem constare dicitur et per supradicta verba Solini, scilicet quod Ianus Ianiculam quae modo Ianua dicitur aedificavit[g], et per cronicas autenticas; sed auctorem sive scriptorem non nominat. Quod Ianus Moisi temporibus regnabat quando populi in deserto tenebat ducatum et quod Roma condita fuit, <si> computabuntur, invenientur[h] anni fluxisse VIIᶜ.VII.[i] quibus Ianuae aedificatio[j] praecessit urbis Romae conditionem. Si autem a Moise usque ad Christi tempora computabuntur, invenientur, ut dictum est, anni qui fluxerunt MDXLVI. Istam autem computationem annorum dicit se fecisse secundum assignationem Hieronymi, qui minorem

---

[a] obscuratis

[b] vella

[c] hedificavit

[d] vocat

[e] hedificata

[f] In the MS the c is written directly above the first V, which is itself inserted between M and X.

[g] hedificavit

[h] invenient

[i] In the MS the c is written directily above the second I.

[j] hedificatio

numerum ponit. Beda enim et Methodius maiorem numerum ponunt, dicentes quod Galli, quorum dux fuit Bellovesius, eam aedificaverunt.[a]

**202.** Titus Livius praeterea non nominat eam Ianuam sed Genuam; dicitque ipsam anno ab urbe condita DXXXIIII a Magone Poenorum duce cum XXX navibus rostratis et multis onerariis in quibus erant duodecim milia peditum et ferme duo milia equitum nullis munitam praesidiis cepit[b] et paene destruxit. Circa quae tempora Mediolanum fuit expugnatum[c] etiam a Marcello, per quod patet quod saltem per annos CCXXX fuit Ianua ante Christi adventum. Alibi dicit quod Scipio, frater puber Scipionis, navibus Genuam venit in occursum Hannibalis Alpes transgressuri. Refert[d] etiam Titus idem quod Lucretio prorogatum est imperium a Romanis, ut Genuam oppidum a Magone pene dirruptum reaedificaret[e] anno ab urbe condita DXLV.

**203.** Et ut ad propositum revertar, in hac autem civitate Kyriacus ipse repperit, Francisco Barbavara ducalibus intercedentibus litteris curante, et praeclara omnia civitatis ornamenta; vidit et insignem illum preciosissima de smyragdo crathera atque C. Marii marmoreum caput. Etenim ibi primarios et inter cives viderat Ioannem Grillum, opulentissimum civem, Franciscum Spinolam, Benedictum Necronem, Paulum Imperialem, nec non doctissimos homines Iacobum Bracellum, Nicolaum Camulium, egregios publicae rei secretarios, quibus a claris viris praedigne in urbe et extra per eximia et ornatissima hortorum diversoria splendide conviva atque perlaute fuerat, et sibi omnia tantae urbis insignia ostentarunt, et amplissimam navistatii portusque murorum molem,[f] naves longas et onerarias ingentes.

**204.** Sed postquam hic omnia viderat, Romam se rursus ad pontificem contulit. Et cum per dies in urbe versaretur, audivit Anconitanos cives, adversus quosdam patriae rebelles concives piraticam exercentes,[g] naves Paliaresio Pisanello praefecto in expeditione parare; et Thomam Blasii filium

---

[a] hedificaverunt

[b] coepit

[c] expugnatam

[d] reffert

[e] rehedificaret

[f] mollem

[g] excercentes

antiquum, qui suam ex[a] Balearibus insulis onerariam navim Caetanum ad portum duxerat, illam hoc in apparatu conducto milite ducere et Paliaresium praefectum ad Illyrici sinus oras expectare, et simul una rebelles impetere cives et in potestatem redactos extremo supplicio afficere debere iussisse.

**205.** Quibus auditis Kyriacus haec omnia moleste ferens, nam potissime verebatur ne quando illa perniciosa coepta civilium discordiarum in civitate tam diu intemeratae[b] unionis integra seminarium denique pestilentissimum essent,[c] quoad licuisset remedia in posterum, una cum Nicolao Petrelli scribae fratre ex urbe se ad Thomam[d] patronum apud Caietam contulit. Qui cum Kyriacum audisset, [et] iuvenis ille generosus non parum laetatus omnia sibi suo de consilio se facturum spopondit.

**206.** Et cum expedita e Caieta navis Neapolim ventura esset, ut interim quid dignum vetustatis inspiceret, Neapolim terrestri itinere petit. Et cum primum per iter Terrecinas, maritimam et antiquam Latinorum urbem, vidisset, DIVI.AVG. marmoreum templum, portumque eximium, et ab urbe Roma ingentia silicum strata viarum conspectare maluerat.

**207.** Sed ex Caieta per Neapolitanum iter Linterneas memorabiles magni Scipionis villas, eiusque marmoream statuam, et ingentia cocto de latere amphiteatra conspexit.

**208.** Inde vero per Suessam turritam Capuam venit, insignem olim Campaneae civitatem, ubi non parva veterum monumenta comperit. Et extra potissime ad tertium ab urbe lapidem inculta inter et silvestria loca maximi amphiteatri reliquias maximorum lapidum vidit, et procul inde antiquas magnae civitatis portas et pleraque subterranea ingentia mirificaque domorum aedificia.

**209.** Exinde per Aversam oppidum Parthenopaeam illam nobilem Neapolitanam regiam civitatem adivit, Ioanna serenissima Karoli regis filia regnantę . . . .

---

[a] et

[b] interatae

[c] esse

[d] Thoma

*[fol. 104 of MS is missing; fol. 105r preserves a Greek inscription:]*

ΤΙΒΕΡΙΟC ΙΟΥΛΙΟC
ΤΑΡCΟC.ΟCΛΙΟΡ
ΟΥΡΟΙC ΛΙΤΗΠΟΛΕΙ
ΤΟΝΝΑΟΝΝ ΚΑΙ.ΤΛΕ
ΗΤΩΙΝΑΩΙΠΕΛΑΓ
ΩΝCΕΒΑCΤΟΓΟ
.ΕΡΟC.
ΚΛΙΕΠΤΙ ΡΟΠΟC.
CΥΝΤΕCΑCΑCΕΡΤΩΝΙ
ΛΙΩΝΡΑΟΙΕ
ΡΩCΕΝ.

[*CIG* 5791; *IG* XIV 714; *CIL* X p. 184]

**210.**      Exinde, Hercule Puteolano praetore ducente, posteaquam ad Caesaream cavam Virgilii divi poetae monumenta viderat, Puteolos venit, et ibi praeclara multa vetustatum Sybillae vidit, templa, Averni lacus, et adusque Misenum celeberrimum montem omnia Cumarum Baiarumque monumenta conspexit, in quis Neroniana Lucullianaque insignia pleraque aedificia nostram ad diem mirifica conspectantur.

**211.**      Inde vero per Neapolim Beneventanam ad insignem Sannitum urbem venerat, ubi ingentia utique multa vetustatum vidit, et maximi sui amphiteatri vestigia, nobilemque Traiani Caesaris arcum praeclarum suo cum epigrammate conspectare maluerat, quod inclytus olim ille S.P.Q.R. fortissimo illi principi ornatissimum dederat.

**212.**      Sub statua marmorea.

T.NONIO MARCEL
LINO.V.C.COS.CAP.<sup>umo</sup>
PATRONO
DIGNISSIMO
OB INSIGNIA BENE
FICIA QVIB.LONGA
POPVLI
TABEDIA SEDAVIT
VNIVERSA PLEBS
BENEVEN
TANA
CENSVIT PONENENDAM      [*CIL* IX, 1589]

**213.** *[no heading]*

D. M
Q.PLOTIVS.Q.F.
QVIR
ROMANVS                [Not found in *CIL* IX]

**214.** De hac[a] urbe reperitur in cronicis antiquis. Beneventum et Arpi[b] Italiae civitates a Diomede constitutae, ut dicit Solinus. Fuit autem Diomedes unus ex principibus Graecorum qui fuerunt in obsidione Troiana, qui ab Illyricis interemptus est, ut scribit Papias, addens quod Diomedis urbs[c] in Apulia, quam Diomedes sub Gargano[d] monte condidit. Ibi tamen non exprimit quod fuit dicta Beneventum, alio autem loco dicit: Beneventum civitas est quae prius dicta est Sanium, et alibi dicit: Sannis civitas est in Apulia et Sanium est Beneventum, et Sanitae gens est quae in CXXX miliario distat a Roma media[e] inter Picenum[f] et Campaniam. Ex historia quoque Longobardorum habetur quod Sannium est quattuordecima Italiae provincia, et in ea Sanium civitas, a qua et tota provincia nomen accepit. In Sanio provincia est civitas ipsa Beneventana; metropolis habetur. Nobilis in Apulia archiepiscopus eius duo et viginti sub se suffraganeos habet. Miletus[g] et Hieronymus scribunt quod Beneventum in Sannio a Romanis conditur anno ab urbe condita CDLXX. Et credo quod illa conditio fuerit reconditio sive reparatio quia sicut dictum est secundum Solinum, Beneventum fuit a Diomede constitutum, qui fuit ante Romam longissimo tempore, et cetera.

**215.** Sed postquam Kiriacus ipse omnia ibi digna litteris commendarat, Neapolim iterum revisit, ubi cum paucos post dies, expedita et completa milite navi, Daniele[h] Parentino episcopo et Ioanne Bosculo Florentino ab Eugenio pontifice ad Alphonsum regem oratoribus Siciliam petentibus acceptis,

---

[a] huius

[b] Arpos

[c] urbis

[d] *corr. in MS from* argano

[e] medii

[f] Picennum

[g] Milletus

[h] Danielis

navigasset, Kiriacus notus et amicissimus illis digna plurima ab iis audierat de rebus inclyto cum rege agendis qui adversus Tuniseum regem Iarbeam tum forte insulam ingenti classe premebat.

**216.**     Et cum tandem navis in Siciliam Messanam ad urbem praeclaram applicuisset, legati illico Syracusas terrestri itinere petiere; et Thomas, Petro Caietano egregio Anconitanorum consule curante, additis expeditioni suae militibus, ut Anconitanae classi obviaret,[a] ad Illyrici sinus fauces navigavit. Ibi die postero non longe <ab> Otranti[b] promuntorio[c] nobili[d] Baleariam navim unamque biremem omnifariam machinis munitam, Paliaresio viro quidem praestante et imperatoria potestate praefecto, adventantes videre, et cum se invicem iunxissent, Tarentinum ad sinum, ubi Calliepolitano in portu piraticam illam navim considere intellexerant, advenere.

**217.**     Sed enim cum inclyta olim regina Maria, Tarentini principis mater, navim illam suo in portu salvam fore <se> permisisse suos per oratores praefecto nuntiasset, non nullas post hinc inde per litteras legatosque contentiones, tandem infecta re classis Anconitanam ad patriam remenso aequore remeavit.

**218.**     Vale, decus saeculi nostri et patriae ornamentum.

---

[a] obivaret

[b] otrenti

[c] promuntorium

[d] nobile

# TRANSLATION

HERE BEGINS THE LIFE OF THE LEARNED AND FAMOUS CIRIACO OF
ANCONA[1]

1.    From Francesco Scalamonti, knight of Ancona, to Lauro Quirini,
patrician of Venice, greetings.

2.    When I was recently at home in Ancona, I read that elegant letter you
wrote from Padua some time ago to our friend, Ciriaco of Ancona, in Florence;
and from it I began to appreciate the nobility of your character. This proposal
of yours to write about the life and career of such an extraordinary man seems
to me well worth while and likely to do honor both to him and to your own
eloquence. Moreover, in the matter of eloquence I did not consider you to be
an idle talent among the learned men of Italy. For who could choose a more
splendid, refined, and happy subject to write about in these days than to hand
down to posterity a record of the life and journeys of this singular figure?
Ciriaco is the only man in thirteen hundred years, since the time of the great
Alexandrian geographer Claudius Ptolemy in the age of Hadrian, whose
expansive nature and high-born temper gave him the courage to travel all over
the world—through Greece, Asia, Egypt, and the Ionian and Aegean
islands—to survey and investigate the sites and characteristics of its territories
and provinces, its mountains, woodlands, springs and rivers, its seas, lakes and
noblest cities and towns. Whatever fine monuments of venerable antiquity he
found worthy of note in these places, he faithfully recorded, not in Italian, but
in Latin or Greek; and, as we have often heard him say himself, his
indefatigable resolve, regardless of all discomforts, toils and sleepless nights
the task involved, was to inspect and examine whatever ancient remains were
to be seen in the world as far as the last rocky heights jutting into Ocean, to the
island of Thule, and any other remote parts of the earth.

3.    Indeed, I recognize that in this matter, Lauro, you who are a
distinguished man and truly a verdant laurel glorifying the Muses, have shown
yourself to be a true Quirinus[2] and eminently worthy to possess and adorn the
name 'Quirinus,' in as much as you have undertaken the honorable and worthy
endeavor to be the first Italian notably to record for all time every notable
achievement of Ciriaco, who himself has worked so diligently to adorn the
Latin name. Accordingly in order to be able to write the life faithfully and as
comprehensively and completely as possible, you asked Ciriaco in your letter
to write out a complete and orderly account of his whole career from the day
of his birth. But when I realized that he was rather slow in complying (for I
know that he is always better at promoting other people's affairs and praise
than his own), and since, from my earliest youth, from my baby toenails as the

saying goes,[3] we have long been close friends and familiar neighbors, honor and decency seemed to lay on me this decent and honorable duty, which it would be very wrong to refuse. In discharge of this obligation, I have therefore taken up my pen and have seen to it that the enclosed materials should be briefly written out and sent to you, giving an account of the lineage, life and travels of our friend, Ciriaco of Ancona, taking my information from his mother,[4] his relatives, and his own mouth and numerous writings. These materials I have arranged and written out as briefly as possible and enclose herewith for your friendly use.

**4.**     Farewell, and read Ciriaco himself.

**5.**     . . . .[5] and did whatever was possible to educate them[6] in good manners and letters. Ciriaco was now about nine years old;[7] born as he was with an immense craving to see the world and impelled by a kind of divinely inspired destiny, he eagerly, against his mother's wishes, accompanied his grandfather, Ciriaco Selvatico, who was then by chance about to make a sea voyage on business up the Adriatic to Venice.

**6.**     For the fates had already fired the boy's young mind with the fame of this great and populous city, and when he first saw it on the 13th of April, Michele Steno being the doge,[8] he was filled with admiration for its marvelous splendor. And just as destiny had decreed that this renowned and important Italian city should be the fit starting-point for a life of such great discoveries, so he always especially loved it and did all he could to exalt and praise it.

**7.**     Next, the young Ciriaco, under his grandfather Ciriaco's guidance, went to Padua, the ancient and noble city of the Eneti,[9] which was ruled by Francesco Carrara.[10] There he looked round the great city, surrounded as it is by triple walls and washed on all sides by a deep river, and he viewed the prince's noble castle with its large painted hall,[11] where, as he used to recall, he saw for the first time the live lions walking around in their cages.[12]

**8.**     After that he returned home to rejoin his relatives and his dearly-loved mother, who had carefully arranged for him to be taught his letters by the schoolmaster, Francesco Zampetta. Nevertheless, before his twelfth year was out, observing evident signs that his grandfather was in a hurry to visit King Ladislao, Ciriaco made up his mind to accompany him on his land and sea journey despite all his mother's entreaties against it.

**9.**     So leaving Piceno he journeyed through the whole of the most noble kingdom of Naples, through the country of the Mauricini, the Bruttians, the Salentines, and of the Apulians, the Samnites, the Lucanians and Campanians. On his way he saw many remarkable cities and towns where he now began to notice their numerous antique monuments, including a marble bust of Achilles that he saw in the ancient city of Thetis. Their first halt in the kingdom itself was at the city of Teano, where they stayed for some days at the court of its lord, Count Geoffredo Alife, the Grand Chamberlain of Naples.[13] They next stopped at Sessa Arunca, where they visited the Duke of Sessa and his aged brother, the count of Squillace, grand admiral of the *regno*. These two lords, of the noble Marzano family,[14] were old and dear friends of Ciriaco the elder, having been with him in Hungary in King Charles' time.[15]

**10.** Finally they arrived at the most noble and royal Campanian city of Naples, where they saw the famous martial prince, King Ladislao, building and fitting out a fleet in the shipyard of the city. After a few days in Naples, where they saw the sights of the great city, setting out for Calabria, they took ship in a merchantman and disembarked at Salerno where they again saw the king with his splendid bodyguard attending a tournament and a horse-race by the sea.

**11.** Then, after viewing the city, they took passage in a small boat, down the Lucanian coast, looking up at the charming sight of the well-cultivated hills of Amalfi and Paestum, until they arrived safely in Calabria, their destination, where they visited the cities of Torpea, Laconia and Maida. At Maida the elder Ciriaco Selvatico settled down, putting his grandson to school to continue his study of letters under the care of his friend, Palfo of Squillace, where the boy first began to learn the rudiments of grammar, the first of the [liberal] arts.[16]

**12.** But then, after a year's stay in Calabria, Ciriaco's grandfather wound up his affairs in Maida (including a complete translation of sacred history into Italian verse) and decided at last to return to his home; so, recrossing the Tyrrhenian Sea, he sailed back to Naples, that they found an Anconitan galley under the command of Marcone Torelliano that had been sent by Ancona to convey Pope Boniface to the baths.[17]

**13.** Having finished their business there, they then returned to Sessa to stay for a few days with the duke, at whose court, the young Ciriaco became such good friends with the duke's young son, Giovanni Antonio,[18] that one could not distinguish which of the two the duke regarded as his own child—for the two boys had soon reached the same degree of maturity, though quite different in education and upbringing. However, the grandfather felt that it was time for them to put these courtesies behind them and to keep his promise to his daughter; so he brought his grandson home to his dear mother who eagerly awaited his return.

**14.** For many days after their return, Ciriaco Selvatico watched his grandson being welcomed and petted by the family. But the boy, he knew, was obviously eager to occupy his mind, and as Ancona was a place wholly given over, not to liberal studies, but to trade and shipping, which had enriched so many of the citizens, and as he wanted to raise the boy from poverty to wealth in that kind of enterprise, he arranged, with his daughter's consent, to apprentice the boy, now aged fourteen, for seven years to a rich merchant relative of his, namely the prominent patrician, Pietro, son of the eminent physician Messer Iacopo. The young Ciriaco applied himself to the business and soon clearly demonstrated that he had learned, not only the basic art of arithmetic, but also geometry and all the mercantile skills; and this he achieved in a very short time, without any teacher, but by studying the way things were done and by relying on his own extraordinary quickness of mind. He labored day and night, regardless of long hours and lack of sleep, and was so trustworthy, diligent, and skillfully attentive to his duties, in and out of the office, in discharging his master's business, that within two years Pietro considered him perfectly capable of looking after the whole business on his own. Pietro had more than once been elected among the six *anziani* and among the three *regolatori*[19] of the city and he now, as a patrician, wanted to have more time and leisure for local politics; so he handed over to Ciriaco the management, not only of all his mercantile business in Ancona, but also of his country estates. The lad manfully shouldered this huge task and for five years conducted the whole complex enterprise so successfully—favored by his divine and catholic genius, Mercury[20]—that he considerably increased his master's wealth, and his fair trading won the praise, not only of his fellow citizens, but of the many outside merchants from Perugia, Florence and Venice who were then doing business with the people of Ancona.

**15.**     Meanwhile, before he had finished his term of apprenticeship and although he was still not of proper age, the young man was raised, with the strong backing of his master, first to consular rank as one of the six *anziani* and later, by exception, to the Senate;[21] and in these offices he never failed admirably to discharge his duty both in peace and war. When the seven agreed years of his apprenticeship were over, Ciriaco's concern for his mother took him back to her simple house, but he never ceased to enjoy the company and kindness of his master.

**16.**     By this time the young man had acquired considerable practical experience in civic affairs, and was perfectly well qualified to take a responsible and useful part in public and private business in Ancona; but now he had a mind to see the world, and to engage in maritime business abroad, so he attached himself as a minor clerk to his relation Ciucio Pizzecolli,[22] who had chartered a merchantman belonging to a certain Alfieri, which was about to start a journey laden with a cargo of fruit.

**17.**    In this good ship, he left Ancona—it was winter time—and sailed down the Dalmatian coast, through the Ionian Sea, had a distant view of Crete, the island of Jove, and finally, after a long crossing through Libyan and Egyptian waters, arrived at the great Egyptian city of Alexandria. There he had his first sight of the huge remains of what was once the tall lighthouse of Pharos,[23] the royal gates of Numidian[24] stone, the great obelisk of King Philadelphus,[25] the tall column of Alexander of Macedon built by the architect Dinocrates, now popularly called the Column of Pompey,[26] and many other remarkable antique monuments;[27] and it was there that for the first time he saw with wonder camels, dromedaries, ostriches, and apes, as well as infidel peoples with their strange garments and accents. In Alexandria, too, he saw the sultan[28] arriving with great splendor attended by a band of eunuch servants of all races[29] and ceremoniously received in the city by his own people and by visiting foreigners.

**18.**    When, through the good offices of Stefano Quirini, patrician of Venice, all the business had been done in Alexandria, he sailed to Rhodes and from Rhodes to Chios; from which noble Aegean island, having now been promoted to senior clerk, the young Ciriaco had a view of the famous islands of Samos and Icaria off the coast of Asia. His next stop, as he came into Ionia, was Miletus, a city once illustrious, but now fallen in ruins, where he viewed the remains of the great theater and of numerous other monuments of its former greatness, which the modern Greeks call palaces.

**19.**    Then, sailing past the coasts of Caria and Cilicia, they arrived at the once immensely wealthy island of Cyprus, where Ciriaco went ashore and visited the ancient cities of Cyrenum [Kirini], Paphos [Bapho], Amacosta [Famagusta] and, inland, the royal city of Leukosia [Nicosia]. They then set sail for Syria, landing in Beirut, and then turned back to make for Gaeta in Italy. On the return voyage they passed the dangerous straits of Scylla and Charybdis and made landfall at the noble and most ancient Calabrian city of Reggio.

**20.**    From there Ciriaco crossed over to inspect the famous and most beautiful city of Messina in Sicily. Finally, sailing up the Tyrrhenian Sea he arrived at the ancient and renowned Campanian city of Gaeta, where they unloaded and repaired the ship and then stood over to Castellamare.

**21.**    There they took on board a cargo of chestnuts and filberts and then set sail again for Alexandria. But on the 26th of February, while they were attempting to cross the Tyrrhenian Sea, they were driven westward by a violent storm through the Lipari (Aeolian) islands by way of the island of Ustica, and during the night they escaped the perils of the sea by taking shelter in the port of Trapani, the ancient and famous city once ruled by the Trojan Anchises, which Ciriaco had much desired to see. Thence, when the sailors, as usual, had said their prayers of thanksgiving in the church of the Annunciata, they set sail without delay and, passing between the island of Vulcano and the northern shore of Sicily, once more navigated the dangerous straits of Scylla and so got back to Alexandria in Egypt.

22.    There they settled their affairs with Giovanni Michiel of Venice and then re-embarked to return home to Ancona. The voyage took them up the Dalmatian coast of Illyricum, giving them a sight of the beautiful ancient city of Ragusa, a colony of Epidaurus; and so, after one and one-half years away, Ciriaco arrived back at the port of Ancona, more experienced and richer than when he had set out, to rejoin his relatives and home. While he was away, his mother had arranged for the marriage of his sister, Nicolosa, who was now of suitable age, and a few days after his return Ciriaco, augmenting her dowry himself, gave her away with due honor to Bartolomeo Brondello, the son of Liborio, to whom she was betrothed, after which he settled down for a time in the city to devote himself to private and public business.

23.    Meanwhile the city was under enemy attack and, on the night of the seventh of October,[30] the upper walls were unexpectedly captured by a surprise stratagem, and Ciriaco, along with other citizens and his own former good patron, Pietro, played an important part in driving back the enemy and safely freeing the city—an event which he not unskillfully recorded in Italian,[31] his first literary composition. For he had already begun to write when he was still in the intervals of learning his trade under his master Pietro and spent a good deal of his leisure reading the poems of Dante, Petrarch, and Boccaccio.

24.    He sometimes had civilized discussions with his more educated friends about poetry writing; and a learned and eloquent citizen of Ancona called Crasso,[32] who admired young Ciriaco's talent, in the course of their poetic exchange sent him the following vernacular sonnet:[a]

(*Siegui il tuo stille e non guardar al folle*)
Follow your style and take no heed of the mad
insensate rabble; follow that excellence,
Kiriaco mine, of those whose splendor
is in itself immortal and fame and time extol.
Abandon concern for these degenerate matters
which it is vile to delight in and futile to love.

---

[a] The Italian poems that follow (para. 25–30, 49–52, and 58) were punctuated and emended, where necessary, by Professor Cecil Grayson, Oxford University. Some additional emendations were suggested by the translator of the poems, Professor Nelia Saxby, of the University of Cape Town, South Africa. Her footnotes, included here, are designated by the initials "N.S."

Follow Nature; your divine authority
in Nature which takes its preeminence from Heaven;
     and Virtue, that one which, bringing honorable repute,
causes man to distinguish himself in arms or science,
and after, Heaven restores him with immortality's sweetness.
     And you, whom the Muses call to join their song,
do not belittle the seed of your divine gift,
to warrant, after, oblivion's all-engulfing shade.

**25.**    To him Ciriaco replied with another sonnet with the same rhyme-scheme:

     *(Non per seguir lo stil che a l'alto colle)*
     Not so as to follow the style which to the lofty hill
of Parnassus urges us - for its excellence
have you ever pursued, and this now does you honor,
like as to him who strove by deserving it -
     do I shed the ink of our ampoules,
but to follow my commercial labor:
I write and cancel out, and the debtor,
instead of poetry, is nurtured in my books.
     The virtue now, which from you alone flows forth
and is bestowed to me by its own clemency,
would show me as exempt from that all-engulfing shade.
     But since a longer form and greater substance
are needed to thank properly Your Reverence,
let my rhyme be here exonerated from that recitation.

**26.**    He also wrote from time to time many other sonnets as well as verses in *terza rima*, songs and sestinas, which he sent to other scholars and poets in Italy, and when an eloquent young local poet, Alberto of Fabriano, heard of this, he immediately wrote him the following elegant sonnet:

     *(Hor serato si vede il fonte Arpino)*
     Now is seen closed the font of Arpino,
of Mantua, Smyrna, Cordoba and Sulmona,
and you, Delphi, Parnassus and Helicon,
silence have imposed on your immortal song;
     for while there lives on earth the mighty Seraphino,
there resounds amongst us such heavenly organ chant,
that makes the brilliance of Athens and Ancona
but a dead spark under a fine ruby.
     Therefore, seize from Daphne the sacred boughs,
and place, in your melodious dance, o divine Apollo,
a sacred diadem upon your most deserving locks.

And you, O Hadrian sea, bestill your waves
and take on tranquil mien, and say, for well you may, "I live
and you, you other nameless waters, are dead in fame."

27.    I will not quote the appropriate sonnet Ciriaco sent back in reply; but
I cannot here omit to cite the one he later wrote to that noble and eloquent
Venetian patrician, Leonardo Giustiniani:[33]

(*Quel che con summa providentia et arte*)
He who with mighty foresight and skill
turns with the utmost power and motion
the holy millstone of the Crystalline Sky,
and moves the other Heavens from side to side,
wishes to surround you with his splendor, like
a fine ruby which is circumscribed in gold,
whence to these heights never could my childish style,
as would be fitting, elevate you so;
because from the Flower of the whole sea-lapped plain
there reaches up to Heaven with loving wings,
the fame of Giustiniani's glorious excellence,
which, like of custom a bright mirror,
reflects the beauty of his human state
and acts as lighted beacon to all others.

28.    To which Leonardo immediately replied using the same rhymes:

(*Quelle ample lode mie che in brieve carte*)
Those ample praises of me which in brief compositions
you enclose[a] with excellent and polished verse,
are here to you alone redressed,[b] for your immortal
intellect shines forth in a thousand parts.
For a long time now, your praises spread,
wherever the lovely Latin land is pressed,
with all my heart have me made close to you,
and with strong desire to love you, eager.
If you search for virtue in me, too far
do you wander fom the truth, for the heavenly Lord
does not, as you say, extend to me his hand.
But if you seek love, an abundant flow
will you find, for your supreme excellence:
by paying honor to virtue, virtue gets back itself.

---

[a] "*conchiude* I have taken this to be 2nd person singular Present Indicative." - N.S.

[b] "*converte* this is a 3rd person singular Pres. Indicative for a plural subject." - N.S.

**29.** And he added the following sonnet:

*(Qual sparir suole matutin pianeta)*

Just as the morning planet is wont to disappear
at the spreading of the golden and yellow locks
of the sun, and to be concealed[a] by the less nocturnal aspect
of the sun's life-giving lantern of the cheering day,

so, overcome by its own sweet verse, is hushed
your own widespread repute, nor yet does it correspond
to the noble rhymes, in which are distilled and fused
the tones of every great and worthy poet.

Such sweet harmony does your voice make,
that hardly Orpheus, Apollo and Amphion
ever did loosen their lips in more beautiful song.

As strongly, therefore, as my first opinion
by truth is overthrown, so strongly is ignited
the love that has long gathered me to your side.

**30.** To which Ciriaco, in his customary fashion, at once replied:

*(In fin che i fiumi al mar seguir lor meta)*

For as long as the rivers do not cease[b] to pursue
their sea-going quest, or to render shade mountains and boughs,
and[c] as long as the sky surrounds[d] the lovely stars,
your fame must needs be like a comet unto the world.

For your noble rhymes so sweet and so replete
of that elevated concord that confounds my senses,
move from the pegasean font waves so enticing
that ever do I thirst to taste them.[e]

---

[a] " have taken *asconde* to mean *i nasconde*. The subject is *pianeta* of v. 1." - N.S.

[b] "*resta* is 3rd person singular Pres. Indicative for plural subjects *i fiumi* (v 1) and *monte e fronde*." - N.S.

[c] "*e che* repeats the sense of *In fin* (v 1)." - N.S.

[d] "*circonde* is 3rd person singular, Pres. Subjunctive and the subject is *ciel*; however, it could also be *stelle*." - N.S.

[e] "The subject is again the plural *unde* = *onde*." - N.S.

But when they descend so lowly
as to praise my base style up to mighty Hyperion,
among the singers that the song extolled,
  they can do me no honor, but they are crowns
and yours, noble virtues, so greatly does that shine forth
which Apollo wished to concede to us here on earth.[a]

**31.**     After nearly two years in Ancona, where he was variously engaged both
in his private affairs and as one of the six *anziani* of the city, he decided to go
to sea again; so having loaded a ship, commanded by Lucinio Brunelli, with
his own and his old master Pietro's merchandise, he sailed via Liburnia,
sighting Tharsaticum[34] and Saevia, and returned once more to the noble island
of Sicily, disembarking on the way at Scilla in Calabria and climbing its
promontory.

**32.**     Then after a distant view of the lofty, smoking volcano of Etna, he
arrived at the steep and ancient town of Taormina, where he inspected many
large, ancient monuments; next, having once more negotiated the dangerous
straits of Scylla, he revisited the splendid city of Messina; and finally, turning
the headland of Pella, he fetched up at the ancient and splendid Sicilian city of
Palermo, where he unloaded his cargo of fir trees and made a stay of many
days. Among the leading nobility of this great city he was honorably and
cordially received by Iacopo Pizinga, Ruggiero Spatafora, knight, and Count
Giovanni da Ventimiglia,[35] in whose humane company we[36] inspected the fine
porticoes known as the Tocci, the richly decorated churches, the splendid
palace of the Grand Admiral Chiaramonte[37] and the remarkable royal Chapel
of St. Peter [38] in the palace with its porphyry marble and marvelously worked
mosaics.

**33.**     At Monreale, in the fertile, mellifluous countryside outside the walls of
Palermo, he visited the remarkable church of the Blessed Virgin and admired
its ornate bronze doors, its noble marble cloister and its fine monuments of
Guglielmo and other Norman kings.[39] He also, in the company of our common
friend, Trintio Foroflaviniano, inspected the monastery of St. Martin in
Chiaravalle[40] and the nearby impregnable town of Alcimon,[41] the seat of
Bernardo Emcaprareo.

**34.**     Finally, they returned to Palermo to find that their ship had been sold
to cover its owner's debts. Four Venetian galleys, however, on their voyage

---

[a]"vv 12-14 I can make no sense of the original and suspect an error here. The simplest and
most economical emendation I can propose is the following for v 13: *a vostre alme virtù* which
is unsatisfactory, as it does not resolve the problem of the shift from the *tu* form of address
which is consistent throughout the sonnet to the plural form." - N.S.

home from England, under the chief command of Niccolò Donato, had just arrived in the port, and Ciriaco as quickly as possible loaded his goods into them, himself boarded the galley owned by Giovanni Magnimperi and thus left Palermo for Venice.

**35.**    On the way home up the Dalmatian coast they stopped at Liburnian Zara and we[42] met and were graciously received by the Venetian representatives there, Santo Venier, knight, and Pietro Loredan,[43] who gave them the first news—a happy augury for the reunification of the Church—of the election of Martin V as pope by the Council of Constance.[44]

**36.**    In Venice he did all he could to get his merchandise unloaded from the ships as speedily as possible and to sell it. This done, he returned safely to his family in Ancona, while his other associates in the voyage had made a hard land journey home by way of Naples.

**37.**    Ciriaco then remained at home with his family for some time, but, desiring at last to see the great Byzantine city of Constantinople, he embarked as clerk on a merchant ship chartered by his relative, Pasqualino. They sailed past Illyria seeing many Liburnian and Dalmatian islands on the way and arrived on the thirteenth of September at Suasna and the Epirote promontory of Acroceraunia, at the jaws of the Illyrian Gulf. The next leg of their voyage gave them views of the Phaeacians' steep and "aery citadels" of Corfu,[45] the islands of Cephalonia and Zante, and the dangerous promontory of Leukas, the Strophades in the Ionian Sea, the fabled, ancient home of the Harpies, which they saw from afar. Then they rounded Cape Mallia and the upland mountains of Arcadia in the Peloponnese, passing Cythera at a distance, and sailing through the scattered islands of the Cyclades in the Aegean, went ashore at Delos, the renowned and holy island of prophetic Apollo. Thence they sailed between Myconos and Tinos, passed close by Lesbos, had a sight of Tenedos and then, during a day and a night, passed through the narrow strait of the Hellespont, where the coast of Asia and Phrygia on the one hand and fertile coast of Europe on the other come close together. At the ancient, ruined city of Sestos, near Gallipoli, on the southern shore of the Hellespont opposite Thrace, they went ashore and Ciriaco had his first sight of the Turks with their turbans and long, pointed shoes; there, having settled their affairs with the aid of the excellent merchant, Lelio Freducio, they re-embarked, saw the marble island of Proconnesus in the Propontis from a distance, and finally arrived safely on the seventh of October at the renowned city of Byzantium on the Thracian side of the Bosporus.

**38.**    The first man they met, after settling down in the great port, was Ciriaco's kinsman, Filippo Alfieri,[46] the consul of Ancona in the city, who showed them some of the sights,[47] a tour during which they saw the emperor, Manuel Paleologus,[48] in all his majesty.

**39.**     Then he viewed the fine brick walls surrounding the two sides facing the sea and the third one facing inland, of the huge, triangular city, and the splendid, royal Golden Gate[49] with its two marble towers built by divine Theodosius and adorned on its external, marble frontispiece with ancient sculptures by Pheidias imported by that emperor from elsewhere. There too he inspected the finely wrought arms made on behalf of Thetis by Vulcan for Achilles flanked by beautiful columns.

**40.**     Next, inside the city, he first inspected its great ornate churches and, especially, the huge and magnificent temple of Hagia Sophia founded by Justinian[50] with its vast dome, its marble-faced walls, its remarkable pavement and its numerous tall, weighty porphyry and serpentine columns, and in front of it the marvelous bronze equestrian statue of Heraclius,[51] conspicuously placed on the top of its high column.

**41.**     A little higher up in the city he saw, too, the noble hippodrome adorned with its convex arrangement of marble columns and architraves at the head, and its stone obelisks and bronze serpents in the middle, and its many marble stands for the spectators; and most of all he admired the enormous obelisk made from a single block of Numidian stone, and inscribed on all sides with hieroglyphs which, as they learned from the Greek and Latin inscriptions below, was erected to the order of the emperor Theodosius by the architect Proculus.[52]

**42.**     And after that he saw the two exceptionally tall and remarkably designed spiral marble columns of Theodosius, one in the Forum Tauri, the other near the hill of Xerolophos.[53] He saw in the city many other great marble and porphyry columns as well as statues of bronze and various kinds of stone, bases and inscriptions, nymphaea, fountains and lofty brick aqueducts.[54] He also saw a number of libraries famous for their many gold-illuminated and pictured Greek manuscripts, both sacred and profane, in diverse monasteries.

**43.**     Then he went over to the farther bank of the port and walked round Galata in Pera,[55] the splendid colony to be seen from the city of Constantinople, across the water, with its turreted walls, its churches, its merchants' warehouses and offices and its many tall public and private palaces. This splendid trading port was crowded with a host of cargo ships.

**44.**     Finally, having finished his business, Ciriaco voyaged back once more in the same ship to his native Ancona, where he stayed for some time. He now had a desire to visit the ancient city of Pola in Istria, close to the Italian

frontier, so embarking in a small ship to cross the Illyrian Sea, he arrived there
to find the city largely ruined. But he did see many evidences of its noble past
including the splendid gates of Salvia Postumia, the daughter of the aedile
Sergius,[56] as well as many large buildings and the fine amphitheater built of
large stones that the people of Pola gratefully dedicated to the imperial
brothers, Lucius Septimius Severus and Antoninus. He also saw, both inside
the city and outside its walls down to the sea, numerous stone tombs, many of
whose epitaphs he transcribed,[57] being accompanied and much helped by
Andrea Contarini, who was then the Venetian governor of the city.

**45.**     Then, after these few days in Pola, he returned home to Ancona, after
which he made a number of voyages to Chios, Gallipoli, and Byzantium,
having previously inspected the coastal city of Albona in Liburnia.

**46.**     While Ciriaco was in Ancona engaged in various business,[58] his old
master, Pietro, being dead, Giovanni di Luca of Tolentino, the leading
spice-dealer in the city, engaged him to balance his books, since Niccolò
Cossi, a Florentine, the former accountant of the firm, was dead, and since
none of his commercial associates was competent to do the job properly.
Ciriaco, young as he was, was a skilled accountant, and though it proved a
particularly difficult and laborious task, since the ledgers had not been
accurately kept and balanced for fourteen years, his superior intellect enabled
him to close the books in a thoroughly true and comprehensive fashion and to
hand them over to the heirs of Giovanni di Luca, who by this time had died.

**47.**     Meanwhile, Gabriele Condulmer, cardinal of Siena and legate of Pope
Martin V, had arrived in Ancona to become rector of the province of Piceno
on behalf of the Holy See;[59] and he very soon resolved to repair the port of
Ancona. This involved introducing better organization of income and
expenditure and of financial officers; and the cardinal caused the city to decree
that one single treasurer should be elected in place of the existing system of
several city treasurers. Accordingly, a board of three men constituted from
among the well-born citizens to control the finances, decreed to elect
trustworthy and experienced accounting officers from among the population,
having already elected Paulo Giuliano to be general treasurer. And the
accounting officers they chose were: Niccolò Luttarelli, who had been an
excellent financial officer for a long time, and the young Ciriaco,[60] who
performed his task with such diligence and foresight, that his colleague stood
down after six months leaving him to carry on alone—a duty he performed to
the satisfaction of all, with the help of assistant clerks chosen by himself, so
long as Gabriele remained in the city as legate of the province. The young
Ciriaco was in this office for almost two years, and during that time he reduced
all the financial records and many of the financial regulations to a better and
more convenient form; and he also, by his extraordinary attention and industry,

with the assistance of a number of leading citizens, freed the city from a large number of unexplained interest charges that had gravely burdened it since the time of Cardinal Egidio.[61]

**48.**    But when Cardinal Gabriele, at Pope Martin's behest, left Ancona for Bologna to become legate in the province of Flaminia,[62] Ciriaco at once tendered his resignation to the six *anziani* of the city; for his noble spirit, no longer content to risk stagnation in these common involvements, now impelled him, rather, to travel and to see the whole world. Shortly before the legate Gabriele departed from Ancona, two of the senior lawyers on his staff, Serafino of Urbino and Memmio Gazario of Siena, with whom Ciriaco had struck up a warm friendship, exchanged Italian poems with him; and these friends further aroused the young man's feeling that his destiny was to explore the world. Here, then, I quote some of the best of these poems exchanged between him and Serafino, beginning with one from Ciriaco:

**49.**          (*Quel Spirito gientil, che amor conserva*)
          That gentle spirit, which Love[a] keeps,
    in his all-seeing mind, on the chosen path,
    urged me to the peak of the Apollonian mount,
    in pursuit of the tracks of a white doe.
          There, Thersicore with her troop
    did I see, round about the Choliambic font
    lead a Seraphim in human guise,
    who was covered in the boughs of Minerva.
          Here it seemed to me that from this font I saw
    naked Diana issue forth with wind-blown locks,
    and underneath a laurel tree Daphne and Apollo;
          then from a thicket Venus and Mars emerge,
    and seeing of the Seraphim the human brow,
    encircle it and crown it with their art.

**50.**    Whereupon Serafino replied with an excellent sonnet:
          (*Le rissonante Rime in chui si serva*)
          The resounding rhymes in which you have enclosed
    every supreme and rare quality
    which encrowns me, and in the company of the Immortals
    with great intelligence, have enshrined me,
          require response from a better lyre and greater vigor,
    like those of Dante and of our Petrarch;
    but as my small intellect is able to do,

---

[a] "v 1 I have taken it that *Amor* is personified, hence the capital letter." - N.S.

I firstly give you thanks, and pray that you[a] may find
     contrary Fortune and Envy so powerless against you,
that future generations will bind your works
and your reputation remain whole and unharmed.
     May your name last in every country
for as long as worldly creation has movement
and may I see[b] you in our lifetime with the laurel crowned.

**51.**    To which, changing the order of the rhymes, Ciriaco rejoined:
     *(Qual circuncinto in oro fin rubino)*
     Like a fine ruby in gold circumscribed,
in which a ray of the flashing sun is locked,
or like a diamond of a great collection,
pearl, spinel, emerald or sapphire,
     like bright stars in azure color,
roses and lilies, green-leaved in grass,
more eagerly are admired[c] with the soul in thrall
     to[d] the first human sense, by the color fine,
     thus to the second one, almost enslaved
are the souls, at hearing the divine and supreme
rhymes of yours, deserving of your immortalization.
     And although to me his voice comes[e] from far away and
from on high,
yet at its resonance did I understand in part
to be its worth much higher than the Mantuan one.[63]

**52.**    And Serafino's answering sonnet followed the same rhyme scheme:
     *(Bench'io comprehenda esser venuto al chino)*
     Although I understand that on the downward slope
our human state is set and in it virtue unnerved,

---

[a] "v 9 Ms v 9 I have taken *te* to be the subject pronoun and have repunctuated thus for vv 9–10. . . ." - N.S.

[b] "I have taken *vegia* to be 1st person singular Present Subjunctive." - N.S.

[c] "I have taken *vaghe* to mean *vagamente* and have followed the . . . ms reading of *si miran*." - N.S. Cf. Footnote to text *ad loc*.

[d] "*Dal* I have taken to mean *Del* as the use of *dal* with the meaning of *del* is common in this area at this time." - N.S.

[e] "v 12 *volli* I have taken to mean *voli*=fly as there are other instances in these sonnets of hypercorrective gemination of the liquid consonant cfr. *stille*=*stile*, style 24, 1." - N.S.

and although I see our age become enslaved
to vice and ignorance, yet do I maintain
    that the Heavenly Force which is all full
of just and holy will, reserves the task to you
of resuscitating the Muses and their[a] company,
by decree of heavenly providence.[b]
    Wherever spread the Adriatic waters,
or even where the oceanic wave might lap,
I see the path to make you in fame immortal.
    Flee from the inert rabble, so insane
that it would engulf you in the waves of other cares,
and let your intellect become of these profane.

These prophetic words of his good friend powerfully strengthened Ciriaco's noble, inborn desire.

**53.**    It was during this time, when the cardinal was still legate in Ancona, that Ciriaco, at the instigation of his close friend, Marco of Pistoia, the secretary of the city, began to pay serious attention to acquiring facility in Latin. He did not start in the usual beginner's way, with the rudiments of grammar, but, having more grown-up ambitions and wanting better to understand Dante's *Divine Comedy*, of which he already had considerable knowledge, he was bold enough to begin by reading the sixth book of Virgil's *Aeneid* with the notable scholar, Tommaso of Camerino,[64] commonly known as Seneca, who at that time was the professor and teacher of literature in the city, where he gave regular public lectures. Ciriaco arranged with Tommaso to become his private pupil, their arrangement being that Tommaso should read Virgil to him, while he read Dante to Tommaso; but before they had come to the end of their mutual agreement, they had to leave Ancona in different directions and part company. Ciriaco, however, found such relish in the divine eloquence of Virgil as far as his study of the poem (with Tommaso) had gone, that he zealously embarked—so keen and capable was his intellectual grasp—on reading the whole *Aeneid* on his own. Thus he not only began to comprehend the elegance and mastery of the poem and to become thoroughly familiar with the poet, but also, from his study of Virgil, he admirably learned both to read and to write Latin.[65] And just as Dante's poems had led him to the knowledge of Virgil, so the reading of Virgil aroused in his mind a noble desire to win knowledge of Homer's great poem and of the Greek tongue.

---

    [a] "I have taken *sua* to mean *loro=their* as is usual in the literary tradition from Dante onwards." - N.S.

    [b] "I would venture to suggest the following emendation: *[Per] decreto [di] spirital distino* and have followed it in the translation." - N.S.

**54.**    Meanwhile he had been diligently and admiringly studying the splendid marble arch[66] of Trajan Caesar, which stands prominently at the port of Ancona, and he recognized that the upper part of it lacked its original golden equestrian statue, which the ancient Senate and people of Rome, with the help of fine architects, had dedicated to this excellent prince, the far-sighted founder of their life-giving port, a statue which was flanked by conspicuous images of his sister, Marciana, and his wife, Plotina. This good emperor, with royal bounty, later bestowed on the citizens of Ancona, which held so prominent a place among the Adriatic ports, the perpetual privilege of bearing a splendid copy of this image as their badge of honor; and we still see it today publicly displayed throughout the city and often adorning the purple standards of Anconitan *podestàs* through the cities of Latium and southern Italy.[67] This is the inscription itself as transcribed from the arch:

[*CIL* IX, 5894]

This remarkable great work of architecture, with its important, well-lettered Latin inscription, was the first seminal inspiration to Ciriaco, as we often heard him say, to search and examine all the other worthy memorials of antiquity in the world.[68]

**55.**    It was not long, therefore, before he eagerly set out for the famous city of Rome in order to view the world's greatest and most significant historical monuments. He arrived there on the third of December, in the eighth year of Martin V's pontificate.[69] Shortly before this, Cardinal Gabriele had himself arrived in Rome from Bologna, his legateship being ended; so Ciriaco visited him at San Lorenzo in Damaso, when he was joyfully and kindly welcomed. He then stayed for forty days as a guest in the cardinal's house, and he daily rode round the city on his white horse closely and diligently inspecting, examining and taking note of whatever venerable antiquities survived in that great city—temples, theaters, vast palaces, marvelous baths, obelisks, and arches, aqueducts, bridges, statues, columns, bases and historical inscriptions. These he faithfully recorded exactly as they were written, so that some day later on he would be able to put them together properly in *Commentaria*.[70]

**56.**    It appeared to him, as he looked upon the great remains left behind by so noble a people, and cast to the ground throughout the city, that the stones themselves afforded to modern spectators much more trustworthy information about their splendid history than was to be found in books.[71] He accordingly resolved to see for himself and to record whatever other antiquities remained scattered about the world, so that he should not feel that the memorable monuments, which time and the carelessness of men had caused to fall into ruin, should entirely be lost to posterity.

**57.**    One day at this time the noble young prince of Salerno, Antonio, the nephew of Pope Martin, rode out with Luigi Verme[72] and a band of other nobles of the city for a hunting expedition near the Salernian Bridge and the cardinal was kind enough to send Ciriaco in the company of his kinsman, Pietro Baduario,[73] to watch it. As they were riding[74] alongside Agabito Colonna, a learned man, they looked up at the arch beside the Capitol of the imperial brothers Severus and Antoninus to whom there was a dedicatory inscription, the latter part of which said:

[*CIL* VI, 1033]

When they had read these words, Ciriaco in his friendly way turned to Agabito and asked, "Could this indolent age of ours have produced any Roman prince worthy of such an inscription?" Agabito glanced over toward the young prince Antonio and replied: "The fates may well have given this young man to our long decayed city, for he springs from a noble Roman family and enjoys the powerful favor of Pope Martin, his uncle." Whereupon that same day, having returned home from the hunt, Ciriaco immediately sent the young prince Antonio, by hand of Agabito, a copy of verses he had composed on this very subject.[75]

**58.**               (*Driza la testa omai, inclyta Roma*)
                    Hold up your head at last, o glorious Rome.
Look upon your Mars and his born twins
who were the first hammers
to fabricate the circle of your hills.
Adorn and gather up your long neglected locks,
for this one wills that in you shall be renewed
Fabii, Scipii and Marcelli,
for whom you have long searched with tear-stained eyes;

9              and wills he too that at last you should regain
that sceptre under which you tamed the world,
which is the gift of mighty Jove to Citharea
and by him promised for Enea.
He wants you, with great guidance, to turn at last full circle
to the time when under every load
of your family, two round Columns

16            held up your outmost reaches.

17            The one in the sacred forum the mighty King
has placed, so that to the ministry
which was conceded to Peter
may come back His bride[a] in the Lateran seat;
so as to congregate again that scattered flock,
for, seeing her in such adultery

---

[a] "v 20 I have taken *sposa* as the subject of *torni* i.e. God's bride = the Church in the Lateran should return to her task, i.e. the *ministero* but the text is ambiguous here." - N.S.

reside, without a true spouse,
it will be dispersed[a] to the ocean's end.

25        Now has He given the ministry[b] into the hands
of Martin V, under whose holy guidance
the long-submerged Fisherman's ship,
together with those great keys
which were to him conceded[c] with the papal mantle,
already have new vigor;
for he will so widely propagate the Christian faith

32     that the profane one will be totally submerged.

33        The other Column in human temporal government
has already directed its gentle offspring
who in his puerile age
gives rare indications of great valor,
glorious, illustrious prince of Salerno
has he been created; in his lordly bent
is discernible the manly
courage to subjugate greater kingdoms;

41        and of no greater worth than he were yet
Caesar and the other bright augustan deities
for valor, should Fortune similarly exert herself.
For should the propitious heavens intend
to exalt him among our kind,
needs must it still be said of him
as of Severus and of Antonin the worthy:

48     "This one has propagated the Roman Empire."

49        This one was to the world given by kindly Jove,
filled with all the goodness and clemency
which the divine Essence
might have to show in creature of our time.
Prudent, just, strong and temperate:
this, from the ten stars which influence him under that power
of the Three, that He irradiates from the divine cloister;

57        under whose splendid purple
quickens in this one such vigorous Hope,

---

[a] "*dispersa* I have taken to refer to *gregie*." - N.S.

[b] "*l'a conducto*: I have made this refer to *ministero* (v 18) but it could apply to *gregie* which is also masculine and postulate that Ciriaco had this in mind." - N.S.

[c] "*fur* is not necessary as there are instances of the singular verb used for a plural subject." - N.S.

burning Charity and uncontaminated Faith,
that to gain for him Mercy
the First Power no longer attempts;
because that scale
that adjusts itself as the universe moves,[a]

64      will never see good become evil.[b]

65          O song, you who still hope to sing as perfect
he who anticipates the mighty task
of the goodly Roman Empire
that from these two Columns awaits its great renewal,
go happily to the youthful Prince,
nephew to Peter's great successor,
and with honest speech
open to him every treasure of your heart.

73          And if of your creation
he should yet wish to know the unknown author,
tell him that a servant of his
born in Ancona, to him sends you

77      for he's a lover of the honor of his crown.

**59.** On Christmas day, the feast of Jove incarnate, he saw Pope Martin celebrate Mass and he was still in Rome on January first, 1425, the day when Jesus, the son of God made man, was circumcised under the Old Law and given his most holy name, a day dedicated by the ancient Romans to two-headed Janus, where he heard a sermon delivered in the pope's presence by the eminent Dominican theologian, Andrea of Constantinople, the master of the papal palace. He then eagerly set off for home.

**60.** On his journey back he stopped at the ancient town of Sutri, inspected the marvelous hot baths in the towered city of Viterbo, and at the venerable city of Orvieto visited the richly adorned marble church of the Blessed Virgin, where he admired its fine, sculptured facade, its beautifully carved choir-stalls, and the statues of the Virgin and angels above its bronze portals.[76]

**61.** So he settled down once more in Ancona, where in the new elections he was appointed one of the six *anziani* along with Pagliaresio Pisanello[77] and other colleagues and thus resumed his active public life. Meanwhile, however,

---

[a] "vv 60-3 the sense here is arduous; I have postulated that the subject of *ricercha* is *la prima possanza*=God and that *aiusta* has the value of a reflexive verb, i.e. adjusts itself and that *billanza* is therefore its subject." - N.S.

[b] "v 64 the literal translation is *will change from white to black*; I have attempted to convey what I think is the sense of the verse." - N.S.

he had received a letter from his kinsman, Zaccaria Contarini[78] in Venice, begging him to be his commercial representative in Piceno or Apulia, but since he was always more interested in grander pursuits than simply financial gain, he preferred to do business in the East, in Greece or elsewhere, which would give him an opportunity to learn Greek and better to understand Homer. Accordingly, as soon as his term of civic office was over, he at once went by overland route to see Zaccaria in Venice. Zaccaria had long-standing commerical interests of various kinds in Cyprus; and when he heard what the young man had in mind, he decided to recall his brother, Pietro, then in charge of affairs in the island, to Venice, and sent Ciriaco with full authority to take his place. This commission Ciriaco took up all the more gladly, because it would allow him personally to meet Janus, the king of Cyprus,[79] whom he had previously known only by reputation, and because it would give him a legitimate opportunity to seek and enjoy the king's gracious favor and company.

**62.** So carrying Zaccaria's letter to the latter's brother, Pietro, he at once returned to Ancona and set sail in a ship owned by Niccolò Corsedacio, which was ready to leave the port, going ashore in Apulia at Monopoli, Bari, and the ancient ruined town of Anterium. He thus arrived at Byzantium, where it did not take him long to learn the rudiments of Greek while he was waiting for a ship bound for Cyprus or Syria.

**63.** Before this vessel arrived, however, he heard that an Anconitan ship, commanded by Benvenuto Scotigolo,[80] had put in at the island of Chios intending to sail on to Syria. Ciriaco, therefore, immediately sailed south to Chios, where he was very cheerfully welcomed by the Anconitan nobles who were taking passage in the ship—the owner himself, a number of merchants, and Francesco Ferretti;[81] and it was through the introduction of the scholarly young Francesco that he now began his close and intimate friendship with Andreolo Giustiniani,[82] a prominent and learned member of the Genoese Mahonensian company on the island, along with whom he recorded in his notebook many antique remains and fine Greek and Latin inscriptions. On Chios, with the valuable help of Andreolo, he was able to buy for twenty gold florins his beautiful Greek codex of the New Testament.

**64.** When the ship was ready to sail and Ciriaco had settled his own affairs with the help of his kinsman, Niccolò Alfieri, they shaped course through the clustered Aegean islands for Syria, landing first at the once-renowned Asiatic island of Rhodes, and thence continuing their voyage without delay before a favorable west wind to Beirut, where the cargo was unloaded. Ciriaco himself immediately struck inland to visit the ancient and renowned Syrian city of Damascus, where, under the guidance of the Venetian patrician, Ermolao Donato, at that time the leading merchant there and a learned man in his own right, he viewed all the important ancient and modern monuments in that magnificent city.[83]

**65.** Outside the walls, also, there are the Street Called Straight and the ruined house of the prophet Ananias, both memorials of the apostle St. Paul, as well as the famous church of the blessed doctor, St. John Damascene; and he saw the fine, high-walled and towered citadel; but nearly all the buildings within the ancient walls had been destroyed by the powerful Persian king, Athemir Bey, and leveled to the ground.[84] He also saw a number of antiquities from the ancient citadel of Sidon along with a beautiful collection of wonderfully wrought Damascene vases inlaid with gold and silver, some of which he purchased for his own collection of *objets d'art* at home, where I have seen them myself. Another sight was the enormous number of camels that had come from Arabia Felix, Saba and Gedrosia, laden with many kinds of spices to be marketed in that remarkable city.

**66.** In Damascus Ciriaco met a rich and prominent merchant called Musalach who regularly sent his two sons to trade in Ethiopia and India. Since Ciriaco very much wanted to visit these places, Musalach introduced him to his sons, who were just then back from Saba. And when Ciriaco asked that he be allowed to associate himself with them (when next they went), Musalach readily complied.

**67.** Instead of this, however, he finished his business in Damascus and returned to Beirut, where he visited his former companions, who soon headed their ship home for Ancona. But Ciriaco himself then boarded a Genoese ship bound for Tripoli and disembarked at Famagusta in Cyprus,[85] where he met the learned natural philosopher (physician), Evangelista de Imola, a great friend of Zaccaria Contarini, who told him that Pietro, Zaccaria's brother, had recently sailed back to Venice leaving things in great disorder. Ciriaco, therefore, on Evangelista's advice, decided to stay in Famagusta until he received word from Zaccaria telling him what arrangements he wanted made. Meanwhile, to fill in the time, he got elected vicar of the Genoese *podestà* of the city, holding office for nearly two months, during which time he took pleasure in his first study of the rules and important opinions laid down in the Roman law books, thereby increasing his skill as a magistrate. He admirably pronounced judgments on the basis of the ancient legal texts alone and skillfully devoted himself to the task of creating concord and peace among the citizens.

**68.** But then Zaccaria's letter at length arrived from Venice, anxiously urging Ciriaco to take his affairs in hand, so he proceeded on to Nicosia having had some difficulty in getting leave to resign his office. His first visit in Nicosia was to King Janus, its serene ruler; and he had only to see and hear the king speak to recognize that his impressive personality outshone the renown of his name, while the king himself, attended in his hall by the royal knights, Badin de Nores[86] and Hugo Saltani and other notables, having listened to Ciriaco's words of praise and his eloquent discussion of the king's recent misfortunes,[87] cheerfully and graciously welcomed him and regally admitted him to the company of his principal courtiers.

**69.**    The king offered all his royal help with those of Zaccaria's affairs that needed settling; and Ciriaco tendered to His Majesty Zaccaria's letter and thanked him for his graceful favor. Ciriaco then, with the authorization of Lodovico Corario,[88] the Vice-Bailie of the Venetians, took over all Zaccaria's and his brother Pietro's business from their agents, Pietro Berardino and Leonello, and administered it so diligently and skillfully, both inside and outside the city, that he completed the whole task within a year, having made an accurate list of debtors and creditors and having reduced them to a very small number.

**70.**    During this period Ciriaco often went hunting with the king and was able to explore most of the island; nor should I omit to mention what a brilliant spectacle this celebrated prince presented on these occasions. For we have Ciriaco's own description of how the king, brightly dressed in gold, and armed with bow and quiver, would ride with his company through fields and hills and trackless glades,[89] startling the birds as he chased his panther prey, just as bright Apollo, armed with his hunting spear, dazzled the eye as he was seen leading his singing band in wintry Lycia or through the Cynthian uplands in days of old.

**71.**    In Cyprus too Ciriaco made a particularly lucky find. After a good day's hunting for panthers, the king, laden with the kill, arrived at a hunting lodge where he conferred knighthood on a Dacian youth; and Ciriaco, on his usual search for books, went to a certain old monastery where, among its squalidly kept and long neglected manuscripts, he was overjoyed to discover an ancient codex of Homer's *Iliad*, which he persuaded an illiterate monk, not without difficulty, to let him have in exchange for a Gospel book. This book afforded him his first great help in overcoming his ignorance of Greek literature. Later on, in Nicosia, from another monk, he also acquired an *Odyssey*, a number of the tragedies of Euripides, and a book of antiquities by the Alexandrian grammarian, Theodosius;[90] and whenever he found a moment of leisure, he would pore over the task of construing and reading them through.

**72.**    At last, when he had finished his business, he decided to leave the island, and as a worthy parting gift he composed the following inscription for a proposed statue of the king:

[Apianus and Amantins, 1534, p. 506]

**73.**     So he left Cyprus by way of Famagusta, where he loaded his own and Zaccaria's goods and embarked on a Genoese ship that brought him to Rhodes. After a few days there he met among other notables the Augustinian theologian, Boezio of Tolentino, metropolitan bishop of Rhodes,[91] who was delighted to greet him as a fellow countryman from the same part of Italy. Boezio in turn introduced him to Fantino Quirini,[92] a worthy member of the religious order of the Knights of Rhodes; and under the guidance of the two men he saw the city and travelled about the island inspecting its ancient monuments, its walls, columns, statues, bases, and Doric-lettered inscriptions.[93] From a Greek monk he bought for himself three recently excavated antiquities, a marble bust of a plebeian priest, a statue of Venus,[94] and another of Bacchus, which he dispatched home to Ancona in the hands of his brother-in-law, Bartolomeo, who had just arrived at Rhodes in an Anconitan ship belonging to [captained by?] Bonifazio, which was bound for Jerusalem. He also admired in Rhodes its lush and charming meadows, its regal parks of fruit-bearing juniper, and its flowery gardens—vegetation very characteristic of the fourth region[95] and the middle of the inhabitable zone of the globe.

**74.**     Making for Thrace, Ciriaco then returned across the Aegean to Chios and his friend, Andreolo, with whom he settled affairs and then left for Gallipoli; but not far from the port a strong northern headwind forced them to put in to the port of Cardamyla on the island, where, while they lay at anchor for several days awaiting a favorable breeze, a party of Genoese noblemen went ashore, some to snare colorful birds in the trees, others preferring to catch fish of various kinds on baited hooks.[96] Meanwhile, Ciriaco did not want to waste every hour of the day in idleness, so he studied the Greek books he had brought with him from Cyprus, and while reading them came upon a life of Euripides that was brief enough for him to put it into Latin;[97] and he sent his translation to his good friend, Andreolo Giustiniani, at Chios.

**75.**     Next day they left Cardamyla with a south wind behind them and arrived at the island of Tenedos, where Ciriaco had the pleasure of viewing the ancient remains of its once noble city and then sailed through the narrow Hellespont to Gallipoli on the Thracian Chersonese. There Ciriaco brought his goods ashore with the help of Pietro Simone Polidori,[98] an Anconitan merchant, loaded them on to camels and set out for the inland Thracian city of Adrianople, where, through the good offices of the royal factor, Juan Rimatres of Tarragona, he had a sight of the Turkish Sultan, Murad Bey,[99] not only holding court in his hall, but also riding on his horse up and down the field in all his splendor, accompanied by his magnificent, mounted bowmen, as he watched a great archery competition for the prize of a silver bowl displayed on a tall standard. The business of selling his merchandise kept him in Adrianople for the winter, and in his leisure he listened to the Greek grammarian, Lio Boles,[100] expounding Homer's *Iliad* and the first part of Hesiod's *Works and*

*Days*; and it was thanks to Lio that he was able to buy a number of Greek manuscripts plundered by the Turks from Salonica,[101] among them being a text of the great Alexandrian geographer, Ptolemy, which was particularly useful to him. In Adrianople, furthermore, he met a well known and learned Genoese merchant called Niccolò Ziba[102] who regularly traded with Persia, Parthia and the territory round the Caspian Sea; and arranged with Ziba one day to visit these countries in his company.

**76.** But now he had finished his business in Adrianople and returned to Gallipoli. At this moment he happened to spy an Anconitan ship owned (or captained) by Tommaso di Biagio passing under sail through the Hellespont, so he at once had himself rowed out to her in a small boat[103] and put on board a consignment of hides and carpets for Lelio to deliver to Zaccaria. On the Turkish slave market in Adrianople he had bought a very intelligent servant girl from Epirus named Clara,[104] whom he wanted to send home to his mother, Massiella, under the care of his cousin, Ciucio;[105] so he put her on board the ship too. Ciriaco himself rowed back with his faithful black[106] manservant, Niccolino, and a number of Turks as his guides, hastened away to visit Macedonia and its important sights; and so, after travelling through the Emathian and Philippian countryside, he arrived at the illustrious city of Philippi itself, where he inspected many fine monuments of antiquity—the ruined marble walls, the theater, and a great number of large tombs of princes and soldiers; and what particularly attracted his attention was a huge monument on the road outside the city fashioned from a single block of stone, which the local Greek inhabitants dubiously call the Manger of Alexander's horse Bucephalus:

[*CIL* III, 642, 7337]

And strewn in the neighborhood around this monument he found many inscriptions which he duly added to his *commentaria*. I know that what particularly inspired the young man to visit this region was the passage he had read in Ovid's *Fasti* about the death of Julius Caesar: "Be witnesses, Philippi and those whose bones are scattered in her soil."[107]

**77.** Then, leaving in the evening, he went on to the noble ancient coastal city of Salonica,[108] among whose excellent monuments he saw the marvelous arch of our own Aemilius Paulus in the main square, and the ruined temple of Diana with numerous marble statues of the gods on its architraves.[109] He also inspected many of the splendid Christian churches, delighting particularly in the big one dedicated to the warrior-martyr, St. Demetrius; the turreted brick walls built by Lysimachus; and many inscriptions relating to heroes and poets,[110] including an inscription on a tripod of the Muses that was brought to Salonica from Mount Helicon, with its extraordinary reference to the date when Homer and Hesiod lived.[111] In Salonica, too, he bought many ecclesiastical and secular manuscripts, which he forwarded by galley to his friend, Andreolo, in Chios.

**78.** He then proceeded, by way of Adrianople, back to Gallipoli, where he found a letter from Ancona informing him that Martin V had died and that Gabriele Condulmer, cardinal of Siena, who—as we have seen—had served in Ancona for two years as papal legate to the province of Piceno, had been elected—on the third of March—to succeed him under the name of Eugenius IV.[112] This admirable election so pleased Ciriaco that he at once, as I came to know, sent letters to Niccolò Ziba in Adrianople, to Giorgio Begna in Zara in Liburnia, and in Italy to Cardinal Giordano Orsini, Leonardo Aretino, and many other influential friends, as well as to myself, to this effect:[113]

> I reckoned that the death of so good a Pope as Martin would be unfortunate for the Church and disastrous for virtually everybody in Italy; but now in the event I see that it was in a sense quite fortunate and timely, rather, in that so responsible, humane, clement, wise and wholly devout a man, as I now learn, has been elected his successor.

And he added:

> For if almighty God[114] wills that Italy and our religion shall be restored by any priest, I am convinced that so excellent a Pope, Eugenius, is the very man to further this great task, because we have already seen how prudently, firmly, justly, devotedly and large-mindedly he has always conducted the important affairs of the Church.

**79.**     These were his own words. At this point Ciriaco decided to give up his idea of exploring Persia, as he had arranged with Niccolò Ziba. His plan now was to get clear of his commercial business, and then, having collected all the intelligence he could concerning a union with the Greeks and the whole Eastern Church[115] and on an effective crusade against the Turks, to hasten home to Italy and to visit the pope in Rome in order, both orally and by written report, to lay before him whatever of importance in his view he had discovered on these matters.

**80.**     To enable him to do this more expertly he visited Memnon,[116] the son of Carlo, the late duke of Cephalonia, a man of parts with military experience, who had just arrived from the sultan's court. Memnon warmly welcomed him, and after a thorough discussion about eastern affairs, they decided to reconnoiter the principal cities and centers of Asia that were under Turkish domination; so they left Gallipoli, sailed through the Hellespont to Asia, and arrived at the royal city of Bursa in Bithynia under Mt. Olympus, which Ciriaco found to be a populous and very wealthy place embellished by remarkable ancient and modern buildings.

**81.**     There he consigned all his own commercial business to the trustworthy hands of the Genoese nobleman, Babilano Palavicini,[117] an excellent
merchant, while he himself went on with Memnon to visit the Turkish
governor of the province, Canuza Bey,[118] who was staying at an inn on the
slopes of Mt. Olympus and who, on learning of their arrival, met them at his
frontier and graciously received them. For Canuza Bey was a Greek by birth
and education and thus able knowledgeably to discuss with Ciriaco the
antiquities of the province, especially the great temple at Cyzicus. Ciriaco had
observed at Mundanya, the port of Bursa, that many dressed marble stones
from the Cyzican temple had been utilized in the erection of modern buildings;
and on the score both of the respect due to antiquity and of the good reputation
of the Sultan himself, lest all trace of the building be lost to posterity, he
persuaded Canuza Bey to forbid any further destruction of the still-standing
walls, columns, and architraves of this spectacular monument. Canuza Bey had
the learning to appreciate this argument and readily promised to do what
Ciriaco advised.

**82.**     Ciriaco then returned to Bursa and, all afire to see the temple, proceeded with a Turkish guide to the noble Asian city of Cyzicus which, as he
says, stands on a peninsula on the southern shore of the Propontis opposite the
island of Proconnesus and is everywhere strewn with the ruins of the huge
stone walls and vast buildings of the ancient city.

**83.**     Prominent among these are the towering remains of the superb temple
of Jupiter with its lofty marble walls which still show the marks of the golden
thread described by Pliny in his *Natural History*: "The temple at Cyzicus also
survives, where the architect inserted a golden thread in all the joints of the
polished stone, etc."[119] Still remaining are various statues of gods on the highly
ornamented facade of the temple and the very wide bases of long rows of
columns; and although the majority of the original columns have fallen to the
ground, thirty-three of them with their architraves are still standing.[120] The
building also bears this Greek inscription, which Ciriaco recorded:
                    [Ashmole, 1956, 187–188]
He also found other inscriptions here and there in the city, as well as huge
marble gates and remains of the amphitheater and a large statue of
earth-shaking Neptune—sights, as he said, that all immensely excited him.
Here he remembered the elegant verses he had read in Ovid: "On this side
Cyzicus, clinging to the shore of the Propontis: Cyzicus, noble creation of the
people of Thrace."[121]

**84.**     He then went back to Bursa, left his unsold goods behind with
Babilano, settled Zaccaria's outstanding business, and decided to return with
Memnon by way of Byzantium to Italy in order to discuss with the pope his
proposals for an expedition against the Turks. On his overland journey to

Constantinople, still with a Turkish guide, he made a detour in order to see the Bithynian city of Nicaea[122]—a towered, brick-walled city situated, as he found, on the edge of a Bithynian lake. There he discovered Greek inscriptions on the gate of Tiberius Claudius Germanicus[123] and on the tower of Trajan and he inspected other ancient monuments of the same quality as well as the great basilica where the celebrated ecumenical Council of Nicaea had met.[124]

**85.**     Then he pressed on day and night through forests and difficult country till he arrived at the ancient ruined Bithynian city of Chalcedon, destroyed by age, which is today known as Scutari, a trading port just opposite Byzantium.[125] Thence he took a boat over to Galata in Pera and the great city of Constantinople, where he found his kinsman, Pasqualino[126] of Ancona, who was proposing to return home a month later in his ship. Meanwhile, so as to lose no time, he decided to look around Asia Minor and to pick up Pasqualino's ship at Chios on its way back through the Aegean.

**86.**     So he took passage in a Taragonian galley to the fine and once powerful city of Mytilene on Lesbos, where, through the kind offices of Giorgio Gattilusio, the lord of the island,[127] he inspected the city's many important sights: its theaters, columns, statues, bases, Greek and Latin inscriptions, and its remarkable marble arch known as the Tetrastyle, dedicated by the ancient ruler of the islands to Flavius Valerius Diocletianus, Constantius, and the most noble Maximianus.
                    [*CIL* III, 450][128]

**87.**     He also looked at the tall ancient stone aqueducts on the island and the fallen stones of the walls of Pyrra and Methymna.[129] Then, armed with letters of introduction from Gattilusio to Turkish authorities in Asia Minor, he crossed the narrow strait in a little boat to the nearest point on the Asiatic shore and took the steep road up to the noble city of Pergamum, once the metropolis of Asia Minor, where with a local Turkish guide he thoroughly investigated the city and its huge ancient remains scattered about it: vast temples, two great amphitheaters,[130] a number of colossal marble statues of gods and famous men and, among its fine tombs, an enormous sepulcher made of great stones rising up like a high mountain. He also saw what was left of all kinds of fine antique structures and many good Greek and Latin inscriptions.

**88.**     Next he came to the long-ruined city of Aeolian Cumae, the birthplace of Hesiod, which, as he learned, the local inhabitants call Chrysopolis; but finding nothing worth recording there, he proceeded to the ancient Ionian city of Smyrna, famous for its connection with the illustrious name of Homer; and indeed he found there on an ancient stone an inscription indicating that Homer was born there. Other evidences he saw of the antiquity of Smyrna were its splendid harbor and a very tall spiral column.

**89.**     Ciriaco then went to old and new Phocaea[131] and visited the big alum mines, where he met their lessee, Federigo Giustiniani, the father-in-law[132] of his friend, Andreolo, who helped him to buy some excellent gold coins of Philip, Alexander, and Lysimachus.[133]

**90.**     Next he came to the coast which is in sight of of the island of Chios, where he took a small passenger boat[134] across to the island. Here he once more visited his friend Andreolo and his black servant Niccolino, who had come from Gallipoli with Ciriaco's remaining goods and book-boxes and was awaiting the arrival of his master. In Chios Ciriaco stayed for several days at Andreolo's house, both reading the Greek books he had forwarded from Salonica and sorting out and packing up all his goods and possessions, while he awaited the arrival of Pasqualino's ship from Byzantium.

**91.**     But the Anconitan ship, captained as we have said by Pasqualino, arrived just at the time when pretty well the whole Aegean was in a state of excitement over numerous reports that a large Venetian fleet was on its way to attack Chios; so the city authorities, fearing that the Venetians might intercept the ship to get up-to-date intelligence about the state of affairs in Chios, forbade Pasqualino to leave the harbor.[135] After four days, however, Andreolo on Ciriaco's behalf was able to persuade the *Maonesi* to allow the ship to leave port, so Ciriaco loaded his goods on board. When they arrived at the port of Cassiope on the island of Corfu, they encountered the Venetian fleet; but when they showed their papers from the Genoese to the Venetian commander, Andrea Mocenigo, he allowed the ship to proceed, and so they at last arrived by way of Illyria at the port of Ancona.

**92.**     There Ciriaco found his family safe and sound. He stayed there only a few days to settle his affairs and then hastened to Rome in the company of Astorgio, the bishop of Ancona,[136] to see Pope Eugenius. An audience was arranged by Aloysius, the papal chamberlain, in the nave of St. Peter's; and on this occasion Ciriaco first presented the pope with a pair of very beautiful Indian porcelain ewers decorated with gold and then clearly and fully put forward his views, both verbally and in written memoranda, concerning the fostering of union with the Greeks, an effective expedition against the Turks, and the payment due to Memnon for his part in this important work. The Holy Father benignly welcomed Ciriaco as a son, and having very judiciously listened to everything he had to say, promised in due course to give it his fullest attention.

**93.**     Ciriaco in the meantime decided to investigate the antiquities in the environs of Rome, and set off for the very ancient city of Tivoli. Here and there along the famous *Via Tiburtina* he found many evidences of the ancient world, and near the Bridge of Lucanus he saw the splendid triumphal monument of Marcus Plautius and the royal gardens of the Emperor Hadrian, where many of its splendid porticoes are still to be seen.

[*CIL* XIV, 3606]

**94.**     Finally he arrived at Tivoli high on its hill, where he viewed its ancient remains and the ruined temple of Hercules Saxonus.[137]

[*CIL* XIV 3543]

**95.**     He saw the colossal marble bust of the Tiburtine Sibyl[138] and the tall aqueduct of Germanicus Caesar which that enlightened prince built at his own expense to bring delicious streams of limpid water into the city. He also viewed the Cimbrian—now called the Salarian—Bridge and the noble mono-lithic tomb of Marcus Antonius Antil., prefect, situated by the Tiber at the fourth milestone out of the city; and, in the company of Cardinal Giordano Orsini,[139] he inspected in another part of the neighborhood the splendid monu-ment composed of four single marble blocks, which Pope Martin, as Ciriaco complained, had allowed to fall into ruins.

**96.**     Next he made an expedition to the port of Ostia, where he examined its principal antiquities and the great shipyard[140] of the emperor Trajan nearby.

**97.**     When he got back to the city, he learned that the Hungarian king, Sigismund,[141] emperor-elect, had arrived in Siena on his way to Rome. Sigis-mund had already sent on his ambassadors, Gaspar, his royal secretary, and the Bishop of Como,[142] to see Pope Eugenius, and the pope, not uninfluenced by Ciriaco, had made arrangements with Cardinal de Conti[143] and Bernardo of Camerino for the official reception of the emperor in the city. The ambas-sadors therefore returned to Siena with Ciriaco in company, and they intro-duced him to the emperor, who graciously received him. Ciriaco then laid before him many cogent arguments as to the deeds to be done only by an emperor of his sovereign authority, dignity, and worth, particularly with regard to a crusade to repel the barbarians; and to give Sigismund an exemplar of a good emperor worthy to be imitated,[144] he presented him with a magnificent gold coin of the emperor Trajan, at the same time reminding him that Trajan had conferred a special lustre on Ciriaco's own native Ancona. At this, the generous prince, attended by his illustrious councillors, Brunoro della Scala[145] of Verona and Battista Cicala of Genoa, magnanimously admitted Ciriaco into the circle of his imperial court.[146]

**98.**     Later, when Sigismund had received from Pope Eugenius in Rome his golden diadem and had begun his important diplomatic negotiations,[147] two Sienese notables, Counts Stefano and Bartolomeo ?Frangipani[148] arrived in Rome from Dalmatia to have audience with him; and in their company Ciriaco again came into the emperor's presence. He then resumed with Sigismund and his prefect, Count Matteo, the subject of their previous conversation, going into greater detail, to which the emperor replied that he and the pope were thoroughly agreed on their plans but that their first task was to get the dangerous council of Basel dissolved.[149]

**99.**     Ciriaco also made a tour of the city with the emperor to view its mighty ruins everywhere thrown to the ground; troubled by the terrible destruction and inspired by the divine presence of the Latins, he stirred the emperor's heart with these words: "I was sure you would be deeply shocked by the way the marble of these huge and elegant buildings throughout the city, these fine statues and columns, which the ancients erected so nobly at such cost, and with such craftsmanship and architectural skill, and these important historical inscriptions,[150] are continually being burnt up into lime by the present inhabitants of the city in so lazy, barbarous, and indecent a fashion, that there will very soon be nothing left of them for posterity to see. What a crime! And may the spirits of the famous Roman dead regard these things and remedy such evils by their superior genius. For these are the shining witnesses the ancients left behind them and they possess particular power to fire the minds of noble men to the greatest deeds and to the pursuit of undying glory." The emperor, too, was disgusted at men's lazy indifference to the preservation of ancient monuments, and applauded the young Ciriaco's close concern for them.[151]

**100.**     Desiring next to investigate other great Italian cities, Ciriaco now went to the ancient and once renowned Etruscan city of Pisa, where he examined all its principal ancient and modern monuments and found many places ruined by time and neglect. The two most noteworthy buildings in Pisa, as he said, were its marble-built cathedral and its remarkable painted cemetery, locally known as the *Campo Santo*.

**101.**     Next he went to Florence,[152] once an illustrious Roman colony and now one of the most flourishing cities in Tuscany and all Italy, where he viewed many of its fine monuments and works of art—its extensive solid stone walls, its regal gates, its broad streets, and its large churches, including the fine great church of S. Reparata lifting its dome to the sky, a marvelous building which he thoroughly inspected under the guidance of the most eminent architect, Filippo,[153] along with its highly decorated marble campanile.[154] He also inspected the remarkable marble baptistery in front of S. Reparata, anciently dedicated to Mars and now to St. John the Baptist,[155] the outside of which is adorned by three very beautifully sculptured bronze doors depicting sacred histories, partly the handiwork of the great artist, Nencio,[156] while its interior is furnished with the gold and purple offerings of subject cities suspended from on high. Nor did he fail to view the lofty, towered palaces of the city-magistrates, the public and private porticoes, the great houses of leading citizens, the fine buildings all over the city, the four wide stone bridges— Rubaconte, Vecchio, Trinità, and Carraia—spanning the Arno, and finally the large iron cages of lions, symbols of popular liberty, in the square.

**102.** But the experience in Florence he had looked forward to even more was that of meeting, among its foremost citizens, Cosimo de'Medici, Niccolò Uzzano, and Palla Strozzi, and among its intellectual leaders, Leonardo Aretino,[157] the most learned man in Italy, Carlo Aretino,[158] and our Picene fellow countryman, Filelfo; while the scholar he recalled having met with special pleasure was the learned book-collector, Niccolò Niccoli, the unrivalled latter-day Ptolemy Philadelphus of Alexandria[159]—a man of immense curiosity who relished discussing with Ciriaco all the antiquities he had discovered over the world, in the great eastern cities of Asia and Europe, and in the islands of Ionia and the Aegean. Niccolò particularly enjoyed Ciriaco's report on the wonderful temple at Cyzicus.[160] Then after inspecting Niccolò's splendid library, his antique coins and sculptures, the remarkable gem by Pyrgoteles, carved of *nicolo*,[161] representing a lupercalian priest, and his bronze statue of a wing-shod Mercury, he went with Carlo Aretino to view the similar precious collections which the wealthy Cosimo had acquired.

**103.** He also saw in the houses of Donatello and Ghiberti many statues, both antique pieces and their own modern works in bronze and marble. Through the good offices of his friend, Leonardo Aretino, he went to the Palazzo Vecchio where, in the presence of the Signoria,[162] he inspected the ancient text of the Pandects brought to Florence from Pisa, and finally he visited the famous Carthusian monastery outside the walls of the city, where he saw many Christian antiquities, the head of the Eastern doctor, St. Chrysostom, and a copy of Flavius Josephus' *Jewish Antiquities*.[163]

**104.** He also climbed the hill to the very ancient city of Fiesole, where he took great pleasure in noting its large-stoned walls and the remains of its big ruined amphitheater.

**105.** He then set off for Milan[164] and arrrived by way of Bologna at Modena, an ancient city of Gallia Togata, where he discovered many evidences of its antiquity, and by courtesy of Scipione its Bishop[165] noted many of its important inscriptions which he recorded in his *Commentaria*.
[*no heading*]:

[*CIL* XI, 832]

**106.** On a marble tombstone:

[*CIL* XI, 863][166]

**107.**    On another tombstone set up in the market-place:
[*CIL* XI, 884][167]

**108.**    On another marble tomb:
[*CIL* XI, 830]

**109.**    In the foundations of the bell-tower with four figures [in relief]:
[*CIL* XI, 855]

**110.**    On an ornate stone in the bishop's residence:
[*CIL* XI, 839][168]

**111.**    Next he proceeded through Reggio to the fine city of Parma and inspected the monument of SS. Largus, Cyriacus, and Smaragdus in the cathedral church of the Blessed Virgin, outside the doors of which he found a monument of Macrobius with a sadly damaged inscription.[169]

**112.**    After leaving Parma he went to Piacenza and Pavia, where in company with Antonio Panormita[170] he found memorials of the holy bishop Augustine and of Severinus Boethius[171] and a few other ancient monuments, and finally arrived at the noble Insubrian city of Milan,[172] his destination. There Ciriaco admired the extensive suburbs, the great and various wealth of the city, and its remarkable ancient and modern buildings.

**113.**    In Milan he met his old friend, Niccolò Fioroflaviano, an official in the ducal treasury, who warmly welcomed him and at once laid before Duke Filippo[173] a letter that Ciriaco had addressed to him; and through the intercession of his secretary, Urbano Iacobo, Filippo gave Ciriaco permission to inspect the ancient monuments of the city. These included a fine series of Latin inscriptions which Ciriaco recorded in his *commentaria* beginning with one on a staircase of the famous courtyard of the ducal palace:
[*CIL* V, 6099]

**114.**    At the ancient shrine of St. Thecla:
[*CIL* V, 6037][174]

**115.**    In a wall of the church, St. Henry Panigarola:
[*CIL* V, 6069]

**116.**    At St. Mark's:
[*CIL* V, 6008]

**117.**    On a bank of the city's earthworks:
[*CIL* V, 5896][175]

118.    In a wall of the city's defenses:
[*CIL* V, 6039]

119.    In a wall of the city's defenses:
[*CIL* IX, 5931]

120.    At the church of the seraphic (St. Francis):
[*CIL* V, 6276]

121.    In a court behind the church of St. Nazarius in a portion of the entrance:
[*CIL* V, 5940]

122.    In a wall of the city's defenses:
[*CIL* V, 6024]

123.    In another location:
[*CIL* V, 6051]

124.    In a wall of the city's defenses:
[*CIL* V, 6045]

125.    In the court of (the church of) St. Simplicianus:
[*CIL* V, 5893][176]

126.    In the church of St. Nazarius:
[*CIL* V, 5859]

127.    In the facade of the governor's palace:
[*CIL* V, 5959][177]

128.    On an ancient statue-base of St. Dionysius:
[*CIL* V, 6041][178]

129.    At St. Peter's:
[*CIL* V, 5905][179]

130.    In the cloister walk behind the church of St. Amabilis:
[*CIL* V, 5906][180]

131.    Beside the church of St. Mark:
[*CIL* V, 6083][181]

**132.**    In the church of St. George on a base:
                         [*CIL* V, 5956][182]

**133.**    On a wall of St. Stephen's:
                         [*CIL* V, 5895][183]

**134.**    At the ?out-of-the-way church of St. Mary, on a base:
                         [*CIL* V, 5762][184]

**135.**    In the church of St. Victor:
                         [*CIL* V, 5942][185]

**136.**    At St. Nazarius, on a base:
                         [*Not Found*]

**137.**    Nearby:
                         [*CIL* V, 6019][186]

**138.**    On a base at the church of St. Donino:
                         [*CIL* V, 5771][187]

**139.**    In the ?Brutian countryside of Milan:
                         [*CIL* V, 6006]

**140.**    On the door of St. Bartholomew's:
                         [*CIL* V, 6100][188]

**141.**    On the door of St. Bartholomew's church:
                         [*CIL* V, 5853][189]

**142.**    In a wall of the city's ?moat:
                         [*CIL* V, 5911]

**143.**    At St. Mark's:
                         [*CIL* V, 5776]

**144.**    At Dertona before the gates of the monastery of St. Martiano:
                         [*CIL* V, 7386][190]

**145.**    In a wall of the city's ?moat:
                         [*Not found*]

**146.**    At Tradate, an old suburb of Milan:
                         [*CIL* V, 5634][191]

**147.** In the woods at some distance from Tradate is seen an inscription:
[*Not Found*]

**148.** In Milan outside the Como gate in the church of S. Simplicius on a decorated tomb:
[*CIL* V, 6128][192]

**149.** On another stone:
[*CIL* V, 5927][193]

**150.** At Dertona, on a marble of the larger church:
[*CIL* V, 7385]

**151.** And outside of Milan, in the castle of Pavia, Ciriaco inspected the famous war-engines going back to the beginnings of the history of the Visconti family, the sumptuous furnishings, the royal gardens, and the huge cages of the menagerie, which was nobly built by the Duke's magnificent father,[194] and he also visited the abbey of Chiaravalle and the great Carthusian monastery in Pavia.

**152.** He then proceeded to Brescia, where he saw many antiquities namely:
[*CIL* V, 4403]
[*no heading*]:
[*CIL* V, 4369][195]

**153.** At St. Julia's, in the wall of the [chapel of?] St. Mary on the outside:
[*CIL* V, 4367][196]

**154.** In another place:[197]
[*CIL* V, 4340]

**155.** On another stone:
[*CIL* V, 4470]
[*no heading*]:
[*CIL* V, 4332][198]

**156.** On another marble:
[*CIL* V, 4368][199]

**157.** In the church of St. Bartholomew on the hill [?mountain]:
[*CIL* V, 4501][200]

**158.** In the church of St. Sandro:
[*CIL* V, 4369][201]

**159.**   On another marble:[202]
[*CIL* V, 4463][203]

**160.**   Near the tower of Palata in the wall of a private house:
[*CIL* V, 4416][204]

**161.**   In the wall of a hospital outside the church of St. Francis:
[*CIL* V, 4676][205]

**162.**   In the church of St. Agatha:
[*CIL* V, 4370][206]

**163.**   In the same place:
[*CIL* V, 4766][207]

**164.**   Outside the church of St. Agatha in the wall:
[*CIL* V, 4460][208]

**165.**   Finally he came to the very fertile and ancient city of Verona, founded by the Gauls, and he found there a considerable number of ancient monuments.[209] The name of the river flowing through Verona, according to Papias,[210] is the Athesis, although some call it the Athax, asserting that it is the same as that mentioned by Lucan;[211] others identify the Athax with the river Ticinus, although Papias says that it is a river between ?Laon and Rheims near the Rhine; however, the river in question is in Verona.[212]

**166.**   In this Ligurian[213] city Ciriaco, as he recorded in his *commentaria*,[214] saw the labyrinth known today as the Arena, which is believed to have been built in the thirty-ninth year of the reign of Octavian Augustus, three years before Christ's birth. The outside of the Arena has been shattered by earthquakes and its whole circuit is seen today to be constructed of large stones and ?perforated, since its interior is ringed about by many caverns and hollow chambers of various shapes. Ciriaco himself records that there are stairways of large stones placed all round the circuit which seem wider and more rotund as they rise in height; and report has it that it is fifty cubits high and had a fine large area of multiform shape, with a marble surround on the topmost level.

**167.**   Another thing he viewed in Verona was the double triumphal gate of the Borsari built of native stone and adorned with twelve windows[215] from which Ciriaco transcribed this Latin inscription:[216]
[*CIL* V, 1. 3329][217]

**168.**   In another place nearby:
[*CIL* V, 3221]

**169.**   In a village:

[*CIL* V, 3338]

**170.**   Above the river Athesis:

[*CIL* V, 3830]

**171.**   In the cemetery of St. Nicholas:

[*CIL* V, 3281]

**172.**   In the cemetery of St. Firmus ?the greater:

[*CIL* V, 3340]

**173.**   [*no heading*]:[218]

[*CIL* V, 3689]

**174.**   In the ?poorhouse:

[*CIL* V, 3257]

**175.**   On a marble tomb located in the major church:[219]

[*CIL* V, 3643]

**176.**   In the church of the first martyr:

[*CIL* V, 3387]

**177.**   In another place, with sculpture:[220]

[*CIL* V, 3734]

**178.**   Elsewhere:

[*CIL* V, 3748]

**179.**   In the shrine of St. Proculus:

[*CIL* V, 3460]

**180.**   Nearby in a garden:

[*CIL* V, 3677]

**181.**   ?Inside the aforementioned church:

[*CIL* V, 3657]

**182.**   On a very old tomb:

[*CIL* V, 3627]

**183.**   In the abbey of St. Zeno:

[*CIL* V, 3628]

**184.**    In the garden of St. Zeno:
                         [*CIL* V, 3419]

**185.**    On a square marble ?pillar:
                         [*CIL* V, 3382]

**186.**    On another side:
                         [*CIL* V, 3382]

**187.**    On the third side:[221]
                         [*CIL* V, 3382]

**188.**    On the other side of the stone:
                         [*CIL* V, 3382]

**189.**    On another stone:[222]
                         [*CIL* V, 3393]

**190.**    After he had carefully investigated all the antiquities of Verona, he returned to Milan and stayed there for several days as a guest of the duke.

**191.**    He then made for Mantua, a most ancient city in the Italian province of Venetia, which the Romans also called Cisalpine Gaul, as I have found recorded in Ciriaco's own *commentaria*; and I cite them here because I am sure they will particularly interest you.[223]

**192.**    Mantua was founded, according to Isidore and Paul the Lombard, by Manto, the daughter of Tiresias; she is said to have come to Italy and to have founded it after the destruction of Thebes. Isidore says that it is called Mantua because it protects its *manes*; it is also named after Manto.[224] But Virgil, who shed great luster on the city by being born there, says that Ocnus, the son of Manto, called the city Mantua after the name of his mother. She was called Manto, or Mantos, because her name was derived from *manes* and *tueor*, since she guarded the *manes*, that is to say, the shades of the deified dead. Other writers say that she had a son by a certain man called Tiberis, who was called Obius or Obnus, and also had the name of Bianor, meaning doubly strong, that is to say, in body and mind; hence Virgil says, "the tomb of Bianor begins to appear." It was this man, as some believe, who founded Mantua, which the Mantuans named after his mother, Manto. Manto's father was the great Theban seer, Tiresias, of whom Statius speaks in his *Thebaid*. So much, then, for what we find in the ancient authors about the origin of the city.[225]

**193.**    From these texts we can deduce the date of its foundation; for the fact that it was founded either by Manto, the daughter of the seer Tiresias, or by her son, means that it is very ancient. For the fall of Thebes and the destruction of its inhabitants was the result of a long siege in which the Greeks, Eteocles and Polinices, the sons of the Theban king, Oedipus, contended for the rule of the city; and that this event preceded the fall of Troy by about sixty years is calculated as follows: Oedipus lived in the time of Abimelech, the judge of Israel. Troy fell in the third year of Abdon, the judge of Israel. Sixty years elapsed from the last year of Abimelech to the third of Abdon. The fall of Troy, according to St. Jerome, occurred 431 years before the foundation of Rome, and according to Orosius, Rome was founded 752 years before the birth of Christ. Thus, not even counting the sixty years that elapsed between the fall of Thebes (after which, as we have said, Mantua was founded) and the fall of Troy, an accurate calculation will show that 1,183 years intervened between the foundation of Mantua and the birth of our Savior. In the chronicles of Miletus or Eusebius, however, we find that Mantua was founded 570 years before the foundation of Rome. For St. Augustine, in Book 18 of his *City of God*, says that the birth of Abraham occurred about twelve hundred years before the foundation of Rome, and if we subtract from these the 530 years that elapsed, as we have said, between the birth of Abraham and the building of Mantua, we are left with 670 years between the building of Mantua and the foundation of Rome; and if to these we add the 752 years between the foundation of Rome and the birth of Christ, our accurate calculation gives us 1422 B.C. (as the date of Mantua's foundation).[226]

**194.**     The river Mincio, a tributary of the Po, flows past Mantua and a surrounding lake strongly protects it and makes it unassailable. In a place outside the city called Pietoli on the shore of the lake it is said that Virgil, the crowning glory of Mantua, was born; and Ciriaco himself carefully searched it to see if he could find any important ancient remains, particularly regarding Virgil.[227] And on the banks of the river Tartaro he found this very ancient inscription:

[*CIL* V, 3827]

**195.**     In Mantua, on a stone at a well:

[*CIL* V, 4066]

**196.**     In another place *[drawing of an arch, under which is the inscription]*:

[*CIL* V, 4072]

**197.**     On the walls of the church of St. Sylvester:

[*CIL* V, 4073]

**198.**     Next he went to Genoa, chief city on the Ligustian coast, which Pliny,[228] in his *Natural History*, locates in the province of Liguria, now called

Lombardy. He writes that this state extends from Ventimiglia and the river ?Merula as far as ?Sestri and the river Macra, and Genoa and the river ?Pulcivere are in the same territory. Paul (the Deacon), the author of the *Lombard History*, says that it is in the fifth province of Italy, called the Cottian Alps, and that, extending as it does from Liguria to the sea and adjoining the frontier of Gaul in the west, it contains Dertona, the monastery of Bobbio, and the cities of Genoa and Saona.[229]

**199.** It is written in the chronicles that Prince Janus, a contemporary of Moses, came to Italy from the East and was the chief ruler there, although other histories assert that he reigned in the time of Abraham. Janus built the city of Genoa and named it Janicula after himself, as is proved by the words of Solinus: "Who does not know that Janicula was built and founded by Janus and Saturnia by Saturn?"[230]

**200.** Another Janus, of Trojan birth, came to Italy after the fall of Troy. Ciriaco says that when this same Janus was sailing with a favorable wind to a place called Albarium, a thick fog appeared of a kind commonly called Albasia (though others call it Cigaria), thus giving Albarium its name. He then proceeded to a place called Galiganum, which he found so pleasantly situated that he called for sails to be lowered, hence the place's name. At a place called Serzanum[231] he jumped ashore and from that leap, or *saltus*, of Janus it got its vernacular name. Arriving in Janicula, Janus built a fortress on the site now called the Castello and erected towers and redoubts on the site of the present archiepiscopal palace, which he fortified with very strong walls; and Janus II similarly added to the city. With the influx of people from various places the city began to grow large. (Ciriaco) says that his remarks about Janus the Trojan citizen were based on popular and ancient oral report alone.

**201.** He adds also that that Genoa was built 107 years before the foundation of Rome and 1,546 years before the birth of Christ in the third age of the world. This statement, he says, depends on the already quoted assertion of Solinus that Janus built Janicula, which is called Genoa, and on authentic chronicles, but he does not name any author or writer. Reckoning from the fact that Janus ruled in the time when Moses was leading his people in the desert and from the date of the foundation of Rome, it will be found that 707 years elapsed between the building of Genoa and the foundation of Rome. Moreover, if one calculates the period between the time of Moses and the time of Christ, one finds, as already said, that 1,546 years elapsed. Ciriaco says that he made this calculation on the evidence of St. Jerome, who gives the smaller number. But Bede and Methodius give a larger number, asserting that the Gauls built Genoa when Bellovasius was their leader.[232]

**202.**     Livy, however, names the city, not *Janua*, but *Genua*, asserting that 534 years after the foundation of Rome the Carthaginian general, Mago, captured and almost destroyed the totally unguarded city with thirty triremes and many cargo ships, with twelve thousand infantry and nearly two thousand cavalry on board. About this time, too, Milan was captured by Marcellus, which clearly shows that Genoa existed at least 230 years before the birth of Christ.[233] Elsewhere he says that Scipio, the younger brother of Scipio, came with a fleet to Genoa to resist Hannibal, who was about to cross the Alps.[234] Livy also reports that in the year 545 after the foundation of the city the command of Lucretius was extended by the Romans so that he could rebuild the town of Genoa, which had been ravaged by Mago the Carthaginian.[235]

**203.**     But to return to our story: Provided with ducal letters of introduction by the help of Francesco Barbavara, Ciriaco acquainted himself with all the principal sights of the city and he saw the famous bowl made of most precious green stone and a marble bust of Gaius Marius. Among the leading citizens he met in Genoa were the wealthy Giovanni Grillo, Francesco Spinola, Benedetto Negrone, and Paolo Imperiale, not to mention Iacobo Bracello[236] and Niccolò Camulio, learned secretaries in the service of the city, who elegantly and sumptuously received him as their guest both within the city and at their beautiful rustic retreats outside its walls, and showed him all the sights of that remarkable city, the massive walls of its shipyard and port, the great galleys and huge merchantmen lying there.

**204.**     After he had seen everything there, Ciriaco then returned to Rome to pay another visit to the pope.[237] Some days after Ciriaco had arrived in Rome he heard that the civic authorities of Ancona were preparing a naval expedition under the command of Pagliaresio Pisanello[238] against certain rebellious citizens who were operating as pirates. They had ordered Tommaso, the eldest son of Biagio, who had arrived with his merchant ship from the Balearic Islands at the port of Gaeta, to join in the expedition when he had taken troops on board and to wait for Paliaresio at the Illyrian Gulf; and together they were to attack, defeat, and destroy the rebels.[239]

**205.**     This news much disturbed Ciriaco, because he greatly feared that these dangerous beginnings of discord in a city that had so long been inviolately united would before long engender worse troubles barring immediate remedies; he therefore, in the company of Niccolò, the brother of the clerk Petrelli, left Rome to see Tommaso at Gaeta; and that noble young man was very pleased to hear what Ciriaco had to say and promised to follow his advice in everything.

**206.**     Since Tommaso's ship would be leaving Gaeta for Naples, Ciriaco meanwhile set off for Naples by land in order to see what he could find in the way of antiquities.[240] The first place he stopped at on his way was the ancient Latin coastal city of Terracina, where he was delighted to see the marble temple of Augustus, the fine harbor, and the wide hard-paved road leading from Rome.

**207.** At Liternum on the way from Gaeta to Naples he viewed the famous country seat of the great Scipio, his marble statue, and the huge brick amphitheater.

**208.** Thence by way of Sessa he came to the splendid towered Campanian city of Capua, where he discovered not a few ancient monuments; and three miles outside the city in a wild, woody setting, he particularly examined what was left of the huge stones of the great amphitheater, and at some distance away the ancient gates of the great city and the many huge and remarkable subterranean remains of ancient houses.

**209.** Then, passing through the town of Aversa, he arrived at the royal Parthenopean city of Naples, which was governed by Joanna, the illustrious daughter of King Charles[241]
[*a folio is missing at this point*][242]
[*CIG* 5791; Kaibel, *IG* XIV, 714; Mommsen, *CIL* X, p. 184]

**210.** Next, with Ercole, the *podestà* of Pozzuoli as his guide, Ciriaco viewed the landmarks of the revered poet Virgil near the imperial cavern and then arrived at Pozzuoli, where he saw renowned Sibylline antiquities and temples and the lake of Avernus; and all the monuments of Cumae and Baiae down to the famous promontory of Miseno, including many splendid buildings built by Nero and Lucullus still to be admired to this day.

**211.** Then he went back through Naples to the famous Samnite city of Benevento, where he saw its huge and numerous antiquities, particularly the remains of its large amphitheater and the fine and noble arch of the Emperor Trajan with its inscription,[243] a highly ornate monument that the ancient Senate and People of Rome dedicated to that powerful prince.

**212.** Beneath a marble statue:
[*CIL* IX, 1589]

**213.** [*no heading*]:
[Not found in *CIL* IX]

**214.** This is what we find written about the city in ancient chronicles.[244] Solinus says that Beneventum and Arpi were cities founded by Diomedes.[245] Diomedes was one of the Greek princes at the siege of Troy who was killed by the Illyrians, as Papias records, adding that Diomedis is a city in Apulia founded by Diomedes at the foot of Mount Gargano. Papias does not mention here that the city was called Beneventum, but elsewhere he says that Beneventum is a city previously called Samnium, while in another place he says that Samnis is a city in Apulia and that Samnium is Beneventum and the Samnite people lived 130 miles from Rome between Picenum and Campania.[246] In the Lombard History we read that Samnium is the fourteenth province of Italy and that Samnium is a city in it from which the whole province took its name. In the Samnium province is the city Benevento itself and it is the metropolitan see.[247] The noble archbishop (of Benevento)has in Apulia twenty-two suffragan bishops under him.[248] Miletus and Jerome record that Beneventum in Samnium was built by the Romans 170 years after the foundation of Rome;[249] but I believe that this was really a refounding or rebuilding of the city, because Solinus, among other things, says that Benevento was founded by Diomedes who lived a very long time indeed before Rome was founded.

**215.** Having recorded all the important sights of Benevento in his notebook, Ciriaco then returned once more to Naples. A few days later, when the ship was ready for sea and the troops were embarked, and when Daniele, the bishop of Parenzo,[250] and the Florentine Giovanni Bosculo, Pope Eugenius' ambassadors to King Alfonso, had come on board on their way to Sicily, they set sail; and the two emissaries, who were already old friends of Ciriaco's, told him a great deal about what they were to discuss with King Alfonso who, with a large fleet, was at that moment attacking the Tunisian sultan on the island of Djerba.[251]

**216.** When at last the ship arrived in Sicily at the famous city of Messina, the ambassadors immediately left for Syracuse by land. Meanwhile, Tommaso, with the assistance of Pietro Gaietani, the Anconitan consul, enlisted further troops and set sail for the mouth of the Illyrian Gulf to join with the Anconitan fleet. The next day, not far off the promontory of Otranto, they sighted a Balearic ship in company with a galley loaded with all kinds of armament, under the general command of Pagliaresio. They then joined forces and arrived at the Gulf of Taranto, where, as they had learned, the pirate ship was at anchor in the harbor of Gallipoli.

**217.** However, the former queen Maria, the Prince of Taranto's mother,[252] sent her representatives to Pagliaresio to inform him that she had given permission for the pirate ship to take safe refuge in the port and so, after many arguments back and forth by letters and messengers, Paliaresio at length had to abandon his plan; and the fleet sailed back home to Ancona.[253]

**218.** Farewell, Lauro. You adorn our age and are a credit to your city.

# NOTES TO THE TRANSLATION

1. The frontispiece of the *Vita* is inscribed: VITA / CLARISSIMI / ET / FAMOSISS. / VIRI KYRIACI / ANCONITANI / FELICITER / INCIPIT. It was probably added by Feliciano. For the letter and its date see the Introduction.

2. The deified name of Romulus.

3. Cicero, *Fam.* 1.6.2: *a teneris, ut Graeci aiunt, unguiculis.*

4. Massiella Selvatico (see next note).

5. The MS lacks the opening folio 21, which would not have run to more than some 220 words, and would have been even shorter if, as is likely, it began with an illuminated initial like the large initial of the letter to Quirini (T, fol. 11r). The missing folio presumably gave particulars of Ciriaco's ancestry, parentage, and birth, and the names of any other offspring of his parents' marriage. Olivieri, 1763, 2, note 6, names two of Ciriaco's fourteenth-century ancestors. The epitaph composed by Ciriaco (Olivieri, 2, and Colucci, 1792, 19–20 = T, fol. 165r) for his mother, himself, and their Greek servant Clara establishes that his mother Massiella was the daughter of Ciriaco Selvatico, with whom the young Ciriaco made his first travels, and that the name of his father—who evidently died when he was very young (N.B. below, no. 5 or para. 5, *invita parente*: singular and feminine, when he was only nine years old)—was Filippo de'Pizzecolli. Ciriaco's birth year must be 1391, since he was thirteen years old in 1404. The date of his birth in 1391 must have fallen after April 13th (see below, note to para. 6).

6. Referring to Ciriaco and his sister Nicolosa, and conceivably to other brothers or sisters as well.

7. For the chronology of Ciriaco's life up to late 1434 or early 1435 see Introduction, 'Chronology of the *Vita.*'

8. Michele Steno became doge on 1 December 1400. Cf. Morozzo della Rocca and Tiepolo, 1957, 185. Therefore, Ciriaco was there on 13 April 1401 at the earliest. If he was nine years old at the time, he must have been born after 13 April 1391.

9. Cf. Livy, 1.1.2.

10. Francesco da Carrara the younger, lord of Padua 1391–1404.

11. For the painted Sala Virorum Illustrium, later the Sala de' Giganti, see T.E. Mommsen, 1952.

12. Gian Galeazzo Visconti (+1402) in Milan, Robert of Anjou in Naples, and Frederick II Hohenstaufen of Sicily all kept lions. The Tower of London had them until the eighteenth century.

13. For Alife as a Campanian name, see *DBI* vol. 2, s.v. 'Ludovico d'Alife.'

14. Giacomo di Marzano, duke of Sessa, and Roberto di Marzano, count of Squillace and grand admiral of the *regno* (Summonte III, 1749, 523, 525).

15. Charles III of Durazzo, king of Naples, 1381–1386, assassinated at Buda on 27 February 1386, where he had gone in 1385 in an attempt to win the crown of Hungary.

16. Latin grammar, the 'first art' of the medieval curriculum. See Grendler, 1991, 13–22, for the communal Latin schools in the Trecento Italy; for the late medieval Latin curriculum and the humanistic alternative, ibid., 162–202.

17. The sick Boniface IX decided at the beginning of 1404 to go to the baths of Pozzuoli and ordered some galleys from different places, including one from Ancona (see Tiraboschi, 1783, VI, I, 158–159, citing the

Chronicle of Teodoro da Niem, itself cited by Rinaldi, *Annales Ecclesiae, ad an.* 1404, n. 1. According to Colucci, 1792, 23, 54, note 18, Boniface later abandoned his plan and died shortly afterwards, on 1 October 1404. Since Ciriaco was thirteen by this time (see above, note to para. 6), he must have been born in 1391.

18. Giovanni Antonio Marzano is named in Ciriaco's account of the battle of Ponza, August, 1435, as duke of Sessa and a participant in the battle on the side of King Alfonso of Naples (T, fol. 116v, Colucci, 106).

19. For the government of Ancona see Peruzzi I, 1818, 276–278. The Latin text here uses the terms, *seviri* and *treviri* for their Anconitan equivalents, the boards of six *anziani* and three *regolatori*.

20. Mercury was Ciriaco's patron 'saint,' to whom he prayed when embarking on a journey. For two variant versions of this formulaic prayer see Bodnar and Mitchell, 1976, 33–34, and Olivieri, 1763, 68 (the latter translated by Mitchell, 1960, 473). For his drawing of Mercury (copies of which are in two MSS, O2, fol. 68r, and M1, fol. 37v, the latter accompanied by still another variant on the prayer) see Mitchell, 1962, 297–298 and Tav. 21; Panofsky and Saxl, 1933, 258–259; Wind, 1958, 121, note 30. See now also Neuhausen and Trapp, 1983, 66–68, and Neuhausen, 1992.

21. *Senator extra comitiorum ordinem.* Cf. the *Oxford Latin Dictionary* s.v. *ordo*, 15b, *extra ordinem*, "in a manner deviating from standard procedure, as an exceptional measure," e.g. *eos ... extra ordinem in senatum legendos curaverat* (Caesar, *Bellum Civile* 3.59.2). Ciriaco was elected senator by exception to the minimum age requirement.

22. Perhaps the name is Cinzio (see Peruzzi, II, 277). Tiraboschi, 1783, VI, 159 gives 'Cincio de' Pizzicolli.'

23. For the medieval state of the Pharos see Fraser, 1972, II, 44, 46.

24. A yellow stone: see Pliny, *N.H.* 36, 49 and Juvenal, 7.182. D.E. Eichholz, editor of the Loeb Pliny, Vol. X, p. 39, identifies it as "a yellow marble with red veins quarried at Simitthus [Henschir Schemtu] in western Tunisia."

25. Either the then standing obelisk of the Temple of Augustus, now in Central Park, New York (another from the Augusteum, then fallen, came to London as 'Cleopatra's Needle'), or one of the obelisks in the Serapeum (see Fraser, I, 24, 265).

26. The column dedicated to Diocletian, standing on the same hill as the Serapeum. Ciriaco wrongly took the fragmentary words [...]ΟΚΡΑΤ[...] and ΑΛΕΞΑΝΔΡ[....] in its inscription to refer to Dinocrates, the architect of Alexandria, and to Alexander the Great, whereas they actually refer to the emperor and to the city: [ΑΥΤ]ΟΚΡΑΤ[ΟΡΑ] and ΑΛΕΞΑΝΔΡ[ΕΙΑΣ] (Fraser, I, 27; II, 89–90).

27. It can safely be assumed that, in 1412, Ciriaco could neither write Latin nor read (or even misread) Greek inscriptions. This account of the sights of Alexandria, seen during the visit of 1412, bears striking verbal resemblances to Ciriaco's account of what he saw there presumably during a later visit, possibly in 1436, as detailed in the '*Itinerarium*' (Vo4, fol. 20r-v, ed. Mehus, 1742, 48–50). For the text of this and other passages of the '*Itinerarium*' related to that of the *Vita*, with coincidences in wording italicized, see Appendix V. For the problems raised by the verbal similarities in these two documents, see the Introduction.

28. Faraj (reigned 1403–1414); see Hill, II, 468. The next sultan, ruling in 1414, was Sheik al Muayyad (ibid., 469).

29. *omnigenum.* This word, especially in this form of the genitive plural, was a favorite of Ciriaco's, owing, no doubt, to his familiarity with book 8 of the *Aeneid*, from which he quotes frequently. Thus, in *Aen.* 8.698: *omnigenumque deum monstra.* It seems likely that the basic meaning, 'of all kinds,' informs readers that the eunuchs who served the sultan's harem were most probably drawn from prisoners of war from various lands.

30. Galeazzo Malatesta of Pesaro attacked Ancona on the night of 6 October 1413 (Leoni, I, 200 [who gives the date as 7 October]; Peruzzi, 1835, 237–239, 279; Tiraboschi, 1783, VI, I, 159–160, prefers the year 1414).

31. Ciriaco's Italian account of this action seems to be lost.

32. Ciriaco addressed a letter to Franciscus eques (probably Scalamonti) and Crassus from Arta, 29 December 1435 (Mehus, 1742, 58–65).

33. For Ciriaco's inspection of Friuli and Aquileia with Leonardo Giustiniani (ca. 1380–1446) see Mehus, 1742, 19–21. Filelfo commended Ciriaco in a letter to Giustiniani of 30 December 1443 (ed. Mehus, 1759, 33r).

34. *Tharsaticum* is modern Rijeka (*Ital*. Fiume) in Croatia (Graesse, 1972, s.v. Flumen S. Viti).

35. Created count of Monteserico and marquis of Gerace in Sicily by Alfonso V; *signore* of Bitonto; captain-general of the Church and viceroy, he accompanied Alfonso of Aragon on his expedition to the island of Djerba in 1432 and was taken prisoner with Alfonso at Ponza in August 1435 (see Ryder, 1976, 98 [ "the premier magnate of Sicily"], 272 [summary of his military career]; Pontieri, 269; and below, para. 215, note).

36. The text suddenly shifts here from the third person singular to the first person plural—perhaps because Scalamonti neglected to alter Ciriaco's diary at this point as he would normally have done.

37. It is uncertain whether this is a reference to the Chiaramonte Palace or to the church of the Martorana (also called S. Maria dell' Ammiraglio). One mosaic of the Martorana depicts King Roger being crowned by Christ and wearing the royal insignia that he had received from Pope Lucius II (cf. Scalamonti's Latin text: *et magnificentissimi Armirati Clari Montis insignia regia*). See Schwarz, 1945, plates 4, 11–15, 52.

38. The Cappella Palatina. For the mosaics see Kitzinger, 1949.

39. William II (reigned 1174–1183) built the cathedral of Monreale.

40. The suppressed monastery of S. Martino delle Scale, thirteen kilometers SW of Monreale.

41. Perhaps the town of Alcamo, 48.5 kilometers SW of Palermo.

42. See note on para. 32 above. Here the text wavers in a single sentence from 'they' (*venissent*) to 'we' (*convenimus*), then back to the third plural again (*perceperant*).

43. Loredan commanded the forces that recovered Venetian strongholds in Dalmatia from the Turks in 1416 (see Spreti IV, 146).

44. Oddone Colonna, elected Pope Martin V at Constance, 11 November 1417, consecrated and crowned, 21 November (Eubel, I, 32).

45. Cf. Virgil, *Aeneid* 3.291: *protinus aerias Phaeacum abscondimus arces.*

46. Filippo degli Alfieri was elected Anconitan consul of Constantinople and of Romania in 1419 at the instance of the Byzantine emperor, Manuel II (Saracini, 1675, 245).

47. For Ciriaco's description of Constantinople see Vickers, 1976[1] ("Mantegna and Constantinople"), who believes that Ciriaco "must have made profuse illustrations of what he saw" and that these hypothetical drawings are reflected in the background of Mantegna's *Agony in the Garden*. Although this is only the first of several known occasions on which Ciriaco visited Constantinople, and there are two other such visits within the scope of Scalamonti's memoir, it is on this occasion only that Scalamonti describes what Ciriaco saw there. As in the case of the visit to Alexandria in 1412, it is difficult to imagine what source

Scalamonti might have used for this description, since Ciriaco was probably incapable of writing a Latin *commentarium* in 1418, and it is tempting to assume that the source is a *commentarium* written during one of his later visits to the Byzantine capital.

48. Manuel II Palaeologus (1391–1425).

49. The Golden Gate was the official entrance of the emperors on their return from military expeditions. It is flanked by two marble towers and fortified with propylaea, to which Ciriaco's "external, marble frontispiece with ancient sculptures" undoubtedly refers. What he thought were the 'arms of Achilles' we have no way of knowing.

50. Either at this time or, probably, later (Ciriaco is known to have visited Constantinople again in 1428, 1431, and several times during the years 1444–1447), he made at least seven drawings of Hagia Sophia, the headings for which are preserved in Parma MS 1191 (Pp), fols. 61v–66v (for the texts of these headings see Appendix VI), the rest of each page being left blank. Two of these drawings, one showing the exterior, the other the interior, were copied by Giuliano da Sangallo, from a source now lost, into his sketchbook, which still survives in the Vatican Library (Vb2, fol. 28r, facsimile edition by Huelsen, 1910). For an interpretation see Smith, 1987.

51. The equestrian statue of Justinian, destroyed in 1540 (Janin, 1964, 74–75). On the drawing, attributed to Ciriaco, of an equestrian figure and its possible identity with the statue of Justinian on the column (Bu, fol. 144v), see Jacobs, 1929, 197–202; P.W. Lehmann, 1959, 39–57 (who argues that the drawing does not fit the literary description of the colossal statue in the Augusteion and suggests it is rather of a medallion of Theodosius I); with a response in the same journal by C. Mango and a reply by Lehmann, 351–356 and 356–358; see also Bodnar, 1960, 67; Babinger, 1961; Babinger, 1962, 322–323; Janin, 1964, 74–75; Vickers, 1976[1], 281, who says that the popular identification of the statue as one of Heraclius goes back at least to 1204.

52. The "convex arrangement of marble columns and architraves at the head" seen by Ciriaco must be the *Sphendone* (Σφενδονή, 'a sling'), a large hemicycle adorned with a colonnade of thirty-seven columns joined together by arches and carrying balustrades on their upper parts. The *spina* of the racecourse was originally adorned with seven monuments, of which three remain today. Ciriaco reports on two of them: (1) the serpentine column, erected at Delphi in 478 B.C. to commemorate the victories of Plataea and Salamis (originally it supported a golden tripod which itself carried a golden vase) and removed by Constantine to Constantinople; and (2) the monolithic obelisk that was brought from Heliopolis to Constantinople by Theodosius and erected with great effort by Proculus in thirty-two days, as the Latin and Greek inscriptions on its base declare. Ciriaco is portrayed as being able to read these inscriptions in 1419. As in the case of the Hagia Sophia drawings, the Parma MS has on fols. 66v and 67r headings for two drawings of obelisks with blank spaces left unfilled. For the hippodrome and its monuments see Casson, 1928, 3–4, 15–20; Mamboury and Wiegand, 1934, 40–42, pls. 102–112; and Janin, 1964, 183–194.

53. The spiral columns of Theodosius, in the Forum Tauri, and of Arcadius, in the Forum of Arcadius on or near the Xerolophos hill, were both inspired by the column of Trajan in Rome (see Janin, 1964, 81–84 and Becatti, 1960, 82–264, pls. 48–63, 73–78).

The expression *mira architectorum ope* is a favorite of Ciriaco's. It occurs again below in para. 54 and in his earliest recorded letter (see Appendix I, para. 7. In his later writings he amended this to *miro architectoris opere*, as in the 'Itinerarium,' (1441): see Appendix V, 2, b, s.v. 'Ancona.' A kindred phrase, *mira fabrefactoris arte*, is reflected in the inscription on Ghiberti's 'Gates of Paradise' in Florence: MIRA ARTE FABRIFACTVM LAVRENTII CIONIS DE GHIBERTIS (Krautheimer, 1970, II, plates 107 and 102).

54. The 900-foot span of Constantinople's main aqueduct, built by Valens in A.D. 368, is standing and still brings water to the city. The *nymphaea* were reservoirs into which the various aqueducts were emptied (Janin, 1964, 198–200).

55. Officially the Genoese colony was called Galata, but the occidentals who lived there habitually referred to it as Pera or Peyre, from the Greek πέραν, meaning "on the other side." For the walls, towers, and houses of Genoese and Byzantine Galata see Janin, 1964, 251–253. For Ciriaco's rhetorical *laus urbis Galatae*, written in epistolary form in 1446 to Baldassarre Maruffo, *podestà* of Galata/Pera in that year, see T. Belgrano, 1877–1884: 979–986 (365–392 in the separate publication).

56. *CIL* V, 50. Her name was Postuma, but the misspelling in the *Vita* combined with the testimony of other copies of the inscription made from Ciriacan sources, particularly VL 6875, no. 1, and Venice, Marc. XIV, 124, no. 1 (Mommsen's 'Iadestinus' and 'Tragurinus'), makes it likely that Ciriaco miscopied the name as 'Postumia.'

57. This is the first mention in the *Vita* of Ciriaco recording inscriptions. *CIL* V, pp. 3–4, lists a number of inscriptions from Pola recorded by Ciriaco (discussed also in *CIL* III, pp. XXII, 271, 272, 631).

58. The *Nova Fragmenta* (ed. Olivieri, 1763)—consisting mainly of Ciriaco's *commentaria* on his North Italian journey of 1442–1443—includes at the beginning a record that Ciriaco was *podestà* of Varano, a township near Ancona, at a time when citizens of Ancona had fled there to escape the plague. This notice is preceded by the inscription Ciriaco composed on that occasion (Olivieri, 1763, 2–3, quoted by Colucci, 1792, 26); and the same note, followed by the inscription, occurs as an isolated fragment in T, fols. 154v and 155r. The following is Olivieri's text, with T's variants recorded in parentheses:

> Apud Varanum in Piceno (T *picenno*) Anconitanae civitatis vicum, ubi Kyriaco (T *Kiriaco*) praetore cives complures vitandae pestis causa (Olivieri *caussa*) convenere; qui postquam se incolumes evasisse cognoverant, Beatae Mariae Virginis, Constantiique (T *Constatque*) et Sebastiani, qui ab omni morbi (T *morbis*) contagie tutelares (T *tutellares*) habebantur, imagines in foro depictas (T *ornatissimas*) imponere religiosissime curavere, quibus et ego (T omits *et*) Kyriacus ipse praetor tale subposueram hypogramma.

The inscription reads:

ANCONITANI.EGREGII.CIVES.QVI.APVD.VARANVM.OPPID.
EX LABORANTE MORBO PATRIA CIVITATE PESTILENTEM
LETHIFERAMQ.(T: *LETI.Q.*)TABEM EVASERE QVORVM SE.NVMINIBUS.
LIBEROS CREDIDERVNT.SACRICOLENDAS.IMAGINES POSVERE

(T has different line-divisions). Saracini, 1675, 246, dated the plague to June and July 1420; and Peruzzi, 1835, II, 277, following Saracini and Olivieri, note 9, makes Ciriaco *podestà* of Varano in 1420. This appointment probably preceded Ciriaco's two-year appointment in the treasury of Ancona (see next two notes).

59. Although he was appointed legate on 7 February 1420 (Eubel, I, 30; II, 4), he may not have arrived in Ancona until autumn, after the plague abated. In any event, work on restoration of the harbor seems not to have begun until 1421 (see next note). Tiraboschi calls him 'Gabriello di'Condulmieri,' Gill, 'Condulmaro.' *Cardinalis Senensis* seems to have been the shorthand for referring to him (just as *Cardinalis Nicenus* was for Bessarion and *Cardinalis Sancti Angeli* for Cesarini), although he had been bishop of Siena for less than a year (30 December 1407–9.May 1408 [Eubel, I, 30]) before resigning from that see when he was appointed cardinal (Gill, 1961, 21).

60. Ciriaco, in his so-called *Itinerarium*, a letter of October 1441 to Condulmer, who was now Pope Eugenius IV, recalled their collaboration in the project to renovate the port of Ancona as having occurred twenty years earlier (*bis denos ante annos*, Vo4, fol. 14v, ed. Mehus, 1742, 38). This would date the beginning of the project to 1421. For the text of this reminiscence see Appendix V, no. 2.

61. Gil (*Ital.* Egidio) Alvarez Carillo de Albornoz, born in Cuenca, Spain, *ca.* 1295; archbishop of Toledo 1338–1350 (Eubel, I, 487; Gams, 81); royal chancellor and ecclesiastical primate; created cardinal 17 December 1350 at Avignon by Pope Clement VI (Eubel, I, 18); made legate in Italy in June 1353 by Innocent VI with extensive powers to prepare the Papal States for the return of the popes; author of a model constitution for Ancona which was later extended to all the Papal States and remained in force until 1816—hence he came to be called their 'second founder.' He died near Viterbo, Italy, on 22 or 23 August 1367 while escorting Pope Urban VI to Rome. For an account of his career see Filippini, 1933.

62. Condulmer arrived in Bologna on 16 August 1423 to replace Cardinal Alfonso Carillo as papal governor (Gill, 1961, 33).

63. Virgil.

64. Perhaps Camerano, near Ancona (see Colucci, 1792, 27).

65. The influence of Virgil on Ciriaco's Latin is already evident in his letter of 15 March 1423 to Pietro de Bonarellis (Appendix I). For an extreme example, see his letter to Giovanni Pedemontano (Bodnar and Mitchell, 1976, pp. 58–60, lines 1098–1142).

66. On Ciriaco's records of Trajan's arch, and particularly the kindred accounts of it in his *Anconitana Illyricaque laus et Anconitanorum Raguseorumque foedus* (June, 1440) and in the '*Itinerarium*' dated October 1441 (ed. Mehus, 35–36; Appendix V, no. 2[b]), see Campana, 1959. As stated in the Introduction, the similarities of this text to those of the later ones does not by itself prove that the *Vita* is later than they are, *pace* Campana, since all three texts could depend on that of the lost *commentaria*. Also, it is clear from these other texts that most of the defects in the *Vita's* copy of the inscription are Feliciano's, not Ciriaco's.

67. On Ciriaco's putative equestrian statute and its heraldic use see Campana, 1959, 496–498.

68. In March 1423 Ciriaco stopped at Fano and Rimini on the way to Venice, a journey not recorded by Scalamonti but documented by Ciriaco's first extant composition in Latin, a letter to Pietro de Bonarellis, from Rimini, dated 15 March 1423 (text and bibliography in Appendix I). It may have been at this time that Ciriaco translated and interpreted for the people of Fano the inscriptions on their prominent ancient monument, the arch of Augustus, erected in A.D. 9–10. His copies of the inscriptions, which date to the mid-fourth century, survives in two manuscripts: Venice, Bibl. Marciana, MS lat. XIV 124 (4404), fols. 142r, 159v, and Bibl. Vaticana, MS Vat. lat. 6875, fols. 68v, 91r. The event is recalled as a boyhood memory by humanist, Antonio Costanzi, a native of Fano, in his commentary on the *Fasti* of Ovid (MS Vat. Urb. Lat. 360, fol. 145v [this page reproduced in A. Campana, 1950, tav. 2], *P. Ovidii Fastorum*, Rome, 1489, fol. qiv [Book IV at the end]), cited here from Weiss, 1965, 352–353:

> [titulum] quem olim Cyriacus ille Anconites vir inclytus ac vetustarum rerum solertissimus indagator magno civium meorum conventu legit nobis pueris facile atque interpretatus est cum exultaret maiorem in modum, perinde ac eius opera semisepulta Fanensium gloria revixisset.

See also De Rossi, 1888, 357, who omits *facile* and adds *si* after *perinde ac*.

69. The MS reads *septimo*, the seventh year of Martin's pontificate, but De Rossi, 1888, II, 357, emends to *octavo*, the eighth year, because Condulmer ceased to be legate in Bologna on 9 June 1423 and did not arrive in Rome before about the middle of that year (Gill, 1961, 34).

70. The first mention of Ciriaco's *commentaria* in the *Vita*; they are later mentioned five more times (para. 76, 105, 113, 166, 199). For occurrences of this word in the '*Itinerarium*' see Mehus, 1742, 23, 36, 38, 52.

71. On the historiographical importance of Ciriaco's preference for the evidence of stones over that of written sources, see Momigliano, 1955, 88, note 37.

72. Luigi dal Verme, condottiere, d. 1449 (Litta, s.v. Dal Verme di Verona, Tav. II).

73. For a *Giacopo* Baduario of Venice see Mommsen, *CIL* V, 1* and Mitchell, 1961, 215.

74. At this point they are riding out from the city on their way to the hunting expedition near the 'Salernian' Bridge. Since none of the known bridges of Rome was called *pons Salernus*, we can only guess what bridge is meant here: perhaps the *pons Aurelius*, near the *porta Septimia* and not far from the Capitol and the Arch of Septimius Severus, the monuments mentioned in the rest of the sentence. See Richardson, 1992, 309.

75. The poem also occurs in Fr4, fols. 68r–69r, under the title: *Ciriacho danchona, chanzone morale* (P.O. Kristeller, I, 1977, 222).

76. For the façade of Orvieto Cathedral by Maitani, see J. White, 1966, 291–302.

77. Pagliaresio di Simolo de' Pisanelli. He was a supporter of Condulmer in Ancona in 1418–1419 (Peruzzi, 1818, II, 249); and soon after Condulmer's election as Eugenius IV, Ancona sent him as ambassador to Rome to ask the pope to restore its castles of Monsanvito and Fiumescino, seized by Malatesta of Pesaro, a request Eugenius granted in a brief of 26 January 1432 (text in Saracini, 1675, 250–252; Peruzzi, ?1818, II, 263–264). A Pagliaresio di Simone de'Pisanelli was on a board of six, along

with Ciriaco, appointed 14 May 1440 to negotiate a new treaty between Ancona and Ragusa (Praga, 1932–1933, 265). See also para. 204.

78. Zaccaria Contarini is also mentioned in the context of a passage on Ciriaco's visit to Padua in the '*Itinerarium*' (Vo4, fol. 10v ed. Mehus, 1742, 29). For the latter text see Appendix V, no. 4.

79. Janus Lusignan (ca. 1372–1432), king of Cyprus, Jerusalem and Armenia (Hill II, 1940, 432, 447–496).

80. Benvenuto Scotigolo is mentioned as the Anconitan captain of the ship that carried Ciriaco to Egypt in ?1436 (Vo4, fol. 20r, ed. Mehus, 1742, 49). Perhaps he is the same person as the ship-captain, Benvenuto di Filippo Scottivolo or Scottivoli, mentioned in contemporary records of sailings from Ancona to the Levant in 1439 and 1440 (Ashtor, 359 and note 517). See also Natalucci, 1975, I, 278, for a Filippo Scotivoli, military architect.

81. Francesco Ferretti, appointed *podestà* of Ancona in 1425, became senator of Rome in 1429 (Peruzzi, 1835, II, 251).

82. Andreolo Banca of Genoa; like most other administrators and shareholders of the Genoese *Maona* (company of merchants) in Chios, he took the name of Giustiniani (see Finlay, 1877, V, 73; Rhodokanakis, 1900, 75–83; Miller, 1921, 303–304; S. Mercati, 1922–1923, Argenti, 1958, II, 222,239; III, 660). Twenty-eight letters from Ciriaco to Andreolo, one dating from 1435, the others from 1444–1447, occur in Fn8 (ed. in part by Targioni Tozzetti, 1773, V, 66–69, 408–461); and a fragment of a letter from Ciriaco, probably to Andreolo, occurs in Lc, fols. 455v–456v (published by Halecki, 86–87; see also Bodnar, 1988, 259, note 46).

83. For the Syrian inscriptions, *CIL* III 160, 206, 16*, 17*, see De Rossi, 1888, II, 258a, note 1, who asserts that *CIL* III, 160 constituted headings of lost drawings of Vespasian and Bacchus.

84. The ungrammatical character of the Latin text at this point (*sunt* with predicates in the accusative [*vicum, casam, arcem*]) is an indication that Scalamonti was working from a first-person record of Ciriaco's which he converted, awkwardly and unsuccessfully in this instance, into a third-person account. Cf. also the wavering between 'we' and 'they' in para. 32 above. Similar mistakes occur in two other Ciriacan texts, the journals recounting (1) his visit to the Cyclades in 1445 and (2) the tour through mainland Greece in 1435–1437, where in each case we have (a) lengthy excerpts from what seems to be the original diary, written in the first person, with dates and personal references; and (2) other MSS in which the same texts have been converted (also by Scalamonti? by Ciriaco himself?) into an impersonal, guide-book style, written in the third person, without dates or personal references (see Bodnar, 1960, 110–114, for examples from the 1435–1437 diary).

85. Since 1383 the Genoese had enjoyed political and commercial jurisdiction, saving the king's rights, in Famagusta, and the privilege was confirmed in 1408; all ships trading with Cyprus were compelled to call at Famagusta, excepting those coming from Turkey, which might put in at Kerynia on the north coast of the island (Hill, I, 1940, 434, 460).

86. Sir Badin de Nores, marshal of Jerusalem, appointed a royal counsellor by Janus in 1425 (Hill, II, 1952, 473, 486).

87. An important passage for dating Ciriaco's visit to Cyprus. The king's 'recent misfortunes' were at the hands of the Mamelukes who, after minor raids in 1424 and 1425, had invaded Cyprus on 1 July 1426 and had defeated and captured Janus at Khirikitia on 7 July, when Badin de Nores (see preceding note) was in command of the left wing. Nicosia was sacked on 15 July and the king and 6,000 of his men and women were carried off to Cairo, where Janus was humiliated on 13 August 1426. Later, when Ciriaco visited Cairo in ?1436, he saw the helmet and shield of Janus hanging in a vestibule of a 'temple,' probably a mosque ('*Itinerarium*,' Vo4, fol. 20v, ed. Mehus, 1742, 50, text in Appendix V, 3). Janus was ransomed on 12 May 1427, and returned to Cyprus (Hill, II, 1952, 467 ff.). His restoration of the ravaged island, commemorated in Ciriaco's inscription, included the building of a new royal palace to replace the one burned by the invaders (Hill I, 1940, 496). Allowing time for the restorations to become noticeable, Ciriaco's arrival in Nicosia must have been well after 12 May 1427 and probably not until some time in

1428. Thus, the period of 'nearly a year' (*nondum expleto anno*) spent there by Ciriaco probably extended over parts of 1428–1429 (see note on para. 75).

Two additional bits of information can then be fitted into the last part of 1427. (1) On 13 May 1427 Ciriaco finished copying Ovid's *Fasti*, which he later carried with him on his journey to the Levant (see note to para. 76 *ad fin.*), so he was still in Italy on that date. Moreover, (2) a letter from Francesco Filelfo to Ciriaco, dated Venice, 21 December 1427 (ed. 1502, I, 12, fol. 2), may imply that Ciriaco did not depart for the Levant until the beginning of 1428, since it seems likely that the encounter between Ciriaco and Filelfo occurred while the traveler was in Venice getting his commission from Zaccaria Contarini and that Filelfo sent his reply (text in Appendix III, no. 1) to Ciriaco' questions to the traveler while he was still in Ancona preparing for the journey to the Levant, early in 1428.

88. For the biographies of several members of the distinguished Correr family see *DBI* 29 (1983): 480–514.

89. The Latin text here echoes three passages from Vergil's *Aeneid*:
    (1) postquam altos ventum in montis atque invia lustra (4, 151);
    (2) qualis ubi hibernam Lyciam . . . Apollo (4.143–144); and
    (3) qualis in Eurotae ripis aut per iuga Cynthi
        exercet Diana choros (1.498).

90. On Theodosius Alexandrinus see Sandys, I, 361–362.

91. Consecrated 11 May 1425 (Eubel, I, 205).

92. For Fantino Quirini see Luttrell, 1978, III, 765; IV, 61; and IX, 377.

93. None of the inscriptions in *IG* XII, 1 (Rhodes) are attributed to Ciriaco.

94. Leoni, 1832, I, 218–219, II, 274–275, reports that Ciriaco gave the Senate of Ancona many manuscripts, which perished on 21 September 1532 when Clement VII seized the city (see Saracini, 1675, 338–342, who only says that public records were destroyed: "... furono le sue publiche scritture della Secretaria, Cancellaria, Ragionaria, d altri Offitii, che fossero, dalle finestre di detto palazzo gettate, e nella medesimo piazza arse, et incendiare"). Leoni adds:
> Fra le altre cose portò una superba statua di Venere al naturale, mancante le coscie e gambe; lavoro del famoso Fidia, ed aciò ogn'uno ne godesse la pose in una nicchia sopra la porta di sua casa, che per lungo tempo fu la delizia degli intendenti; ma invaghitosene il cardinal di Mantova, non potendola ottenere con preghiere ed oro, di notte armata mano la tolse dalla nicchia, e la spedì al marchese di Mantova suo fratello nel 1503; donando agli eredi Pizzecolli ottanta ducati d'oro.
>> [Leoni's references are to L. Ferretti, lib. IX, Francesco Filelfo; Leandro Alberti, Storia, etc.; Bartolomeo Alfeo, Pietro Razzano, Carolus Moronus, pg. 34, Cod. Chart. Bibl. Riccardiana cc. in 4, N. III Cod. XXIX.]

Mantua had no cardinal in 1503. Cardinal Francesco Gonzaga (1444–1483), raised to the cardinalate in 1461 (Eubel II, 14, 185), was indeed a collector of art and antiquities; and the *marchese* of Mantua in his time was Lodovico Gonzaga (1444–1478 [b. 1414]), his brother. The next Mantuan cardinal was Sigismondo Gonzaga (b.1469–d.1525), who received the red hat, but not until 1505 (Eubel III, 11, 234), at which time the *marchese* was *his* brother, Francesco II Gonzaga (1484–1519 [b. 1466]). See the fold-out genealogical table in Brinton, 1927. For the Gonzaga family's patronage of the arts see Woods-Marsden, 1988, 72–87, 215–225 (Lodovico's patronage of Alberti, Mantegna, and Pisanello) and Lightbown, 1986, 81–97, 257–258 (Mantegna).

95. This sentence is clearly a misunderstanding, either by Scalamonti or by Ciriaco himself, of a passage in Buondelmonti's *Liber Insularum Archipelagi*, a copy of which Ciriaco carried with him on his travels (Mitchell, 1962). A. Luttrell, who noticed the misreading (*The Maussolleion*, 211, n. 64), attributes it to Ciriaco, adding "such are the dangers of using guide books as historical sources," but the error may very well be Scalamonti's, since Ciriaco, who often included in his notebooks *testimonia* regarding a particular place, habitually marked these off from his own text.

96. This same phraseology occurs also in Ciriaco's letter of 29 December 1435 to Francesco [Scalamonti] and Crasso (Vo4, fol. 30v, ed. Mehus, 1742, 60):

Hic primum nautae adducta e sylvis materie ignem e silicibus excitant, tum vero generosus ille Venetus vir Thomas praefectus noster . . . suos discreverat iuvenes. Nam *alii per* dumos *pictas* quaeritant avibus *aves, alii quidam escatas* [read *escatis?*] *sub undas hamis varigenos laqueare pisces amabant,*

whose next sentence is also echoed in the passage of the '*Itinerarium*' cited below in the next note:

Sed animi praestantiores alii ad altos per invia lustra montes (Itin. colles) *orthoceros insectare cervos plerisque venalibus* [read venabulis] *armis canibusque* cucurrunt (Itin. percurrunt).

97. The Latin translation of the life of Euripides mentioned here in the *Vita* seems to be lost. This same language occurs in the '*Itinerarium*,' with a slight change at the end (Vo4, fol. 10v–11r, ed. Mehus, 29; for the text, with verbal similarities italicized, see Appendix V, no. 4). Writing there in the context of a visit to the country estate of Zaccharia Contarini near Padua, Ciriaco says in almost the same words as Scalamonti does here that, to avoid wasting time while others engaged in hunting and fishing, he studied the Greek MSS that he had brought with him and came upon a work that was short enough for him to translate into Latin. This translation of the pseudo-Aristotelian opusculum, *De Virtute*, with its dedicatory letter to Paolo da Pergola (ed. Mehus, 29–30), has survived in four MSS and has been published (from FL11, fols. 40r–45v, by Spadolini, 1902, 179–185). Ziebarth, 1901, 157–159, and Nardi, 1957, 137–138, published the letter only, Nardi basing his text on Vu2 collated with V12 and Vo1.

98. Perhaps the cousin of Paolo di Onofrio de Polidori, who with Ciriaco and four others, was one of the six *regolatori* of Ancona who represented the city at the renewal of the commerical pact between Ancona and Ragusa in 1440 (see Peruzzi, 1818, II, 235–236; Praga, 1932–1933, 263–280, who gives the names of the other four: Niccolò di Leonardo de Bonarelli, Pagliaresio di Simone de Pisanelli, Antonio di Bertuccio degli Amandulani and Stefano di Tommaso de Fatati).

99. Murad II.

100. E. Trapp et al., *(PLP)*, do not list an exact equivalent of 'Boles.' Harlfinger, 1990, 226, note 4, cites Βούλλης (nr. 3078) and Βουλλωτής (nr. 3079–3088) as possibilities.

101. Salonica was captured by the Turks on 29 March 1430 (see Nicol, 1972, 366–367, who draws from the eye-witness account and Monodia of John Anagnostes, in the Bonn edition of Sphrantzes, 1838, 483–534). It follows that Ciriaco's purchase in Adrianople of MSS plundered from Salonica occurred in April 1430 at the earliest. Since Ciriaco is described as having spent the winter *(per hiemem)* in Adrianople, this must have been the winter of 1429–1430. Thus the period of almost a year passed in Cyprus *(nondum expleto anno)* must have been 1428–1429 and the progress from Ancona to Cyprus (leisurely though it was, via Constantinople, Chios, Beirut, and Damascus) could not have begun any earlier than January 1428 (see above, note on para. 68).

102. Probably Niccolò Ceba, of the Grimaldi family, to whom Filelfo wrote many letters including one of 1441 referring to a voyage of his to Persia (Tiraboschi, 1783, VI, I, 163; Filelfo, *Epistolae*, ed. 1502, 31r; the letters of Filelfo to Ceba span the period 1441–1454).

103. The Latin term used here, *peranterea scapha,* may be derived from the Greek word, πέραν (see above note to para. 43) and could possibly mean 'ferry-boat.'

104. See note to para. 4 above. For the buying and selling of slaves by Italian merchants in Ciriaco's time and the probability that they purchased slave-girls to serve as their concubines, see Ashtor, 1983, 408; and in reference to Ciriaco's Clara, Colin, 1981, 52–64 and 184–185. For the practice of slavery in contemporary Genoa and Chios see Argenti I, 615–623.

Murad II had swept down into Epirus and Albania after his capture of Salonica (29 March 1430). It seems likely that Ciriaco's 'Chaonian' (= Epirote) slave-girl had been caught up in that sweep, although the capital city of the Despotate of Epirus, Ioannina, had capitulated (on 9 October 1430) only after the Turks had agreed beforehand in writing that no one would lose his freedom and no children would be abducted (Nicol, 1972, 367–368).

105. With whom Ciriaco sailed to Egypt *ca.* 1412 (para. 16 above).

106. If *libertus* means a freed slave, the presumption is that Niccolino, like the slave-girl Clara (Chiara?), had no family-name, which would suggest that *nigro* in the Latin text means 'black' and is not a surname. Colin, 186–187, takes it in this sense.

107. Cf. Ovid, *Fasti* 3, 707–708 (where the received text reads *albet*, not *habet*). In his own copy of the *Fasti*, VL11, which he copied out himself (signed 13 May 1427), Ciriaco added inscriptions of Philippi in the margin of fol. 31v (see Banti, 1939–1940, 213–220 and Berra, 1914, 461–462).

108. For Ciraco in Salonica see Vickers, 1976[2].

109. It is unlikely that a triumphal arch would have been erected in the provinces as early as the time of Aemilius Paullus (victor at nearby Pydna in 168 B.C.). Vickers held briefly to the view that Ciriaco was misinformed by local inhabitants about a likely-looking monument in the middle of the city (*medio in foro*) (1976[1]), but later (1976[2]) 224–230) decided that the Arch of Galerius must be meant, even though it is on the eastern edge of the ancient city and not in its center. Vickers, 1976[1], 76–77, identified the 'temple of Diana' as an elaborate portico known as *Las Incantadas*, which stood in the center of the city on the southern edge of the ancient forum until 1864, because of its numerous statues of deities on its architrave (see Guerrini, 1961, 40–70).

110. St. Demetrius, just north of the ancient forum, was the metropolitan church of Salonica in 1431 when Ciriaco visited it. The walls Ciriaco saw are from the fifth century A.D. and the extant inscriptions that contain the name Lysimachus (*IG* X, 2, 1, nos. 27, 97, 113, 243, 635), refer to private individuals and not to the Hellenistic king. See Vickers, 1976[2], 78–79, and his bibliography there.

111. I.e., that the two poets were contemporaries. Cf. *Anthologia Palatina* VII, 53, and see Bodnar, 1960, 154–155 and 159–160; Robert, 1961, 123–124, no. 15; and Vickers, 1976[2], 78–79.

112. Martin V died 20 February 1431 (Gill, 1961, 36, 40; Eubel, II, 20). For the reference to Condulmer as 'the Sienese cardinal' see above, para. 47.

113. The letter survives only in this fragmentary form. For another letter of Ciriaco's to Giorgio Begna of Zara, dated 1 December 1435, see Moroni, 3; Mehus, 1742, 56–57; and Bodnar, 1960, 25–27, 102. Ciriaco presumably met Cardinal Giordano Orsini (d. 1439) and Leonardo Bruni Aretino (1370–1444) when he visited Rome in 1424. See Appendix II for an exchange of letters between Bruni and Ciriaco that falls within the time-span of the *Vita*. For Giorgio Begna, see Venice, Bibl. Marc. Lat. XIV, 24 (4044), written in large part by Begna himself and later acquired by Bernardo Bembo around 1457; De Rossi II, 359, n. 3, 360; W. Henzen, 1866; G. Praga, 1932–1933, 212–213.

114. *Divum pater et hominum rex* (*Aen.* 1, 65; 2, 648; 10, 743).

115. See Iacopo Zeno's eulogistic letter to Ciriaco, 13 June 1442 (Bertalot and Campana, 1939, 374):
> Quid enim utilius, quid praeclarius et gloriosius universo christiano nomini afferri potuit quam excellens illa Graecorum unio conciliatio atque concordia et cum recta atque sincera universorum fidelium veritate redintegratio? Ad quem sane tu tantum operae studii ac diligentiae adhibuisti, ut maxima ex te pars tam sanctissimi et divini operis emanasse videatur. Tu enim hac dumtaxat ex causa privatis tuis rebus omnibus derelictis profectus in Graeciam tantum apud imperatorem (John VIII Palaeologus) suavissimis orationibus tuis et vehementissimis suasionibus valuisti, ut ad sanctissimum et immortali memoria dignum opus, ad difficilimum iter et provinciam obeundam miro illum desiderio, miro ardore concitares incenderesque.

These exhortations to the Emperor are not otherwise recorded, but there is room in the chronology of Ciriaco's travels for a journey to the Peloponnesus at precisely the time when Emperor John VIII Palaeologus was making his desultory and possibly reluctant way toward Italy and the council of union by leaving at Cenchreae the papal ship sent to fetch him and crossing the Peloponnesus by land to Patras by way of Mistra (late November 1437 to 3 January 1438). For the emperor's route see Gill, 1959, 89. This would do much to explain Ciriaco's return to the Peloponnesus after completing a strenuous tour of the mainland just the previous year (see Bodnar, 1960, 45–50). Ciriaco was in the Peloponnesus as late as 24 December, 1437, the date of a letter he sent from there to the authorities in Venice (Archivio di Stato, Archivio di S. Maria de Rosario, b, 29, ed. M. Morici, 1898).

116. One of five bastard sons of Carlo I Tocco, count of Cephalonia. He had received only one-fifth of Acarnania on Carlo I's death in 1429 and had appealed to Sultan Murad II for aid in recovering what he considered to be his whole heritage, most of which had gone to his cousin, Carlo II, the nephew of Carlo I. After the fall of Salonica in 1430 the Sultan used Memnon's appeal as a pretext for sending an army to Ioannina, which capitulated and thenceforth became part of the Turkish Empire (see Miller, 1908, 395–397; Ziebarth, 1926, 110–119; Bodnar, 1960, 28–29, note 1). Memnon is mentioned in Ciriaco's letter of 17 September 1437 to a priest called Daniel (Moroni, 40; Bodnar, 1960, 48).

117. Babilano Pallavicini (d. 1488) was one ot the leaders of the Genoese commercial colony in Galata Pera, which he later saved from destruction when he paid homage to Mehmed II in 1453 (see Litta, s.v. 'Pallavicini di Genova').

118. T. Reinach, 1890, 521, note 2, says that Canuza Bey is the same person as Hamza Bey, a well-known personage of the reign of Murad II, and that he is here wrongly said to be a Greek.

119. Pliny, *N.H.* 36, 98. The golden 'thread' (*filum*) occurs in only one MS of the *N.H.*

120. Ciriaco visited Cyzicus again in 1444, when he lamented the further ruin of the temple since his first visit (T. Reinach, 1890; Saxl, 1940–1941; Ashmole, 1956; Lyttelton, 1974, 261–263, pls. 178, 180, 181); Bodnar and Mitchell, 1976, 27–31. Today there is nothing left of the temple except its vaulted foundations, barely discernible in the brambles that cover and surround it.

121. *Tristia* I, 10, 29–30.

122. Modern Iznik.

123. The inscription on the lintel of the south gate (Yenishehir) states that the arched structure was erected under Claudius Gothicus at the end of A.D. 268, not by Tiberius Claudius Germanicus.

124. Hagia Sophia, the seat of the second Council of Nicaea, A.D. 786.

125. Scutari (Uskudar) is not the actual site of Chalcedon, which is the nearby district of Kadikoÿ.

126. Pasqualino Mucciarelli. An evaluation of the ships of Ancona, drawn up in 1430, names Pasqualino as the owner of a *navetta* worth 200 scudi (Saracini, 1675, 249).

127. The lord of the island of Lesbos at this time was not Giorgio, but his uncle, Dorino I Gattilusio, who had succeeded his brother, Jacopo, by 1428 and continued to rule until 1455. It is hard to say in what sense Giorgio was *praeses* of Lesbos when Ciriaco visited the island in 1431. Either Scalamonti got the name wrong or *praeses* here means something like 'acting governor,' or 'in charge of the garrison (from *praesidium*).'

128. Other inscriptions of Lesbos attributed to Ciriaco are: *CIG* 2171, 2173, 2190, 2211, 2194, 2172; Kaibel, 1875, 1–24; and *CIL* III, 455, 456.

129. Methymna is modern Molivos.

130. There are two theaters in Pergamum; the smaller, Roman one (capacity 3,500) is in the Asklepieion (Bean, 1966, 88).

131. Called Foglia Vecchia and Foglia Nuova by the Genoese (modern Foça and Yeni Foça). Dorino I Gattilusio was also lord of Foglia Vecchia. where his family had a factory for the production of alum. It remained united with the Lesbian branch of the family till 1455 (Miller, 1913, 419, 423).

132. According to Rhodokanakis, 1900, 80, the father-in-law of Andreolo was Errico Simone Giustiniani-Longo. He also calls Andreolo's wife 'Clarissa,' whereas Ciriaco consistently refers to her as 'Clarentia' in his letters to Andreolo.

133. These coins Ciriaco later showed to Ambrogio Traversari in Venice, who wrote in a letter to Niccolò Niccoli:

> offendi Cyriacum antiquitatis studiosum. Ostendit aureos et argenteos nummos, eos scilicet, quos ipse vidisti. Lysimachi, Philippi et Alexandri ostendebat imagines. Sed an Macedonum sint, scrupulus est. Scipionis Junioris in lapide onychios, ut ipse aiebat, effigiem . . . vidi summae elegantiae . . . . eam tibi nequaquam conspectam adseverat, sive sponte subtraxerit, sive illam, posteaquam profectus a vobis est, nactus fuerit (quoted by Tiraboschi, VI, I, 1783, 168, from Mehus, 1759, Book 8, letter 45 [#46 in Luiso's chronological reordering]).

The sense calls for *vobis* rather than the *nobis* of the printed text. For the year of this letter, and presumably of Ciriaco's encounter with Traversari, see note to para. 97, *ad fin.*

134. *perenteream scapham*: see note on para. 76, where the adjective is spelled with an 'a': *peranterea scapha.*

135. The events here narrated occurred after 31 October 1431, when the Genoese government learned of the Venetian preparations, and before 6 November, when the Venetian fleet arrived off Chios (see Argenti, 1958, I, 176–181; II, 391–416. For the Venetian attack on Chios see Lane, 1973, 229–230).

136. Astorgio Agnesi, consecrated bishop of Ancona on 6 March 1419 (Eubel, I, 87).

137. Probably the so-called temple of Vesta or the Sibyl, the dedication being to Hercules Saxanus (see Dessau, *CIL* XIV, 3543).

138. Not identified.

139. On Cardinal Giordano Orsini as a collector of manuscripts, see the inventory of Orsini's library in Cancellieri, 1786, 909, 910.

140. *navistatium*: possibly a coinage by Ciriaco. Taken by itself, it should mean 'harbor,' 'anchorage,' 'roadstead' (*navis + stare*, Greek ναύσταθμον), but the connotation of shipyards (Greek ναυπήγιον, νεώριον, νεώσοικος, Latin *navalia*) may be inferred from the existence of guilds of shipbuilders, *fabri navales* in both Ostia (Meiggs, 1973, 323 and passim) and Portus (the imperial harbors and the settlement that grew up around them: ibid., 324); one of these guilds may have had its own temple in Ostia (ibid., 327–328). At Ostia Ciriaco recorded *CIL* XIV, 1, 401 and 298.

141. Sigismund (1361–1437), king of Hungary, arrived in Siena on 8 July 1432 and remained there until 25 April 1433 (Gill, 1961, 48). For arguments that the events narrated in par. 204–216 (southern Italy) belong chronologically between para. 96 and para. 97, see our notes to para. 215–217.

142. Gaspar Schlich, chancellor, and Francesco Bossio, bishop of Como, 1420–1435 (Eubel, I, 225; II, 156). Pall, 1937, 15, note, referring to Martène and Durand, 1733, col. 531, says the *Comus pontifex* of our text should be *Curiensis pontifex*, i.e. the bishop of Chur.

143. Lucio Conti, protonotary apostolic; created cardinal, 1411, died in 1437 (Eubel, I, 31–32).

144. Cf. Petrarch's gift of gold and silver coins bearing the image of Augustus Caesar to Charles IV of Bohemia, Sigismund's father, when they met in Mantua in December, 1354, and Charles was on his way to be crowned emperor (see Gregorovius, 1898, VI, 380):

> Itaque peroportunum aggredi visum est quod iandudum facere meditabar; sumpta igitur ex verbis occasione, aliquot sibi aureas argenteasque nostrorum principum effigies minutissimis ac veteribus literis inscriptas, quas in delitiis habebam, dono dedi, in quibus et Augusti Cesaris vultus erat pene spirans. 'Et ecce' inquam, 'Cesar, quibus successisti; ecce quos imitari studeas et mirari, ad quorum formulam atque imaginem te componas, quos preter te unum nulli hominum daturus eram. Tua me movit autoritas; licet enim horum mores et nomina, horum ego res gestas norim, tuum est non modo nosse sed sequi; tibi itaque debebantur' (*Le familiari*, ed. Rossi, III, 315 [Book XIX, no. 3], para. 14–15).

In 1444 Ciriaco also gave a silver coin of Vespasian to Raffaelle Castiglione to remind him of the destruction of the Temple in Jerusalem in A.D. 70 that avenged the death of Christ (see Colucci, 1792, 131–132; Bodnar and Mitchell, 1976, 33) and in 1445 he gave a Rhodian Greek silver coin to Bandino of

Rhodes (Mitchell, 1962, 289).

145. Brunoro della Scala, died in Vienna 1434 (Litta, s.v. Scaligeri di Verona).

146. Ciriaco probably remained in Sigismund's court from this point on until the coronation, accompanying the emperor-elect on his journey to Rome (25 April 1433), and participating as one of his honorary courtiers in the ceremony in St. Peter's on 31 May 1433. If so, his encounter with Ambrogio Traversari in Venice, mentioned in the letter quoted above (note to para. 89 *ad fin.*), has been wrongly dated in the literature. Written from Venice on 29 April, the year not given (Mehus, 1759, book 8, letter 45, #46 in Luiso's reordering), it is assigned by Mehus to 1433. Stinger, 1977, 41f. (following Luiso) dates it to ?30 May 1433, and locates Traversari's encounter with Ciriaco in Venice to May–June 1433, when Traversari spent forty days there. He supports this date with references to two other letters of Traversari, dated 6 June and 20 June (Mehus, 1759, 8, letters 46 and 47, 47 and 48 in Luiso) and to Traversari's *Hodoeporicon* (text in Dini-Traversari, 1912, 61–69, separate pagination). It is unlikely, however, that Ciriaco was in Venice at the very time when he was deeply involved in diplomatic preliminaries to the coronation of Sigismund as emperor, which took place in Rome on 31 May 1433 (below, para. 97–98). Moreover, Ciriaco did not begin his northward journey, in the course of which occurred the meeting with Niccoli in Florence mentioned in Traversari's letter, until after the coronation in Rome (see Introduction, 'Chronology'); and the second letter of Traversari cited above, assigned to 20 June of the same year (ed. Mehus, 1759, Book 8, letter 47, Luiso 48) says that Ciriaco after their meeting went from Venice to the *East* : *Cyriacus Anconitanus hinc abiit Orientem petiturus.* Ciriaco's next trip to the East did not start until November 1435 (Bodnar, 1960, 23ff.), so it is likely that his meeting with Traversari took place in Venice in the Spring of 1435, not 1433.

147. Sigismund was crowned on 31 May 1433. See Appendix II for an exchange of letters between Leonardo Bruni and Ciriaco, written some time after the coronation (probably 13 December 1433), in which Ciriaco complains that Sigismund, out of ignorance of Roman usage, was holding the title of *imperator* to be higher that that of *rex Romanorum.* Ciriaco's letter was published by Mercati, 1894, 337–338; Bruni's reply was published by Mehus, 1741, Lib. VI, Ep. 9, and by Mercati, 1894, 337–338.

148. MS Phrygipenates.

149. See Gill, 1961, 48–49; even after Eugenius officially transferred it to Ferrara on 18 September 1437, it continued as a 'rump council' (Gill, 157).

150. On Ciriaco's collection of inscriptions from Rome see de Rossi, 1888, 359–360.

151. There is a most striking verbal agreement between the texts of the *Vita* and the '*Itinerarium*' at this point. For the corresponding passage in the latter document (Vo4, fols. 7r–8r, ed. Mehus, 1742, 2122), see Appendix V, no. 5.

152. Ciriaco's visit to Florence must have occurred *before* Cosimo de'Medici's exile from the city (September 1433 to 6 October 1434 [Rubinstein, 1968, 1]).

153. The name of the old cathedral was often applied to the new one (founded 1296: Paatz, 1952, III, 321). Brunelleschi's dome was still under construction in 1433; it was not finished finally until 1436: Paatz, III, 333; Saalman, 1980, 134, 137–141. For the state of the cupola at the time of Ciriaco's visit, see Saalman, 132–133.

154. *marmoream ornatissismam Cienceriam turrim*: evidently the campanile, though the meaning of *cienceriam* is unclear. For the campanile see Trachtenburg, 1971; for a study of the iconographical program of the sculptures see von Schlosser, 1896, 13 ff.

155. For the tradition that the baptistery (actually built between 1059 and 1150) was originally a Roman temple of Mars rededicated to St. John the Baptist (a confusion echoed in Dante's *Divina Commedia, Inferno* 13, 143–146; 19, 17, and *Paradiso* 16, 22 ff., repeated by Ciriaco's friend Leonardo Bruni, *Historiarum Florentini Populi* I, 60, and lasting until the nineteenth century) see Paatz, 1952, II, 211-212; Krautheimer, 1970, I, 31; Trachtenburg, 6.

156. Of the three bronze doors, Andrea Pisano's south door (on the story of St. John the Baptist) was set up in 1338; Ghiberti's present north door (scenes from the New Testament) was installed in 1424; but the panels of his second door, the 'Gates of Paradise,' (scenes from the Old Testament) were not cast until 4 April 1436 or 1437 and its frame not until 1445, and the completed door was not set up until the summer of 1452, when it was placed at the east entrance of the baptistery, facing the cathedral. Cf. Paatz, 1952, II, 195–199; R. and T. Krautheimer, 1970, I, 32, 112, 159, 164–168; R. Krautheimer, 1971, 3–9 (where he gives the date of Pisano's door as 1330).

A problem is created by Scalamonti's reference to *three* bronze doors on the occasion of Ciriaco's visit to Florence in 1433 (*Baptistae Ioannis sanctissimi delubrum, tribus aeneis ornatissimis divinae historiae portis exornatum, partim eximium Nencii nobilis fabrifactoris opus ... .*). If the chronology of the doors given above is correct, the third door could not have been seen by Ciriaco in 1433; and they were not set in their frame, much less *in situ*, until after the last of his recorded visits to Florence, in 1441. This anachronism, apparently introduced into the text by Scalamonti and not based on Ciriaco's notebooks, seems to indicate that this part, at least, of the *Vita* was not written until after 1452.

157. Ciriaco's earliest recorded encounter with Leonardo Bruni. See Appendix II for an exchange of letters between them that falls within the time-span of the *Vita*.

158. Carlo Marsuppini, 1390–1453, from Arezzo; member of the Florentine circle of humanists. He succeeded Filelfo in the chair of Greek at Florence in 1431, served for a time as a papal secretary, and, at the end of his life, as chancellor of Florence. Highly respected for his command of Greek, he translated Book I of the *Iliad* into Latin (Vespasiano da Bisticci, *Le vite*, ed. Greco, 1970, I, 591–594). Marsuppini also composed a poem in praise of Ciraco which occurs frequently in the MSS. For Marsuppini, Cosimo de' Medici, Donatello, and Ghiberti as art collectors, see Alsop, 1982, 352–357.

159. Ciriaco here compares Niccoli, who promoted the library of S. Marco, to the founder of the library of Alexandria. For another characterization of Niccoli as a connoisseur of antiquities see Vespasiano da Bisticci's memoir of him (*Le Vite*, ed. Greco, 1970, II, 225–242). Ciriaco later sent Niccoli a copy of the hieroglyphs on the biggest pyramid he saw in Egypt (Mehus, 1742, 52). See also Alsop, 1982, 329.

160. See above, para. 83.

161. A bluish onyx. The expression, *cavata ex nicolo*, is a confusing play on the great collector's name. See B. Knox in Alsop, 1982, 347, 354. For Ghiberti's cornelian showing Apollo and Marsyas, which he also thought was the work of Pyrgoteles see R. and T. Krautheimer, 1970, I, 13, citing from Ghiberti's autobiography.

162. *apud amplissimum ordinem.* Perhaps the Council of Ten, as in the expression, *ex amplissimo decemviratus ordine*, which occurs in a letter Ciriaco sent to Francesco Sforza from Florence in 1441 (T, fol. 129r; Colucci, 1792, 112).

163. For a nearly contemporary commentary on the notable statesmen and humanists visited by Ciriaco see the Memoirs of Vespasiano da Bisticci (*Le Vite*, ed. Greco, 1970, s.vv. Cosimo de' Medici, Palla degli Strozzi, Bruni, Carlo Marsuppini, Filelfo, and Niccoli).

164. On the inscriptions recorded by Ciriaco during this north Italian journey in 1433–1434 see de Rossi, 1888, 360.

165. A crux. G. Mercati, 1894, 328–332, argued from a seeming anachronism here that the *Vita* could not have been written until after 17 October 1436, when it is thought Mainenti actually became bishop of Modena; and that probably its composition should be dated after 21 October 1442, the next time Ciriaco visited Modena. (Olivieri, 20–22, where some of the same inscriptions reappear in the diary of that trip, but the wording of the journal itself for that visit does not coincide with that of the '*Itinerarium*' or the *Vita* and there is no mention of Mainenti).

Mercati's argument for 1436 as the year of Mainenti's consecration is based on (1) a letter of Antonio Beccadelli Panormita dated 1437 (*Literas ad Guarinum dedimus Scipioni Ferrariensi utriusque nostrum amantissimo, nunc ut audio, Pontifici Mutinensi* [cod. *Utinensi*]); (2) a letter of B. Alberto da Sarteano written in 1436 or 1435 which refers to Mainenti simply as *Scipioni Ferrariensi* without mention of any episcopal title (whereas later, in 1443, he gives him the full title, *Scipioni Mutinensi Episcopo*); and

(3) the letter of congratulation that Poggio wrote Mainenti on the occasion of his elevation to the episcopate, in which he says that he himself had some time ago chosen the secular life, a choice which was made at the *end* of 1434.

Moreover, according to Ughelli, 1717, II, 131, followed by Eubel, 1913, II, 218, s.v. "Mutinen" (Modena), "Scipio de Maynentibus, legum doctor," was not consecrated bishop of that see until 17 October 1436 and died in 1444.

Mercati is willing to go further and to accept from Tiraboschi and degli Agostini their opinion that the *Vita* was written *ca.* 1455, after Ciriaco's death, though he admits in a footnote that there is no evidence for this in the document Tiraboschi and Olivieri cite, Scalamonti's dedicatory letter to Lauro Quirini (para. 1–4 above).

On the other hand, the date of Mainenti's consecration may not be so clearly established as Mercati supposed: Tiraboschi, 1783, VI, I, 166 (on Ughelli's date for the death of Mainenti's predecessor, Bojardo [Eubel II, 131]); Bormann (on *CIL* XI, 1, 148); and Gams, 1873, 758, date the consecration to 1431 (Tiraboschi, followed by Bormann) or 1433 (Gams). Gams' date seems to be based on two other publications by Tiraboschi.

Mercati also argued to a date later than 1442 from the apparent fact that Ciriaco himself seems to have committed the same anachronism in his '*Itinerarium*' (written after October 1441) when referring to the same visit to Modena (Vo4, fol. 10r, ed. Mehus 27: text in Appendix V, no. 6) and that Scalamonti fell into the same error, influenced either by his conversations with Ciriaco or by the '*Itinerarium*.' If our view of the '*Itinerarium*' is correct, however, Ciriaco's arrangement in that letter of the account of his travels is not chronological at all, but logical and rhetorical, so that nothing can be deduced from this 'anachronism' in his reference to Mainenti. If Scalamonti's reference here to Mainenti is in fact anachronistic, the anachronism was not necessarily caused by a dependence on the text of the '*Itinerarium*.' And as we have already seen above (para. 101, note), Scalamonti has already been guilty of at least one anachronism — regarding the doors of the Florence baptistery, the third of which was not hung until 1452.

166. Also in *Nova Fragmenta*, Ciriaco's northern Italian journal of 1442–1443, ed. Olivieri, p. 20, n. 33. Referred to henceforth as *NF*.

167. Also in *NF* p. 20, no. 32.

168. Also in *NF* p. 20, no. 31.

169. See *NF*., p. 23):

> *Apud Aedem B. Virginis Cathedralem* vidimus antiquum SS. Martyrum *Largi, Cyriaci, et Smaragdi* Sepulcrum, *et ante* faciem eiusdem Ecclesiae conspexi praeclarissimi *Macrobii nostri* tumulum ex marmore peromatum, in quo Phy(sici) Parm(ensis) ossa posita sunt (*emphasis added*).

Both Ciriaco and Flavio Biondo (*Italia illustrata*, cited by Olivieri, p. 23, note 120) interpreted the tomb of the philosopher Biagio Pelacini of Parma (+1416) as the tomb of Macrobius, to which they thought the remains of Pelacini had been added. The tomb had on it busts of Pelacini and Macrobius, who was believed to have been born in Parma: A. Mancini, 1928, cited by Weiss, 1969, 121. For the inscription see *CIL* XI, 1122.

170. 'Panormita' (Antonio Beccadelli, 1394–1471, so called because he was a native of Palermo, Lat. *Panormus*) taught at the *Studi* in Pavia in 1430–1431 and again in 1432–1433. This dates Ciriaco's arrival in Pavia to the end of 1433, since Panormita left there at the beginning of 1434 to enter the service of Alfonso V of Aragon in Naples (G. Resta, in *DBI* 7 [1965]: 401–402). He composed a distich as an epitaph of Ciriaco's mother:

ANCONIS SPLENDOR IACET HOC MASIELLA SEPULCHRO
UNA PUDICITIAE KYRIACIQ. PARENS

(*NF*, p. 2, who says [note 8] that it recurred at the end of his MS, where the word *VETUSTATIS* was substituted for *PUDICITIAE*; this latter version also occurs in T, fol. 164v [cf. Colucci, 20, note 13]. appended to a letter, undated, of Francesco Filelfo to Panormita urging him to be kind to Ciriaco [the letter, without the appended epitaph, is also in Rome, Bibl. Casanatense, MS 3636, fol. 122v. and *NF*, p. 63; for its text see Appendix III, no. 4]).

171. Cf. *NF*, p. 26): Vidimus ad aedem Aurelii Augustini Doctoris SS. eiusdem et Monachae beatae matris suae conspicua de marmore atque ornatissima monumenta, Severinique Boetii serenissimi sarcophagem, non tamen quantum sua dignitas merebatur ornatum. Vidimus et insignem arcem tantae civitatis, nobile

159

opus incliti Galeacii *[Giangaleazzo Visconti]* equitis nobilissimi, et aeneas insignes machinas ac monumenta antiquae ab origine gentis quamplurima.

172. The corresponding passage of the *'Itinerarium'* regarding Ciriaco's visit to Milan again has many phrases in common with the account in the *Vita*, para 112–113 and 151 (Vo4, fol. 8r, ed. Mehus 22). For the *'Itinerarium'*'s text see Appendix V, no. 7.

173. Filippo Maria Visconti (1392–1447), duke of Milan 1412–1447.

174. Also in *NF* p. 32, n. 65.

175. Also in *NF* p. 35, n. 77.

176. Also in *NF* p. 34, n. 70.

177. Also in *NF* p. 30, n. 51

178. Also in *NF* p. 30, n. 53.

179. Also in *NF* p. 30, n. 52.

180. Also in *NF* p. 32, n. 60.

181. Also in *NF* p. 36, n. 80.

182. Also in *NH* p. 36, n. 82.

183. Also in *NF* p. 32, n. 61.

184. T reads *Mariae templum secretum* in the heading, not *Mariae Secretam* as reported by Mommsen in *CIL*.

185. Also in *NF* p. 35, n. 78,

186. Also in *NF* p. 29, n. 47.

187. Also in *NF* p. 35, n. 79.

188. Also in *NF* p. 30, n. 54.

189. Also in *NF* p. 30, n. 55.

190. Mommsen, *CIL: Examinavi titulum hodie male instauratum.*

191. Also in *NF* p. 60, no. 160; cf. p. 59, no. 158 *fin.*

192. Also in *NF*, p. 33, no. 69.

193. Also in *NF* p. 34, no. 72.

194. Filippo Maria Visconti's father was Giangaleazzo Visconti, duke of Milan 1395–1402. A genealogical table of the Visconti family can be found at the end of the *Storia di Milano* VI, 1955.

195. Also in *NF* p. 66, no. 189.

196. Also in *NF* p. 66, no. 181.

197. Later MSS locate this inscription "at the church of St. Andrew outside the walls near the entrance to the aforesaid church (Mommsen in *CIL).*"

198. Mommsen found this inscription buried beneath a pile of ruins (*sub aggere*) in an ancient temple to Diana. Only the three lines copied by Ciriaco stuck out (*eminuisse*) from the wall (*CIL ad loc.*).

199. Later MSS, from Feliciano on, locate this inscription "in the church of saints Faustinus and Lovita near the altar of St. Honorius at the foot of the bell-tower (*sub campanile*)" (Mommsen, *CIL, ad loc.*).

200. Also in *NF* p. 66, no. 186.

201. Also in *NF* p. 66, no. 189.

202. *NF* p. 67, no. 190: *Cippus Brixiae ad S. Georgium.*

203. Also in *NF* p. 67, no. 190.

204. Also in *NF* p. 62, no. 191.

205. Also in *NF* p. 65, no. 174.

206. Also in *NF* p. 65, no. 176.

207. Also in *NF* p. 65, no. 177.

208. Also in *NF* p. 65, no. 178.

209. This is the only recorded occasion when Ciriaco investigated the antiquities of Verona. Whereas Scalamonti, whose ordering of Ciriaco's itinerary is consistently chronological, puts the visit to Verona *before* the visit to Mantua, the corresponding passage on Verona in the '*Itinerarium*' (where the order is rhetorical: see Introduction and note to para. 206) is placed *after* an account of Ciriaco's visit to Mantua (Vo4, fol. 10r-v, ed. Mehus, 1742, 28–29; for the text see Appendix V, no. 8). In the case of Verona, the language of the *Vita* has nothing in common with that of the corresponding passage in the '*Itinerarium*.'

210. Papias, *De linguae Latinae vocabulis*, 1476 etc., s.v. *Athesis: Athesis flumen Veronae.*

211. *Phars.* 1, 403.

212. Scalamonti's source for these topographical remarks about the Adige in Verona—as well as for his tedious accounts of legends about the foundation of Mantua and the origin of its name (below, para. 192) and his murky calculations about the date of Mantua's foundation (para. 193); his confused summary of legends about Genoa's foundation, name, and date (below, para. 198–202); and his jumble of lore about the foundation and original name of Benevento (para. 214)—was probably one of Ciriaco's notebooks of *parerga* and extracts from ancient and medieval sources about the particular places he was visiting, which the traveler kept *pari passu* with his journals, occasionally entering a few of the ancient *testimonia* into the journals themselves at the appropriate places (e.g., in the Cycladic diary he places quotations from Solinus, Virgil, and Ovid about Naxos at the end of the section on Naxos, along with the description of a Rhodian coin depicting, he thought, the head of the colossal Apollo set up at Delos by the Naxians [M1, fol. 40v; Bodnar, 1972]). We have one such notebook, fortunately preserved in Ciriaco's own hand, MS Berol. gr. qu. 89 (B4): see Maas, 1913, 5–15 and Bodnar, 1960, 21n, 23n, 24n, 25, 32, 34, 35n, 45n.

At this point it begins to look as if Scalamonti, growing tired of his task and perhaps despairing of ever reaching the end of it, figuratively emptied out his Ciriacan files, including the traveler's notes on Verona, Mantua, and Genoa garnered from ancient and medieval sources. Other signs of careless haste toward the end of the *Vita* will be pointed out as they occur.

213. Verona was in Gallia Cisalpina, not Liguria, which is farther to the west.

214. The Veronese section of these *commentaria* is partially preserved, explicitly identified as such, in Sarayna, 1540, 13 (partially quoted by Mehus, 1742, xxvi–xxvii). Verbal agreement with the text of the *Vita* is indicated here by italics:

> De Amphitheatro etiam legitur in quibusdam chronicis Amphitheatrum, quam arenam vulgo appellant, anno XLII Imperii Augusti extructum fuisse, et Cyriacus Anconitanus in quodam itinerario sic scriptum reliquit: *Et denique Veronam feracissimam et antiquam civitatem venit, ubi non exigua monumenta comperit, praesertim Labyrinthum* quod *Arena nunc dicitur, et habetur quod constructum fuerit anno* imperii *Octaviani trigesimo nono ante* natalem *Christi* diem *tertio cuius pars exterior terraemotibus corruit et nunc* conspicitur *locus rotundus Arenae per totum magnis saxis undique constructus est* ut ita dicam *perfilatus* quum *intus cubalis* vel *antris multiformiter redimitus* sit. *In huius autem rotunditate extant scalae magnis lapidibus appositae, quae, quanto magis in* amplitudine protenduntur, tanto magis *in* rotunditatem *videbantur ampliari et*, sicut nonnulli referunt, *quinquaginta cubitis in* altitudinem *extenditur, in cuius summitate quidam locus magnus et nobilis multiformis* elaboratus *marmoreo lapide* circumcirca *redimitus erat....*

A comparison of Sarayna's quotation from the *commentaria* of Ciriaco with the text of the *Vita* (see Introduction, where the two texts are placed in parallel columns) shows how closely Scalamonti adhered to the text of Ciriaco's *commentaria* on at least this one occasion, when he expressly refers to his written source (*ut in commentariis suis reposuit*). The differences between Sarayna's text and Scalamonti's are minor, but in a few cases Scalamonti's apparent substitutions (e.g. of *altitudine* for *amplitudinem*) tend to obscure the meaning of the original.

215. A drawing of the Borsari gate in the hand of Felice Feliciano, showing the two arches and twelve windows, figures in MS 992 (α.L.5.15), Modena, Bibl. Estense., fol. 124 (see Huelsen, 1907, 11 and 13, fig. 10, and Mitchell, 1961, 218, Pl. XLIa).

216. Faenza, Bibl. Comunale, MS 7 is a much fuller *sylloge* of Veronese inscriptions, with drawings of most of the monuments on which they appear; it is in the hand of Felice Feliciano, who seems to be copying Ciriaco's own lost *sylloge*, without any connecting narrative, of the stones he inspected during this visit (see Mitchell, 1961, 214–215, Pls. XXVIIb, XXIVb, XXXVIIIa). The *Veronensia* are discussed by Mommsen in *CIL* V, 1, pp. 319, 321, 322. We await the publication of A. Campana's paper on this MS, listed in the program of a conference on Felice Feliciano held in Verona in June 1993; and another, by Gian Paolo Marchi, "Ciriaco negli studi epigrafici di Scipione Maffei" delivered at a congress held at Ancona in February 1992 to commemorate the 600th anniversary of the birth of Ciriaco (see Bibliography, *ad fin.* for a list of papers of both congresses germane to this study).

217. Mommsen, who examined the inscription *scalis admotis: literae olim aere expletae videntur fuisse ... lectio hodieque perspicua est exceptis paucis litteris ... quae iam aegra agnoscuntur (CIL, ad loc.)*.

218. *CIL: Veronae in contrata S. Andreae antiqui*.

219. Ciriaco missed or was unable to see another inscription on the back of this stone.

220. In later MSS (Feliciano, Marcanova, etc.), this inscription is located *prope Sanctum Salvatorem ubi coria conficiunt (CIL)*.

221. *CIL* locates this inscription *in postica*.

222. Later MSS locate this stone *in moenibus vetustissimis S. Michaelis a porta loco privato (CIL)*.

223. When Scalamonti says he found the following material (para. 192–193) in Ciriaco's *commentaria*, he may be referring to one of the traveler's commonplace books, such as the one he kept *pari passu* with his journal of the visit to mainland Greece in 1435–1436 (see above, note on para. 165, *ad fin.*).

224. Isidore of Seville, *Et.* 15, 59: *Manto Tiresiae filia post interitum Thebanorum dicitur delata in Italiam Mantuam condidisse: est autem in Venetia, quae Gallia Cisalpina dicitur: et dicta Mantua quod manes tuetur.* This extract would especially interest Lauro Quirini because he was a Venetian.

225. Cf. Virgil, *Aen.* 10, 198–200:

> Ille etiam patriis agmen ciet Ocnus ab oris,
> fatidicae Mantus et Tusci filius amnis,
> qui muros matrisque dedit tibi, Mantua, nomen

and *Ecl.* 9, 59–60:

> namque sepulcrum
> it apparere Bianoris

with Servius' commentary on both passages identifying Ocnus and Bianor (an indication that Ciriaco perhaps knew Servius); see also Paul the Deacon, *Hist. Langob.* 2, 14; Statius, *Theb.* 4, 406 ff.; Isidore, *Et.* 15, 59.

226. Orosius, *Hist. adversus paganos,* 7, 3, 1 (date of the foundation of Rome); Augustine, *City of God* book 16 (not 18, as in the text), para. 17 (date of the birth of Abraham). The references to Jerome and to the chronicles of Miletus and Eusebius are too vague to recover.

227. Scalamonti's text and the pertinent passage in the '*Itinerarium*' (Vo4, fol. 10r, Mehus, 1742, 27–28, see Appendix V, no. 9) have nothing in common except for the mention of Pietoli.

228. Pliny, *Natural History* 3.5.48.

229. *Hist. Langob.* 2, 16.

230. Solinus, *Collectanea rerum memorabilium* (ed. T. Momsen, Berlin, 1895), 2, 5.

231. Albarium, Galiganum, Serzanum: none of these place-names appear in Graesse, 1971.

232. The statements attributed to Jerome (on Moses and the foundation date of Rome) and Bede and Methodius (on the founding of Genoa) could not be traced. The legend of Bellovesus, the son of a Celtic king, who was led by augury to found Mediolanum, is told by Livy, 5, 34, but he does not speculate on the date.

233. Livy, 28, 46, 7.

234. Publius Cornelius Scipio, consul 318 B.C., younger brother of Gnaeus Cornelius Scipio Calvus: Livy, 21, 32, 5.

235. Livy, 30, 1, 10.

236. Francesco Barbavera was lord of Gravellona and other places, a courtier of Giangaleazzo Visconti who married Antonia Visconti (Spreti, 1931, s.v.). Ciriaco saw the precious crater, a spoil from the sack of Caesarea in Syria, in the treasury of S. Lorenzo in Genoa (Mehus, 1742, 17, n. 4). The pertinent passage in the '*Itinerarium*' (Vo4, fol. 6r-v, ed. Mehus, 1742, 16–18) mentions the precious bowl and many of the same names. For the text see Appendix V, no. 10.

In a letter written in August 1446, Ciriaco refers to this visit as having taken place *bis senis iam annis exactis*, i.e., in 1434 (see Belgrano, 1877–1884, 984); here also the names of Francesco Spinola, Benedetto Negroni, and Giovanni Grillo are mentioned in connection with the bowl of precious green stone, which he said he recorded in his *per Ligustiam commentaria*. We have also a letter of 13 January 1443 from Ciriaco to Benedetto Negroni, which mentions Iacopo Bracello (Maom, Miscell. n. 44; see Montevecchi, 1939, 80–82). In Ciriaco's account of the battle of Ponza, 5 August 1435, Francesco Spinola is named as admiral designate of the Genoese fleet (ed. Sabia, pp. 163, 165, and 174–175, with note 17, and 177; one of several versions is in T, fols. 109r–119v ed. Colucci, 1792, 100–108). A poem written by Ciriaco's friend, Andreolo Giustiniani-Banca, on the Venetian attack on Chios in 1431 is dedicated to Iacop Bracello (see Porro-Lambertenghi, ?1865).

237. If this visit had occurred in 1434, it would have had to be before 18 May 1434, when Eugenius IV fled Rome for Florence, where he stayed until 19 September 1443 (Eubel, II, 29, n. 30). However, it is much more likely that it was a continuation into early 1432 of the 1431 visit. See Introduction, 'Chronology,' and the notes to para. 206 and 215–217 of this translation for a discussion of the chronological anomalies presented by these final paragraphs.

238. On Pagliaresio di Simolo de' Pisanelli see above, para. 61, note.

239. For the practice of piracy in the Mediterranean by both Christians and Moslems at this time see A. Tenenti, 1973, and Ashtor, 1983, 391.

240. For the text of the pertinent account in the '*Itinerarium*' of Ciriaco's travels in south Italy (Vo4, fols. 8r–9v, ed. Mehus, 1742, 23–25), see Appendix V, no. 11. This portion of Ciriaco's letter to Pope Eugenius IV, which occurs immediately after the account of the visit to Milan, corresponds so closely to the record given in the last pages of Scalamonti's *Vita* in wording, observations, and date (both mention Joanna II of Naples, who died on 2 February 1435, as still on the throne) that, with a few exceptions that will be noted, the two accounts must refer to the same tour. They differ, however, in the order of presentation. The '*Itinerarium*' has Ciriaco travelling hither and thither on the following improbable course: Naples - Pozzuoli - Literno - Terracina - Benevento - Gaeta - Capua - Sessa, after which he takes ship with the bishop of Parenzo and with Boscolo to Sicily, which he circumnavigates clockwise, and then proceeds to Reggio Calabria, Barletta and Manfredonia (visits to Manfredonia and Barletta are dated to July 1437 in Moroni, *Epigrammata*, p. 37). The *Vita*, on the other hand, gives a more reasonable itinerary: Gaeta - Terracina - Gaeta - Literno - Sessa - Capua - Aversa - Naples - Pozzuoli - Naples - Benevento - Naples, whence he sails with the bishop and Boscolo to Sicily, where he lands in Messina.

As we have seen (see Introduction), the difficulty of reconciling the '*Itinerarium*' with the *Vita* (see Tiraboschi, 1783, VI, I, 165; Colucci, 1792, 32–36; de Rossi, 1888, 361) arises only if we assume (wrongly, we believe) that the letter to Eugenius IV was intended as a chronologically consecutive travel-journal. Once it is seen that connectives like *deinde* do not mean 'next' in *time*, and that the organization of the letter is logical and rhetorical rather than historical, the apparent discrepancies disappear. There is a problem, however, about the *year* in which these travels took place and the '*Itinerarium*' may be right in placing them right after the Milan visit. See note on para. 215.

241. Joanna II died on 2 February 1435 (Giannone, 1731, II, 318).

242. This torn-out folio (104) presumably referred to Ciriaco's welcome by Joanna as a grandson of Ciriaco Selvatico, his obligation to Giovanni Caracciolo, and his visit to the temple of Castor and Pollux, as described in the '*Itinerarium*' (see text in Appendix V, no. 11b). Perhaps there was a drawing of the temple, which would account for the removal of the folio. For the dedicatory inscription on the temple see Campana, 1973–1974, who characterizes Felice's orthography as *cattiva*.

Campana, ibid., 89, points out the chronological difficulty created by the mention of Giovanni Caracciolo (died August 1432) in the '*Itinerarium*' in connection with the visit to Naples. In this case, however, the chronological problem is not confined to the '*Itinerarium*,' since most of the events mentioned by Scalamonti in connection with this journey are commonly dated from other sources as having occurred, not in 1434, as one would expect, but 1432: see below, note on para. 215.

243. *CIL* IX, 1558.

244. As with Mantua and Genoa, this intercalated 'historical' section indicates that Scalamonti was utilizing Ciriaco's *parerga*.

245. Solinus, 2, 10.

246. Papias, s. v. Diomedis, Samnis, Samnium, Samnitae.

247. Paul the Deacon, *Hist. Langob.* 2, 20.

248. The archbishop of Benevento was Gaspar Colonna, consecrated in 1429, and he did have twenty-two suffragans (Eubel, I, 137, 576; II, 313).

249. References to Miletus and Jerome not found.

250. Although we should now be in late 1434 or early 1435, the events referred to in these last paragraphs seem to belong to the year 1432. The reference to Daniele de'Rampi (Tiraboschi, 166, calls him Daniello), as *Perantinus* is a case in point: consecrated bishop of Parenzo on 7 January 1426 (Eubel, I, 409), he left that diocese when he was made bishop of Concordia on 7 January 1433 and he died later that same year (Eubel, II, 149, based on Ughelli, 1717—see Mehus, 1742, 24, note). Add to this the facts that Alfonso's attack on Djerba took place in the summer of 1432, not in 1434 (see the next note) and that the Giovanni Caracciolo who, according to the *'Itinerarium'* received Ciriaco in Naples (see text, Appendix V, no. 11), died in August 1432 (F. Petrucci, *DBI* 19 [1976], 374) and we have a chronological crux that can be solved only if we place this whole south Italian journey in the first months of 1432, immediately after Ciriaco's visit to the new Pope Eugenius IV and his exploration of Tivoli and Ostia at end of 1431, i.e., after para. 96. See Introduction, 'Chronology,' under the year 1432.

251. Off the coast of Tunisia. Alfonso attacked the sultan's forces in the summer of 1432 (*DBI* II, 324–325, s.v. Alfonso V d'Aragona; Pontieri, 1975, 257; Ryder, 1976, 272). The king of Tunisia was Abu Fâris `Azzûz, who reigned from 1394 to 1434 (Pontieri, 259). Alfonso's ongoing naval war against the sultan of Egypt, Barsbay, went on until the summer of 1435, when Alfonso, in an all-out effort to gain the throne of Naples, withdrew his ships to Gaeta, where they were engaged by the Genoese on 5 August 1435 off the island of Ponza and Alfonso was captured (Ashtor, 1983, 301–302). It may be significant that the item that appears immediately after the *Vita* in T is Ciriaco's *Naumachia Regia*, an account of the battle of Ponza, which he wrote in Ancona on 13 September 1435 and dedicated to Francesco Scalamonti (for an excellent edition of this text, which Ciriaco revised several times, see Sabia, 1977–1978).

252. Maria d'Enghien, *ca.* 1370–1446, queen of Sicily, wife of Raimondo del Balzo Orsini and then of King Ladislao of Naples. Taranto, which was her fief, she passed on to her son, Giovannantonio del Balzo Orsini, who sided with Alfonso of Aragon in the latter's attempt to gain the throne of Naples. For the prince of Taranto in the battle of Ponza see T, fol. 116v, ed. Colucci, 1792, 106 and Sabia, 1977–1978, 167, 180–181.

253. The text of the *Vita* seems to imply that Ciriaco returned to Ancona *with the fleet*. Granted that the *'Itinerarium'* is not arranged chronologically (see Introduction), we need not attribute to this same journey the circumnavigation of Sicily, the visit to Reggio Calabria, and the return *overland* through Apulia to Barletta and Manfredonia at the end of his south Italian tour, as the *'Itinerarium'* seems to say (text cited in Appendix V, 11f.). A confirmation of this view may be found in Ciriaco's other record of the visits to Barletta and Manfredonia, also fragmentary, which the text as published by Moroni, p. 37, from a lost MS (see Bodnar, 1960, 45–49), dates to 1437, just before he set off for the Peloponnesus that year:

MCCCCXXXVII

Ad X. K. Iulii [*22 June*] venimus Manfredoniam Apuliae Dauniae civitatem inter Sipum [*i.e. Sipontum*] antiquam urbem et Gargani montis promontorium sitam, in qua nil memorabile videtur praeter magnam ex aere squillam. Vidimus et Sipum dirutam civitatem, quam Sipatum vocant.

MCCCCXXXVII

Ad VIII K. Iulias [*24 June*] venimus Baroletum, nobile Apuliae Dauniae oppidum, secus Ionicum mare, iuxta Salpias civitatem maritimam atque Canusium mediterraneum oppidum. In Baroleti maritimo foro vidimus colosseam Herculis imaginem aeneam magnam, quam Heraclem incolae vocant.

It seems likely, therefore, that Ciriaco's visit to Manfredonia and Barletta occurred later, in 1437. As we have seen (note to para. 165 *ad fin.*), this last part of the *Vita* seems fragmentary and patched together and it appears rather to stop than to come to a conclusion. Even when we re-date paragraphs 204–217 back to the year 1432, bringing Scalamonti's account to an end with Ciriaco still in Genoa (para. 203), followed by the one-sentence valediction to Lauro (para. 218), the ending feels abrupt and unfinished.

# APPENDIX I

## Letter of Ciriaco
## to Pietro di Liberio de Bonarellis, Rimini[1]

## 15 March 1423

This is Ciriaco's earliest known work, written during an otherwise undocumented journey in 1423 from Ancona to Venice by way of Fano and Rimini.[2] In it he justifies his attention to pagan authors by reference to Dante, *Purgatorio* VI, 119–120, where Christ is called *Giove crocifisso*.[3] The literary form is that of an imagined dream in which the debate takes place, with Mercury pleading Ciriaco's cause. Thirteen years later he returned to this form and repeated some of the same phraseology in a letter to Leonardo Bruni of 30 January 1436 in praise of Caesar.[4]

The poetic cast of the language and numerous grammatical errors typical of the autodidact fully bear out Scalamonti's report (*Vita*, para. 53) that Ciriaco had only recently begun to learn and write Latin by close study and imitation of Virgil. Virgilian and Ovidian echoes are identified in the apparatus.

Regarding the many errors of spelling and grammar, since this is of the work of a beginner in Latin and the only extant copy is not in Ciriaco's own hand, we have tried in our edition to distinguish between errors probably committed by Ciriaco and those that seem attributable to the scribe of VL9. The latter we have corrected, indicating the reading of the MS in the apparatus.

As in our edition of the *Vita*, we have employed modern capitalization, punctuation and numbered paragraphing. Abbreviations have been expanded without use of brackets unless the expansion is an interpretation of the editor: e.g., In para. 1 below: *clar.*° is written *clarissimo*, without brackets, whereas the next word, *P<etro>*, is a conjectural expansion of '*P*'. following Morici's suggestion that *P. de Bonol.* is Pietro de Bonarellis. As in the text of the *Vita*, we have written *ae* or *oe* instead of the scribe's usual *e* where the diphthong is meant.

# TEXT[5]

**1.** Kiriacus de Picenicollibus Anchonitanus viro clarissimo P<etro> de Bon<ar>el<lis>[a] Liberii filio Anchonitano salutem plurimam dicit.

**2.** Cum Venetiarum ad urbem profecturus iter haberem et ad vetustissima Fauni moenia ventum[b] consisterem, huc ubi iam dies coelo concesserat alma,[c] occeano[d] cadente Phoebo, placidum per membra soporem tacitae sub noctis curriculo carpere placuit.[e] Sed paulo antequam cristatus ales vigili ore tepidum provocaret diem,[f] necdum in luteis aurora fulgente bigis[g] astra fugarat Olympo, et ecce iamque in ipsa, ut videbatur, aula Fauni obtulit se mihi in sonnis[h] ante oculos insignis forma[i] et maiestate puer pluribus undique comitatus claris equestris iurisve consulti ordinum viris spectatissimis aliisque civibus ornatissimis. Hic ea forte tempestate adolescentulus, amisso genitore, huiusce praesul urbis considebat. At ego itaque dum tantorum coetum diu admirans

---

[a] P. de Bonol, with a horizontal line through the 'l.' Colin, 472, writes, de Bo[na]rel[li].

[b] Construe as = <postquam> ventum <est>. Cf. e.g. Virgil, *Aeneid* 4.151: postquam altos ventum in montis atque invia lustra, / ecce ferae etc.

[c] cf. *Aen* 10.215–216: Iamque dies caelo concesserat almaque curru / noctivago Phoebe medium pulsabat Olympum.

[d] This spelling occurs in Ciriacan autographs.

[e] cf. *Aen.* 4.522–523, Nox erat, et placidum carpebant fessa soporem/corpora per terras . . . ; and 8.405–408, placidumque petivit / coniugis infusus gremio per membra soporem. / Inde ubi prima quies medio iam noctis abactae / curriculo expulerat somnum.

[f] Cf. Ovid, *Fasti* 1.455–456: nocte deae Nocti cristatus caeditur ales, / quod tepidum vigili provocet ore diem. A favorite allusion of Ciriaco's. It occurs later, in his 'Caesarean' letter to Leonardo Bruni, 30 January, and in a relatively late letter to Giovani Pedemontano, dated January 1445 (Bodnar and Mitchell, 1976, p. 59, lines 1105–1106).

[g] bigiis MS. Unless otherwise stated, the variants listed in this apparatus are the actual readings of the MS that have been corrected in our text.

[h] frequent in Ciriaco for somnis

[i] The Virgilian formulaic language in this sentence is borrowed from various parts of the *Aeneid*: 7.25–26, Iamque rubescebat radiis mare, et aethere ab alto / Aurora in roseis fulgebat lutea bigis; 5.42–43, postea cum primo stellas Oriente fugarat / clara dies . . . ; 4.556–557, huic se forma dei vultu redeuntis eodem / obtulit in somnis . . . ; 2.270–271, in somnis, ecce, ante oculos maestissimus Hector / visus adesse mihi . . . ; 5.295, Euryalus forma insignis viridique iuventa.

hominum perlegerem oculis,[a] vir ex his quidam eques ad me magna se gerens gravitate conversus, talibus me vehementer obiurgando dictis visus est:

**3.**     "Unde haec[b] tam caeca tamque obscena, Kiriace, obumbraris[c] caligine, qui Cristiano indutus habitu, sacris almae fidei nostrae amissis[d] codicibus, tanta cum tui frequentia et curiositate diu gentiles lectitare poetas insudando magno cum labore contendis, cum praesertim, ut sane intelligis, tam a nostra penitus religione alieni sint, ut Iovem ipsum Cretensem multum pollutum vitiis hominem et mortalem deum esse omnipotentem variis undique carminibus cecinere;[e] quin etiam innumeros e fide devios infandosve errores in suis ut patet operibus inseruere[f].

**4.**     "Sed quid plura? Quaerendo tempus in verbis, deducemus quod[g] ut de totius summa rei sententiam dicam. Quis neget maximus[h] Latinorum ille poetarum, quem tu tam grandibus[i] excellere facis laudibus, Maro, in suo posuisse nobiliori volumine alios inter errores humanas[j] corpore iam solutas[k] animas iterum nova ad corpora redituras? Ut Lethaei ad fluminis undam per Anchisem filio sciscitante canit: 'animae quibus altera fato corpora debentur.'[l]

---

[a] cf. *Aen.* 6.34: perlegerent oculis

[b] Construe as = hac.

[c] obrumbaris

[d] amisis; Morici corrects to ommissis

[e] Construe as = ut . . . cecinerint.

[f] inserere

[g] Construe as = quid.

[h] Construe as = maximum . . . illum . . . Maronem . . . posuisse.

[i] grandis

[j] humanos

[k] solutus

[l] *Aen.* 6.713–714

Quantisque utique[a] in locis Iovem ipsum vocet 'omnipotentem divum patrem ac hominum regem' praetereo."[b]

5.        Vix haec ubi tandem dicta[c] conticuerat, cum omnes ei simul ore frementes annuere. Ast ego ubi verba haec tam temere a rei quidditate[d] dissentire accepi, moleste ferens, dumque multa in pectore volvens[e] pluribus munire suasionibus vocem, magno tuendi mei vatis amore summopere animi vires excitare cogor. Sed cum tam maxima responsurus tantorum in conspectu virorum ingenii diffidens vis et eloquentiae subnubilus formidarem, Elyconeas[f] ubi ad auxilium proposcere[g] coepi deas, ecce iamque adventare mihi ex alto vidi, Urania concitante, Caliopem et perdulcissime suam pulsantem[h] liram. Meam ocius in cantu rapuit mentem et coelum alte petens ad magni Iovis solium se supplicem[i] contulerat, quem lacteo sic ore coepit obsecrare: "O divum pater optime aeterneque rerum opifex, namque omnia potes,[j] ne, pater, absiste petenti auxilium praestare tuum. Disice[k] telo nephas. Nam vides in ipsa cornigeri[l] aede indignos[m] nostros ab omnibus lacerari[n] vates."

---

[a] corrected in MS from undique

[b] pater omnipotens occurs nine times in the *Aeneid*: e.g., 1.60; divum pater atque hominum rex, four times, e.g., 1.65.

[c] cf. *Aen.* 8.175, haec ubi dicta, dapes iubet. . . . The full Virgilian expression is haec ubi dicta *dedit* (e.g., 2.790).

[d] quiditate

[e] cf. *Aen.* 1.305: at pius Aeneas per noctem plurima volvens

[f] Morici reads Elyconas.

[g] = poscere

[h] pulsante

[i] suplicem

[j] cf. *Aen.* 10.18, o pater, o hominum rerumque potestas; 6.117, potes namque omnia; and 8.39, ne absiste.

[k] discice; Morici corrects to disice.

[l] an epithet of Faunus, a play on the name of the city, Fano: cf. above, para. 2, and below, para. 7.

[m] Morici indigne

[n] lacerare

**6.** Dixerat. At ille genitor alte syderea in sede obnixus, oculos[a] per omnia lustrans, qui nutu vibrante coelum annuerat precanti[b] divae, protinus ad accitum sic alloquitur Cilleneum: "Vade, nate, cape virgam et optimos nostri numinis auxiliare praecones, Calliope monstrante viam."[c]

**7.** Dixit. Tum ille, magni parentis imperio parante, aurea munitis thalaria pedibus[d] et baculum[e] gerente manu, aethereumque tonante[f] cursum et littora radente[g] Piceni,[h] Musa duce, in praefata consedit aulea Fauni. Huc vero Mercurius ubi me ex abdito[i] cava occulerat nube,[j] suisque exuens divinis ornamentis mira ope vultu et[k] habitu induerat[l] se meo. Hic autem primum meae responsionis officium summens et ad praelibatos conversus viros, divino afflante spiritu placido sic pectore coepit:[m]

---

[a] Construe as = oculis and see next note.

[b] In the 'Caesarean' letter *lustrans* is changed to *volvens* and *precanti* to *poscenti*.

[c] cf. *Aen.* 10.2–3, concilium vocat divum pater atque hominum rex / sideream in sedem; 4.607, Sol, qui . . . opera omnia lustras; 9.106 and 10.115, adnuit et totum nutu tremefecit Olympum; 7.752, intentos volvens oculos; 4.222–223, tum sic Mercurium adloquitur ac talia mandat: 'vade, age, nate, voca Zephyros et labere pennis; and 1.382, matre dea monstrante.

[d] cf. *Aen.* 4.239–240, dixerat. ille patris magni parere parabat / imperio; et primum pedibus talaria nectit / aurea . . .

[e] bacculum

[f] Construe as = tonando or tonans.

[g] Construe as = radendo or radens.

[h] Morici reads picem and corrects to Piceni.

[i] Construe as = *in* abdito.

[j] cf. *Aeneid* 5.809–810: Aenean . . . / nube cava rapui

[k] etiam

[l] cf. *Aen.* 684, falle dolo et notos pueri puer indue vultus; and 1.315, virginis os habitumque gerens

[m] cf. *Aen.* 1.521, maximus Ilioneus placido sic pectore coepit

**8.**       "Magnam quidem, o viri, ut accipio, tantorum oppinare[a] vatum dementiam temere praesumpsistis. Aspicite ergo namque omnem, quae nunc obducta tuentibus vobis mortales hebetat visus, nubem eripiam.[b] Videbitis[c] autem, viri boni, optimus ille magni numinis poeta Mantuanus[d] suis nonnullis in divinis carminibus, quamquam[e] sub Iovis nomine, veram aeternam ac omnium causarum causam deitatem divina cum mente intuendo, sublimare. Videtur autem multis in locis peroptime se nostrae conformare[f] religioni vetustaeque[g] primordialis Pentatheuci legi, ut in VI° inquit per Anchisem: 'Principio coelum ac terras camposque liquentes / lucentemque globum lunae thitaniaque astra / spiritus intus alit, totamque infusa per artus / mens agitat molem et magno se corpore miscet,' et continuo subdit: Inde hominum pecudumque genus, vitaeque volantum, / et quae marmoreo fert monstra sub aequore pontus.'[h] Patet ergo sane divinus ille vates[i] verum intellexisse deum, quem[j] a principio universarum opificem rerum omnem a se nutu condiderat mundum, quamvis ille pluries id nomen poetice Ioviali[k] nomine cecinisset.

**9.**       "Quin etiam ut de varietate dei nominum diceret, ostendendo quem praedominaretur deum[l] in loco ubi rerum inclita Roma condenda fuerat,[m] per Evandrum ait in VIII°: 'Hoc nemus, hunc,' inquit, 'frondoso vertice collem, /

---

[a] Construe as = opinari.

[b] cf. *Aen.* 2.604–606: aspice (namque omnem, quae nunc obducta tuenti / mortalis hebetat visus tibi et umida circum / caligat, nubem eripiam.

[c] Morici corrects to videbitur.

[d] Construe as = optimum illum . . . poetam Mantuanum.

[e] Morici reads quaquam.

[f] confirmare, corrected by Morici to conformare

[g] vetustateque

[h] *Aen.* 6.724–729

[i] Construe as = divinum illum vatem.

[j] Construe as = qui.

[k] Iovialis

[l] Construe as = quis . . . deus.

[m] fierat

quis deus incertum est, habitat deus; Archades ipsum / credunt[a] se vidisse
Iovem, cum saepe tonantem / aegida concuteret dextra nymbosque cieret.'[b]

**10.**     "Sed cur tantis percurramus in verbis, cum sacer maximus ille fidei
catholicae princeps Augustinus ad nostram maxime tuendam religionem suos
codices huiusce nostri vatis carminibus roborare summopere laboravit?[c] Idem
Hieronymus Lactantiusque fecere.

**11.**     "Videtur an vobis satis manifestum perpulcre nostrae fidei inhaerere
poetam, quando ad beatos Elysii posuerat sedes felices optimorum animas
omni cum gaudio aeternis frui amoenissimo in loco bonis?

**12.**     "Et primo, ut martirum defingeretur paritas, inquit in VI° praefati: 'Hic
manus ob patriam pugnando vulnera passi, / quique sacerdotes casti dum vita
manebat,[d] quique pii vates et Phoebo digna locuti,[e] inventas aut qui vitam
excoluere per artes,'[f] viros ut activarum rerum optimos repertores cultoresque
simularet.

**13.**     "Alia vero ex parte ad impia posuit Tartara monstra inter immania
Thesiphonem sceleratas acerrime ferro lacerare animas, necessariamque[g]
adiecit, ut nostrae magis conveniret se legi, iudice sub aequo scelerum
confessionem. Nam inquit subinde per Sibillam Phoebi vatem canens:
'Gnoscius haec Radamantus habet durissima regna / castigatque auditque
dolos subigitque fateri / quae quis apud superos, furto[h] laetatus[i] inani, / distulit
in seram commissa piacula mortem.' / Et hic, ut severissimas ad moerentem
culpam poenas religiose tribuerat, immediate subdiderat: 'Continuo sontes

---

[a] creditur

[b] *Aen.* 8.351–354. The received text reads nigrantem, not tonantem.

[c] corrected in MS from laudavit

[d] manebant

[e] Morici's addition of 'et deinde addit' at this point is not in the MS.

[f] *Aen.* 6.660–663

[g] necessariasque

[h] furtu

[i] laetatur

ultrix accincta[a] flagello / Thelsiphone quatit insultans, torvosque sinistra / distentans angues vocat agmina saeva sororum.'[b]

**14.**     "Sed quid enim divinus iste vates de divino ignoverat misterio, cum de adventu sacratissimi humanae pientissimae culpae redemptoris mirifice suum per fatidicum carmen vaticinatur[c] canens suo in pastorali libello: 'Ultima Cumaei venit iam carminis aetas. / Iam redit et virgo, redeunt Saturnia[d] regna / iam nova progenies coelo demittitur[e] alto.'[f]

**15.**     "Praeterea vos dum obiicitis illi posuisse animas corporibus iterum redituras, hoc autem potissime videtur se nostrae conformare[g] legis opinioni, cum firmiter habetis in fide coelicolum animae[h] novissimo in die inire corporibus glorificatis uniri. Quid enim aliud infert cum cecinerit inde: 'Has omnes, ubi mille rotam volvere per annos, / Lethaeum ad fluvium[i] deus evocat agmine magno, / scilicet inmemores supera ut convexa revisant, / rursus et incipiant in corpora velle reverti?'[j]

**16.**     "Quas ob res optimus ille vetustarum conmentator rerum Macrobius ad huiusce altissimi poetae de deorum religione peritiam comprobandam, haec suis in Saturnalibus verba conseruit dicens: 'Videturne vobis probatum sine divini ac humani iuris scientia non posse profunditatem Maronis intelligi?'[k]

---

[a] accinta

[b] *Aen.* 6.566–572. The received text reads intentans.

[c] vaticinantur

[d] redeunt et saturnia

[e] demictitur

[f] Virgil, *Ecl.* 4.4, 6–7

[g] confirmare

[h] Construe as = animas.

[i] fluvitum

[j] *Aen.* 6.748–751

[k] Macrobius, *Saturnalia*, Liber tertius, cap. IX, *ad fin.*

**17.** "Sed ut ne per talia[a] omne datum duceremus tempus, finem faciam et solum pro rei summa dicam quod ille utique noster[b] catholicus Maronisque imperator et materni eloquii[c] poeta Dantes[d] in suo Christianissimo volumine[e] exclamavit summum Iovem ut verum humani generis redemptorem in terra crucifixum esse secunda in parte carminis:[f] 'Et se licito m'è, o summo Jove, / che fusti in terra per noi crucifixo, / son li justi occhi[g] tuoi revolti altrove?'[h]

**18.** "Patet namque nescia mens hominum veri, cum sacratissima divinarum rerum archana misteria honestissimo sub velamine fictionis ab excellentissimis operta poetis insane variis incusando[i] calumniis elaborare.[j] Proh[k] scelus! Hii quidam fuere qui, suis divinis momentis atque optimis institutis, hominibus, ad bene beateque vivendum lumen, doctrinam, et honestissimis moribus disciplinam dedere."

**19.** Nam haec ubi caducifer dicta dedit, me aperta nube ad locum referente meum, divinam resummens formam, et magno corruscante lumine, ubi mille Dei volantum vitae[l] gloriam almae Trinitati cecinerant, in tenuem auram[m]

---

[a] italia

[b] vester

[c] eloghii

[d] Morici writes ille utique *vester* catholicus *Maro et* imperator materni eloquii poeta Dantes.

[e] corrected in MS from poeta

[f] canitis

[g] ochie

[h] Dante, *Purgatorio* 6.118–120. The received text reads *sommo Giove, fosti, crucifisso, giusti,* and *rivolti.* Sinclair, 1961, *ad loc.*, reports the suggestion that perhaps Dante thought that *Jove* and *Jehovah* were the same word.

[i] Construe as = ut incuset.

[j] Construe as = cum . . . elaboret.

[k] Prho

[l] Cf. *Aen.* 6.728 (cited above, para. 8).

[m] auram: aulam

nostris ex oculis evolavit.[a] Exim[b] ego excutior e sonno[c] membra; tibique optimo Pieridum cultori portentuosam hanc scribere visionem ut dignum amicitiae nostrae munus existimavi.[d]

**20.** Tuque iam vale. Ex itinere[e] apud Ariminum Idus Martias MCCCCXXIII°.

---

[a] Cf. et procul in tenuem ex oculis evanuit auram: *Aeneid* 4.278 (of Mercury) and 9.658 (of Apollo).

[b] There is a dash over the 'm.' Morici reads Exinc.

[c] Cf. *Aen.* 2.302, excutior somno.

[d] In the 'Caesarean' letter, where these expressions are used again, *Trinitati* is changed to *trini numinis maiestati* and *dignum to praedignum*.

[e] intinere

# TRANSLATION

**1.** Greetings from Ciriaco de' Pizzecolli of Ancona to the illustrious Pietro di Liborio de Bonarellis of Ancona.

**2.** On my way to the city of Venice, I broke my journey at the ancient walls of Fano. The fostering day had already withdrawn from the sky and the sun was setting into the sea when I decided to snatch peaceful sleep beneath the chariot of the silent night. But shortly before the crested cock aroused the warming day with its waking cry, when Dawn in her saffron-colored car had not yet put the stars to flight in the shining heavens, behold a boy, distinguished in beauty and dignity, appeared to me in a dream, in Fano's very palace, it seemed, surrounded by a numerous company of notable knights and lawyers and other prominent citizens. This mere lad chanced to be presiding at the time as head of this city in the absence of his father.[6] As my eyes swept in wonder over this gathering of great men, one of the knights turned to me, quite serious in his demeanor, and delivered the following strong rebuke:

**3.** "Why are you overshadowed by this dark and dreadful cloud, Ciriaco? Why, though dressed in Christian attire, do you abandon the sacred books of our fostering faith to spend so much of your time struggling with eager attention, sweat, and toil, to read pagan poets, especially since, as you know well, they are so utterly foreign to our religion? For instance, they proclaimed in poems of all different kinds that the Cretan Jove, himself a mortal man much defiled by vices, is almighty God; and furthermore, they inserted numerous unspeakable errors divergent from the faith, as is evident from their works.

**4.** "Need I say more? In the interest of brevity, I shall lay out what I intend to say as my opinion on the whole matter. Who will deny that Maro,[7] the greatest of the Latin poets,[8] whom you exalt with great praise, wrote in his most important work,[9] among other errors, that human souls,[10] once they have been set free from the body, will come back again to new bodies? For instance, in answer to Aeneas' inquiry at the bank of the river Lethe, <the poet> sings through Anchises: '<these are> the souls to whom fate owes other bodies.' I pass over the numerous passages in which he calls Juppiter himself "the almighty father of gods and king of men.'

**5.** Barely had he lapsed into silence, when all expressed noisily their agreement with him. But when I perceived that these words differed radically from the truth, taking it ill and all the while pondering in my heart the many ways to buttress my speech with persuasive arguments, greatly desirous as I was to defend my poet, I was strongly compelled to stir the powers of my mind. But now that I was about to make such an important reply in the presence of these gifted men, I was afraid, lacking confidence in my innate powers and somewhat overshadowed in eloquence. As I began to pray to the goddesses of Helicon for help, at that very moment I beheld Calliope coming to my aid from on high at the urging of Ourania and plucking sweetly on her lyre. Swiftly she caught up my petition in song and, making for the heavens on high, betook herself as a suppliant to the throne of mighty Jove, whom she began to implore with milk-white lips: "O good father of the gods and eternal craftsman of the universe, you can <do> all things: do not, father, fail to grant my petition. Destoy injustice with your shaft. For you see our poets being attacked by everyone in the very temple of the horned god."[11]

6.       When she was finished, the father <sat> steadfast on his starry throne, scanning everything with his eyes. He nodded to the praying goddess with the nod that causes heaven to shake, and summoning the Cyllenian one,[12] addressed him as follows: "Go, son, take your wand and help the excellent heralds of our divinity. Calliope will show you the way."

7.       When <Jove> had finished speaking, then <Mercury>, as the power of his mighty father prepared the way, donned his golden winged sandals and, wand in hand, thundered his way through the sky along the shores of Piceno with the Muse as his guide, and perched in the aforesaid palace of Fano. Here Mercury secretly concealed me in a sheltering cloud, doffed his divine trappings, and, by virtue of his wondrous power, assumed my features and garb. He took over my function of responding, turned to the men, inspected[13] them, then, divinely inspired, began calmly as follows:

8.       "Gentlemen, as I see it, you have rashly taken it on yourselves to assume that highly accomplished bards are quite mad. Well, look, for I shall remove all of the cloud that is now drawn over your gaze blunting your mortal vision. You will see, good men, that the excellent Mantuan poet of great inspiration, in some of his divine poems, though he calls the godhead 'Jove,' still, gazing at it with prophetic vision, exalts it as the true and eternal cause of all causes. Moreover, he is seen in many passages to conform perfectly to our religion and to the primordial Law of the Pentateuch. For example, in the sixth book,[14] he says: 'First, the spirit within nourishes heaven and earth and the flowing plains and the bright sphere of the moon and Titan star;[15] and mind, spreading through the limbs <of the universe>, sets in motion the entire mass and mingles with the vast frame;' and he adds immediately: 'From this <commingling> comes the race of men and beasts and the lives of birds and the curious creatures that the sea bears beneath its bright surface.' Thus it is quite clear that the inspired poet, although he sang <of the divinity> frequently under the name of Jove, meant the true God, the craftsman of the universe, who[16] constructed the whole world by himself, with a nod.'

**9.** "Nay more, to speak of the variety of the names we give to God, <the poet>, when showing what god prevailed in the place where world-famous Rome was to be founded, says through Evander, 'A god (what god we do not know) dwells in this grove, this hill with its leafy crest; the Arcadians believe they have seen Jove himself whenever he shakes with his right hand the booming aegis and summons the clouds.'

**10.** "But why should we run through passage after passage when the foremost churchman of the Catholic faith, Augustine, to defend our religion most effectively, took great pains to reinforce his works with <citations from> the poetry of this our bard? Jerome and Lactantius did the same.

**11.** "Is it not sufficiently clear to you that the poet adheres magnificently to <the tenets of> our faith since at the blessed dwellings of Elysium he maintained that the fortunate souls of the just enjoy eternal goodness in a most beautiful place?

**12.** "And first, to give equal status to the martyrs, he says in the aforesaid sixth book: 'This group <consists of > those who were wounded fighting for their country and priests who were unstained throughout their lives and the poets/prophets who were upright and uttered <words> worthy of Phoebus or those who enhanced life by discovering new skills.' <This he said> so as to equate the great practitioners of practical skills with the great inventors of those skills.

**13.** "From another standpoint, he wrote that Tisiphone afflicts the souls of sinners most harshly in wicked Tartarus, among savage monsters; and, to be more consistent with our Law, he added a required confession of sins before a fair judge. For he says right after, singing through Phoebus' prophet, the Sibyl: 'Cnossian Rhadamanthus rules this harsh realm and reproves <sinners> and hears about their falsehoods and forces each person to confess to what he did in the world above, gloating over some vain deceit, while he put off making atonement for his sins until death, too late.' And here, when <Virgil> has scrupulously assigned the harshest penalties to the sinner who is grieving for his sin, he immediately adds: 'Without delay, vengeful Tisiphone, armed with a whip, makes them writhe as she leaps upon them and, holding the grim snakes in her left hand, summons her savage company of sisters.'

**14.** "But what did that divinely inspired bard not know about the divine mystery, since, remarkably, he predicted in prophetic song the coming of the most holy redeemer of mankind's fortunate fault?[17] For he sings in his book of pastoral poetry: 'The last age of Cumaean prophecy has come. Now returns the virgin, the reign of Saturn returns; now a new offspring is being sent down from high heaven!'

**15.**    "Moreover, although you fault him for writing that souls will return again to bodies, this <teaching> especially seems to conform to the belief of our Law, since you firmly believe that the souls of the heaven-dwellers begin to be united with their glorified bodies on the last day. What other inference can be drawn from the following lines? 'A god summons all these <souls> in a great company to the river Lethe when they have rolled the wheel <of time> for a thousand years, so that—forgetting <their out-of-body experience>, of course—they may revisit the vault of heaven and begin to wish to return to bodies.'

**16.**    "For these reasons that excellent interpreter of antiquity, Macrobius, to prove this most exalted poet's knowledgeability regarding the worship of the gods, composed these words in his *Saturnalia*, 'Does it seem proved to you that without a knowledge of divine and human law Maro's depth cannot be understood?'

**17.**    "But lest I use up all my allotted time on such matters, I shall end my speech and say only by way of summary that our catholic expert on Maro and poet of our mother tongue,[18] Dante, in the second part of his most Christian work, cried out that supreme Jove was crucified as true redeemer of the human race on earth, <saying>: 'And if I may <ask>, supreme Jove, who were crucified on earth for us, are your just eyes turned elsewhere?'

**18.**    "For it is a mind clearly ignorant of the truth about humanity that strives in its madness to attack with varied calumnies the best poets when they conceal the sacred, secret mysteries of the godhead beneath the legitimate veil of fiction. How criminal! These <poets> are the ones whose inspired influence and excellent moral teachings, a light to a good and happy life, have instructed and trained humanity in honorable behavior."

**19.**    When the wand-bearer finished speaking, the cloud opened and restored me to my place while he resumed his divine shape, and, as a multitude of God's flying creatures sang glory to the fostering Trinity, flew with a great flash of light from our presence into thin air. Thereupon I shook off sleep from my limbs and decided to write down this portentous vision for you, excellent devotee of the Pierides, as a gift worthy of our friendship.

**20.**    And now, farewell. Rimini, 15 March 1423, <while> en route <to Venice>.[19]

## NOTES

1. Edited by Morici, 1899, from the unique MS, *Vat. lat.* 8750 (VL9), fols. 125v-128r. Transcribed from VL9 by G.B. De Rossi in *Vat. lat.* 10518 (VL10), fol. 312v. Additional bibliography: De Rossi, 1888, 357; Morici, 1896, 102, note 1; 1897; and 1898. French translation in Colin, 1981, 471-475. The name of the addressee (P. de Bonol. in the text) is read as 'Bonoli' by De Rossi; Morici suggests 'Bonarelli' or 'de Bonarellis' referring to G.F. Lancellotti in Colucci, *Antichità Picene*, vol. 27, 289. See also Morici, 1897.

2. See note to our translation of the *Vita*, para. 54 *ad fin.* An undated event in Fano recalled many years later by Antonio Costanzi may have occurred at this time (ibid.).

3. See note to text *ad loc.*

4. Two drafts of the 'Caesarian' letter to Bruni exist: Berol. gr. qu. 89 (B4), fols. 6r–18v (unfinished draft, in Ciriaco's hand); and Vat. lat. 13497 (VL12), fols. 10r–19v (complete letter, in a hand similar to Ciriaco's, but probably not his). Maas, 1915, 7–8, 11–13, published excerpts from the text in B4 (fols. 6r–7v, 9v, 11v) but did not mention the version in VL12. See Fava, 1944, 300, on VL12.

5. Our edition is from VL9 but we have consulted Morici's throughout.

6. The lad was Sigismondo Malatesta, son of Pandolfo Malatesta (+1427), lord of Fano. Sigismondo (b. 1417) was only six years old in 1423.

7. Virgil's cognomen

8. Colin translates this obscure passage freely as follows: *Mais pourquoi insister? Ne perdons pas le temps en discours et retenons, pour porter un jugement global, que le plus grand des poètes latines . . . , personne ne peut le nier*, etc.

9. the *Aeneid*

10. reading humanos as a mistake for humanas

11. Faunus. Cf. note to the Laltin text ad loc.

12. Mercury

13. *praelibatos*

14. of the *Aeneid*

15. the sun

16. *quem* = *qui*?

17. taking *pientissimae culpae* in the sense of the *felix culpa* of the Easter liturgy.

18. Morici's text would mean, "your Catholic Virgil and master of our mother tongue, the poet Dante."

19. See above, para. 2.

# APPENDIX II

Correspondence with Leonardo Bruni, 1431–1433
1.
Ciriaco to Bruni, Florence, 13 December ?1431, ?1432, ?1433.[1]
Text[2]

1.     Leonardo Aretino Kiriacus Anconitanus.[a]

2.     Cum hisce diebus ad urbem, Leonarde praecelentissime,[b] litteras[c] quasdam ab inclito Pannoniae rege sive imperatore[d] Sigismundo cardinali cuidam missas e[e] Senis legerem, in iis Romanum se regem inscribere animadverti,[f] ut forte minorem[g] imperatoris[h] titulum capescere[i] videretur. Ego sed[j] enim vero[k] maius longe ambitiosiusve[l] nomen regium in Romanos sumpsisse videbar[m] quam imperatorium[n] Caesaremve aut augustale,

---

[a] Ciriacus Anconitanus Leonardo Aretino sal. p. d. V11

[b] praecellentissime V11

[c] literas V11

[d] sive *designato* imperatore V11

[e] e corrected from esse V11

[f] audivid corrected to animadvert V22

[g] maiorem V11

[h] imperatore V11

[i] capessere V11

[j] sed: secundum? V11

[k] non V11

[l] ve repeated, then crossed out V11

[m] videbatur V11

[n] Imp. V11

quamquam etenim[a] magis errore[b] et[c] imperitia rerum Romanarum a suis iam diu praecessoribus hoc in consuetudinem ductum putarim, quam animi nova aliqua elatione aut insolentia. Qua quidem in re tuam velim[d] hac in parte[e] sententiam habere.

**3.**       Vale ex fluentinis scenis Idibus decembribus[f] Olympiadis autem DLII anno 3°.[g]

## 2.

Leonardo Bruni to Ciriaco, after 31 May 1433.[3]

### Text[4]

**1.**       Leonardus Kyriaco salutem.[h5]

**2.**       Melius erat, o Kyriace, non tantum sapere quantum sapis, siquidem te scientem aliorum errata conturbant, quae ab ignorante nulla molestia praeterirentur. Habet enim ignorantia multis in[i] malis quiddam boni, quod minus angitur quia minus sentit. Atque, ut ad postulata veniam tua, admiratum te dicis in hoc novo Sigismundi principis adventu quod, qui ante coronationem se regem sciberet Romanorum, post coronationem vero, quasi maius quiddam et dignius exprimere volens, imperatorem se nuncupabat, non[j] regem, quod tu

---

[a] etenim V11 et eum Ma3

[b] errorem V11

[c] V11 omits et.

[d] volumus corrected to velim V11

[e] in hac parte V11

[f] idibus decemb. 1433 V11

[g] V11 omits Olympiadis . . . 3°.

[h] FL8 and Mehus; Ma3 has Leonardus Aretinus Kyriaco responsiva.

[i] in FL8, Mehus; Ma3 omits.

[j] Ma3 omits non.

perperam[a] factum arbitraria. Itaque te id reprehendisse ais et quaeris a me num idem sentiam quod tu, an contra putem.

**3.**       Ego vero et[b] in his[c] et in aliis permultis plurima quotidie[d] mihi videor errata cognoscere. Sed utor Democriti regula: rideo enim illa, non fleo. Quid enim mea refert[e] quemadmodum barbari loquantur, quos neque corrigere possim, si velim,[f] neque magnopere velim si possim? De rege tam[g] et imperatore idem sentio quod tu, et iam pridem ridens barbariem istam, hoc ipsum[h] notavi atque redargui.

**4.**       Tres enim gradus maiorum dignitatum apud Romanos, de quorum principe loquimur fuere: rex, dictator, imperator. Ex his suprema[i] omnium potestas rex est. Post regem vero secundum tenuit dignitatis[j] locum dictatura. Post dictaturam imperium tertio gradu consequitur. Huiusce rei probatio est quod Octaviano[k] imperatori, optime se gerenti, volens senatus populusque Romanus dignitatem augere, pro imperatore dictatorem eum[l] facere decrevit; quod ille non recepit, sed flexo genu recusavit quasi maioris fastus maiorisque invidiae dignitatem, existimans imperatoris nomen modicum ac populare, si ad dictatoris fastigium compararetur. Inferioris ergo dignitatis imperator est quam dictator, ut patet ex hoc.[m] Maiorem vero esse regiam potestatem quam

---

[a] perperam FL8, Mehus; Ma3 omits, leaving a blank space.

[b] FL8 omits et.

[c] iis Ma3

[d] quottidie Ma3

[e] refer Ma8

[f] vellem Ma3 FL8, Mehus have velim.

[g] Ma3 omits tam.

[h] Ma3 omits hoc ipsum; FL8 and Mehus include it.

[i] supprema Ma3, FL8

[j] FL8 omits dignitatis.

[k] Octavio Ma3 Octaviano FL8, Mehus

[l] Ma3 and Mehus omit eum.

[m] ut patet ex hoc FL8, Mehus; ex hoc patet Ma3

dictaturam[a] ex eo potest intelligi quod Iulius Caesar, dictator quum[b] esset, affectavit regem fieri, cuius gratia interfectus est, non ferentibus civibus ut regiam assumeret potestatem, sed dictaturam, utpote minorem,[c] aequis animis in eo patientibus.[d]

5.     Haec igitur quae adhuc dixi, etsi nulla penitus alia super adderentur,[e] ipsa per se vel sola probant[f] abunde[g] regium nomen quam imperatorium esse praestantius, nisi forte aut senatum dum pro imperatore dictatorem facere volebat, aut Caesarem dum ex dictatura rex fieri cupiebat, non intellexisse vim istarum dignitatum existimemus.[h] Sed nolo his[i] esse contentus, praesertim ad te scribens, cuius aures, novi, quam avidissimae sint vetustatis simul ac veritatis. Explicemus ergo singulorum naturam, qua[j] cognita et inter se comparata, differentiam sui dilucide[k] nobis ostendent.[l] Regem omnes sic accipiunt quasi suprema[m] quaedam et absoluta sit potestas, supra quem in suo regno nemo sit, sed ipse praesit omnibus; ex quo fit ut rex nisi unus dumtaxat esse non possit. Plures enim reges simul[n] eidem regno praesidentes sese mutuo impedirent naturamque perimerent regis, quae non omnibus praeesset, sed haberet paritatem.

---

[a] dictaturam FL8, Mehus; dictatura FL8

[b] quum FL8, Mehus; cum Ma3. Ciriaco in his autographs prefers quum.

[c] minorem Ma3, Mehus; maiorem FL8

[d] pacientibus Ma3

[e] aderentur Ma3; superadderentur, *tamen* Mehus

[f] probant Ma3, Mehus; probabat FL8

[g] habunde Ma3 FL8

[h] existimemus FL8, Mehus; existemus Ma3

[i] his FL8, Mehus; iis Ma3

[j] qua FL8, Mehus; quo Ma3

[k] dilucide FL8, Mehus; dillucide Ma3

[l] ostendent FL8; ostendant Ma3, Mehus

[m] supprema Ma3

[n] simul FL8; Ma3, Mehus omit.

**6.** Patet hoc in antiquis modernisque regibus. Neque enim Numa[a] neque Hostilius neque Ancus[b] neque alii deinceps Romani reges consortem aut socium regni habuere. De Romulo et Tatio[c] ferunt,[d] sed alter Sabinorum, alter Romanorum rex erat, et in[e] propinquo collati repugnante natura sese passi non sunt. In modernis[f] quoque regibus hoc idem[g] apparet; neque enim Francorum neque Anglorum plures simul reges regnum gubernant, sed unus et solus, cui fratres, cui patrui, cui propinqui omnes genua submittunt.[h] Cessit[i] iam quandoque apud hos filio pater, ac regiam potestatem se[j] vivo transferre in filium[k] voluit, ipse dimisit, quoniam duos simul regiam potestatem habere contra naturam est huius dignitatis. At imperatores simul plures saepissime fuerunt. Non est[l] enim suprema[m] potestas imperium, sed salva re publica, salva[n] auctoritate senatus, et populi salva libertate, imperator creabatur. Est enim[o] imperium armorum exercituumque[p] ad tutandam augendamque rem

---

[a] numma FL8

[b] Antus Ma3 anous FL8

[c] Tatio Ma3; tacio FL8, Mehus

[d] ferunt FL8, Mehus; ferut Ma3

[e] in Ma3, Mehus; FL8 omits.

[f] in modernis FL8, Mehus; inodernis Ma3

[g] regibus hoc idem Ma3; FL8, Mehus omit hoc.

[h] submictunt Ma3 FL8

[i] Cessit FL8, Mehus; Cessis Ma3

[j] si Ma3

[k] filium FL8, Mehus; flio Ma3

[l] est FL8, Mehus; Ma3 omits.

[m] supprema Ma3 FL8

[n] salva re publica salva Mehus; salva rei publicae salva Ma3; rei publicae salva omitted by FL8

[o] est enim FL8, Mehus; et enim Ma3

[p] exercituumque Ma3, Mehus; exercitumque FL8

publicam commissa auctoritas. Itaque imperatore existente, nihilominus[a] consules praetoresque ac ceteri magistratus in re publica manebant,[b] rege autem existente manere non poterant, quod patet ex dictatura. Illa enim, quod vim quandam regiae potestatis habere videbatur, simul atque inducta fuerat in rem publicam, ceteri magistratus[c] interibant, et abrogati per creationem dictatoris censebantur[d] praeter tribunos plebis. Et in hoc differebat[e] dictator a rege quod dictatore existente plebs plebeique magistratus vim auctoritatemque suam[f] retinebant; rege autem existente, tribunicia[g] potestas[h] plebisque auctoritas omnis omnino solvebatur. At enim cum[i] imperatore cuncti simul magistratus in re publica perstabant,[j] et auctoritas vigebat senatus, et populi libertas servabatur.[k] Ex quo apparet imperatorem non esse dominum sed legitimam[l] potestatem, nisi forsan[m] Crispum Sallustium[n] ignorasse vim dignitatemque[o] imperatorii nominis arbitremur,[p] qui inquit: nam cum tute per

---

[a] nihilominus Ma3; nichilomenus Mehus; nihil hominum FL8

[b] manebant FL8, Mehus; erant Ma3

[c] magistratus *omnes* Ma3, Mehus

[d] censsabantur Ma3

[e] differebat Ma3, Mehus; differebant FL8

[f] suam Ma3, Mehus; FL8 omits.

[g] tribunitia FL8

[h] potestas Ma3, Mehus; FL8 omits.

[i] cum Ma3, Mehus; cui FL8

[j] perstabant Ma3, Mehus; praestabant FL8

[k] servebatur Ma3

[l] legiptimam Ma3 FL8

[m] forsan FL8, Mehus; forsitan Ma3

[n] Sallustium FL8; Salustium Ma3, Mehus

[o] vim potestatemque Mehus

[p] arbitremus FL8, Mehus; arbramur FL8

mollitiem agas[a] exercitum supplicio cogere, idem[b] dominum non imperatorem esse.

7.  Volo insuper unam vel alteram rationem inducere, quo maioris dignitatis regium nomen esse[c] ostendam. Imperium enim quibusdam magistratibus recte tribuimus. Nam omnes, qui iurisdictionem[d] exercent ac punire et coercere[e] possunt,[f] imperium habere dicimus. At regnum habere illos nunquam diceremus, quoniam nomen imperii legitimam[g] potestatem significat; regnum autem habere supra leges esset.

8.  Praeterea quae Deo tribuimus vocabula, ea praestantissima sunt existimanda.[h] Cum enim Deus ineffabiliter excellat, nec ulla humana reperiri[i] digna possint eius maiestate, illa Deo tribuimus, quae apud nos sunt maxima,[j] quoniam maiora tribuere non habemus. Dum autem regem nuncupamus ac regnum caelorum dicimus, ut sacrae litterae poetaeque testantur. Imperatorem vero qui deum vocaret, vix quisquam reperiretur,[k] propterea[l] quod[m] rex potestatem supremam[n] absolutamque significat; imperator vero longe inferior est.[o] Ex his omnibus luce clarius apparet, qui imperatorium nomen regio nomini anteferunt, eos in maxima ignoratione versari.

---

[a] agas Ma3, Mehus

[b] idem Ma3; idest FL8, Mehus

[c] esse FL8, Mehus; Ma3 omits.

[d] iurisdictionem FL8, Mehus; iurisditionem Ma3

[e] coercere FL8; cohercere Ma3, Mehus

[f] possunt FL8, Mehus; possent Ma3

[g] legiptimam Ma3 FL8

[h] ea . . . existimanda Ma3, Mehus; FL8 omits.

[i] reperiri Ma3, Mehus; imperii FL8

[j] sunt maxima FL8, Mehus; maxima sunt Ma3

[k] repiritur Mehus

[l] praeterea FL8; propterea Mehus; popterea Ma3

[m] quia Mehus

[n] suppremam Ma3 FL8

[o] inferior est FL8; inferiorem Ma3, Mehus

**9.**      Sed heus! Tu qui hunc errorem notasti, cur alium huic annexum[a] tacitus[b] praeteristi? Coronari enim imperatorem ubinam gentium mos fuit? Quis imperatorem Romanum antiquis illis temporibus coronatum fuisse[c] unquam audivit aut legit? Non Augustum, non Tiberium, non Caligulam,[d] non Neronem (cum praesertim hi duo extremi intolerandae[e] superbiae ac[f] luxuriae forent): non Traianum,[g] non Hadrianum,[h] non Antoninum;[i] nemo, inquam, istorum coronam imperii unquam suscepit aut habuit aut usus est, nisi forte lauream, quum[j] triumphasset[k] aut rostratam quod classem hostium cepisset, quae duae coronae non imperatorum erant magis quam quorumcunque triumphantium[l] aut vincentium. An ergo, quod illi tantam imperii magnitudinem habentes non faciebant, hi quatuor iugerum possessores coronabuntur? Enim vero, non ut imperatores, sed ut reges, Romani coronantur. Cur ergo se post coronationem imperatores scribunt, non reges? Deinde totum hoc ignorantiae[m] est, cum ne reges quidem[n] Romanos unquam

---

[a] annexum FL8, Mehus; anexum Ma3

[b] tacitus FL8, Mehus; Ma3 omits.

[c] coronatum fuisse FL8, Mehus; Ma3 omits.

[d] Caligulam FL8, Mehus; Gallicolam Ma3

[e] intolerandae Ma3, Mehus; intollerandae FL8

[f] ac FL8; aut Mehus

[g] Traianum FL8, Mehus; Tayanum Ma3

[h] Adrianum FL8, Mehus; Hadrianum Ma3

[i] Antoninum Mehus; Antonium Ma3 FL8

[j] quum FL8; cum Ma3, Mehus

[k] triumphasset FL8, Mehus; triumphaset Ma3

[l] triumphantium Ma3, Mehus; trihumphantium FL8

[m] ignorantiae Ma3, Mehus; ignoratione FL8

[n] quidem FL8, Mehus; Ma3 omits.

coronari mos[a] fuerit. Romulus enim et hi[b] qui post eum[c] fuerunt reges numquam coronam receperunt[d] aut gestarunt aut usi sunt. Idem quoque observatum est a Tuscorum regibus, ut numquam corona uterentur, sed trabea dumtaxat[e] et palmata[f] tunica. Quare hanc barbariem, quaeso, cum sua ignorantia valere sinamus, et nos antiquis doctissimorum virorum scriptis, quod unicum est refugium, oblectemur, non curiosi quid agant isti aut quemadmodum loquantur. Vale.[g]

## NOTES

1. This letter occurs in two manuscripts: (1) Milan, Ambros. R 21 sup., saec. XV? (Ma3), fol. 174r.; paper, in 4to, except for parchment leaves at beginning and end. This is a miscellany of transcripts by Giacomo Morelli, who took this letter from MS 257, saec. XV, from the library of St. Giovanni in Verdara, Padua. (2) Venice, Marc. lat. 14, 221 (4632), paper, in 4to, saec. XVIII (V11), fol. 174v, "Ex cod. ms. sec. xv. n°. 257 in Bibliotheca Patavina S. Joannis in Viridario." The MS is a miscellany of *Epistolae, carmina, et orationes variorum auctorum ex codicibus MS exscriptis a Jacobo Morellio, maiori ex parte inedita.*

Bibliography: The first publication of this letter was by Luiso, *Studi su l'epistolario di Bruni*; see also De Rossi, 1888, 358b, note 6; Gill, 1961, 48; G. Mercati, 1894, 337-338 (=1937, 126-127).

The date: De Rossi knew the letter only from V11, which gives the year as 1433. But since Sigismund was no longer emperor *designatus* in December 1433, having been crowned in Rome on the previous 31 May, De Rossi argued that the date of the letter must be 1432, when Ciriaco was in Siena with two papal ambassadors to meet the emperor-designate (*Vita*, para. 97-98). Mercati argues from Ma3 that the year given there for the letter (*Olympiadis autem dLij anno 3°*) is 1431, but that this also is wrong; that Bruni's reply (see next letter) was written *after* the coronation and presupposes that Ciriaco's letter was also written *after* the coronation. He places great weight on Bruni's expression, *imperatorem se nuncupat non regem.*

The different datings in the two MSS and the reading *designato* in V11 indicate that the two texts derive from separate versions of the letter. Bruni's reply [below] summarizes Ciriaco's argument and makes clear that Sigismund's coronation as emperor in Rome on 31 May 1433 preceded Ciriaco's letter. The date given in V11 can therefore be taken as correct only if *designato* is translated 'elected.' For the difficulty of making out the meaning of Olympiads in

---

[a] mos FL8, Mehus; mox Ma3

[b] hi FL8, Mehus; hii Ma3

[c] eum FL8, Mehus; Romulum Ma3

[d] receperunt FL8, Mehus; ceperunt Ma3

[e] dumtaxat FL8, Mehus; Ma3 omits.

[f] palmata FL8, Mehus; paliata Ma3

[g] Vale FL8, Mehus; Ma3 omits.

fifteenth century Florence cf. R. and T. Krautheimer, 1970, vol. 2, 353-358.

2. The basic text used here is that of Ma3, with variants from V11 noted in the apparatus.

3. Mercati et al. assume—from its position in Ma3—that this is Bruni's reply to letter #1, above. It is found in three MSS: (1) Florence, Laur. Gaddian. lat. 90 sup. 55 (FL8), a miscellany of humanist letters, etc. (Bandini, 1776, 635–639), fols. 52v–55r; (2) Milan, Ambros. R 21 sup. (Ma3), fols. 174r–177r; and (3) Turin, Bibl. Nazionale J III 13 (To), vellum, misc., XVI C., fols. 400r–401v (not seen).
      Bibliography: Baron, 1928. 210–211; Bruni, L., *Epistolae*, ed. Mehus, 1741, II, Lib. VI, Ep. IX, pp. 57–61; Luiso, 1898–1903; Mercati, 1894, 337–338, (= 1937, 126–127)
      The date: Since the wording of the text assumes the coronation of Sigismund as emperor has taken place, it must be dated after 31 May 1433. Baron dates it 13 December 1433 / beginning of 1434, relying on Luiso's argument against Beck's date of summer 1433.

4. The basic text used here is that of Ma3, with variants from FL8 and Mehus noted in apparatus. In a few cases, where the reading of Ma3 is clearly wrong, we have replaced it with a reading from V11 or FL8, indicating that in the apparatus.

5. Mehus follows the greeting with a summary of the letter's argument: *Regis nomen maius esse, quam Dictatoris. Dictatoris autem praestantius Imperatoris nomine fuisse docet.*

# APPENDIX III

## Letters of Francesco Filelfo written to or about Ciriaco, 1427–1434

### 1.
### From Venice, 21 December 1427[1]

Singularem tuum erga me amorem, si non vehementer amem, ingratus sim. Amo te, inquam, mi Kyriace, cum ob tuam in me benivolentiam, tum ob eam inquisitionem atque diligentiam, qua uteris maxima, in earum rerum inventione, quae vel nimia vetustate vel patrum nostrorum negligentia apud nos perierant. Incumbe igitur, ut facis, in tam liberale tamque laudabile munus renovandae vetustatis, vel ab interitu potius vendicandae. Non enim parum et voluptatis et commodi, prae se ferunt istiusmodi eulogia, atque epigrammata, quae tanto cum studio et labore, undique ex universo prope orbe, in Italiam advehis: et horum quidem gratia, non solum vivos tibi concilias, sed mortuos quoque tibi reddis obstrictos beneficio sempiterno. Et hac de re satis ac super.

Petis a me ut tibi declarem quae Publij Virgilij Maronis sententia fuerit in scribenda *Aeneide*. Nam communem illam opinionem quam ludi magistri afferunt, voluisse Virgilium et imitari Homerum et laudare Augustum nequaquam tibi admodum probari. Non mediocrem profecto rem petis neque brevis orationis opus, a me praesertim, qui hoc tempore otiosus non sum et angor animi non iniuria, cum ob hanc pestilentiae acerbitatem, qua me Venetiis obsessum intueor, tum quia hic inutiliter tempus tero, ab ijs delusus a quibus minime conveniebat. Sed ne me difficilem voces aut in amore tibi minus respondentem, dicam brevi quod sentio.

[The rest of the letter is his interpretation of the *Aeneid*.[2] The letter ends:]

. . . Et haec sunt quae mihi ad tuas litteras in hac temporum difficultate respondenda occurrrerunt. Vale.

Ex Venetijs, xii. Kal. Ianuarias. M.cccc.xxvii.

### 2.
### Filelfo to Ciriaco, from Venice, 28 January 1428[3]
### Franciscus Philelfus Kyriaco Anconitano Sal(utem) dicit.

Placuisse tibi litteras meas et quae de Virgilii Maronis sententia scripsimus in *Aeneida*, gaudeo. Quod autem petis qua ratione Neptunus ab Ovidio Nasone cognominatus sit Amphitrites et fortuna Rhamnusia, paucis accipe. Rhamnusia quidem non est fortuna, ut vulgo exponunt magistri ludi, sed indignationis dea, qua graeci tui νέμεσιν (nemesin) vocant. Nam cum Narcisus formae bonitate abuteretur superbius, recte fingitur eiusmodi dea

191

adversus illum indignata iustis precibus assensisse. Est enim indignatio animi aegritudo adversus eum, qui bonis praesentibus sit indignus, nemesis inquam indignationem significat. Rhamnusia vero dicta est a Rhamnus, qui est atticae vicus, ubi colebatur. Cuius quidem deae simulachrum eo in loco pulcherrimum fuisse tradunt, factum a Phidia ulnarum in altitudinem decem illudque marmoreum. Neptunus autem nequaquam est Amphitrites cognominatus. Dictio illa depravata est apud Ovidium librariorum inscientia. Est enim foeminini generis declinaturque more graeco. Nominativo Amphitrite, Gentivo Amphitrites. Fingitur autem a poetis esse Neptuni uxor. Unde Claudianus *de raptu Proserpinae* ita cecinit: Etiam "Nereia glauco, / Neptunum gremio complectitur Amphitrite."[a] Nam Amphitrite mare significat dicta illa quidem ab ἀμφί (amphi), circum, et τρεῖν (trin), terrere. Mare enim circum se navigantes pereundi terrore insequitur. Ex Amphitrite autem et Neptuno, Triton natus fingitur a poetis. Si quid est quod aliud a me velis, nunquam frustra requires officium meum. Vale ex Venetiis quinto kal. Februarias. M.cccc.xxviii.

### 3.
### From Bologna, 7 July 1928[4]

1.     Franciscus Philelfus Kyriaco Anconitano S.

2.     Vix profecto credi queat et praecipue ab indoctis quam ipse tuis his epigrammatis delectatus quae ex Aegypto in Italiam reportaras et in praesentia dedisti ad me ...

Ex Bononia nonis iuliis MCCCCXXVIII.

### 4.
### From Florence, 7 March 1431.[5]

1.     Φραγκίσκος ὁ Φιλέλφος Κυριακῷ[b] χαίρειν.

---

[a] Claudian, *De Raptu Proserpinae* 1.103-104.

[b] Κυριακῷ Legrand

2.     ['Ε]γώ[a] σου τὴν περὶ λόγους δύναμιν καὶ πάλαι θαυμάζων, νῦν οὐκ ἔχ' ὅπως ἂν τοῦτο δρασαιμι[b] προσηκόντως οὕτω με τὸ τῶν σῶν ἐπιστολῶν κατὰ τὴν ἑλληνικὴν γεγραμμένων φωνὴν ἐξέπληξε κάλλος, καί σε οὐκ ἐν τῇ Κωνσταντίνου [?πόλει] ποτὲ τοὺς λόγους μαθεῖν, ἀλλ' ἐν 'Αθήναις ἐκείναις περιφανῶς ἐμήνυεν. ἡ γὰρ ἐνοῦσά σοι χάρις τῷ λέγειν, ἐκεῖθεν.

3.     ἐγὼ μὲν οὖν οἶμαι τὴν τῶν μουσῶν πρώτην, εἴπερ ἂν αὐτῇ σωματικῶς ξυνέβαινεν ἐντυχεῖν σοι, διαπορευμένην τε καὶ[c] σου τὸ ἐπαφόδιτον τῶν λόγων θαυμάζουσαν, τὸ ὁμηρικὸν ἐκεῖνο ἐρέσθαι

Τίς πόθεν εἰς ἀνδρῶν; πόθι τοι πόλις ἠδὲ τοκῆες;
καὶ γὰρ ἐρῶ σ' ἄγη μ' ἰχει[d] ὡς ὑπὸ θνητοῦ τοσσον
νικῶμαι πασάων θεάων ὑπέρτατος.[e]

4.     ὑγιαινε[f] τοιγαροῦν ὡς ἂν ἡμᾶς τε καὶ τοὺς πρὸς τὴν σὴν ἀρετὴν ἡμῖν ὁμοίως διακειμένους, τῇ θεόθεν ἐνούσῃ σοι εὐμουσίᾳ καὶ μᾶλλον εὐφραίνειν ἔχοις. ἐγὼ δέ σοι ἐπὶ τούτοις καὶ τὸ τοῦ Νέστορος γῆρας ἐπεύχομαι, ὡς οὐ μόνον τοῖς καθ' ἡμᾶς ἐπὶ σοφίᾳ, ἀλλ' ἤδη καὶ τοῖς πάλαι διατρέψασι,[g] μηδ' ὁπωσοῦν τῶν πρωτείων παραχωρήσαντι.

5.     ἔρρωσω, τῶν μουσῶν τέμενος (?), καὶ τὸν σὸν Φιλέλφον φίλει, ὡς εἴωθας, ὃς ὑπέρ σου[h] καὶ τῶν σοὶ[i] συνοισόντων κἂν εἰς πῦρ ἄλοιτο[j] τὸ τοῦ λόγου προθύμως.

---

[a] The capital E is omitted, with a small ε written in the margin, indicating that the space was to have been filled by an artist or calligrapher as an illuminated initial.

[b] δράσαιμι Legrand

[c] καί Legrand

[d] ἔχει Legrand

[e] ὑπερτάτη Legrand

[f] ὑγίαινε Legrand

[g] διαπρέψασι Legrand

[h] ὑπὲρ σοῦ Legrand

[i] σοι Legrand

[j] ἄλοιτο Legrand

7.     Φλωρεντίαθεν, ταῖς νώναις μαρτίου ἔτει α<sup>ω</sup> υ<sup>φ</sup> λ<sup>φ</sup> ά<sup>φa</sup> ἀπὸ Χριστοῦ γεννήσεως.

### 5.
### Filelfo to Panormita, 1433 or 1434[6]

Franciscus Philelphus Antonio Panormitae, ἀνδρὶ ἀρίστωι καὶ ποιητῃ καλλίστω<sup>b</sup> salutem dicit.

Salve, dimidium animae meae. Si vales, ita est ut opto. Ego autem perbelle valeo. Kiriaci Anconitani singulare studium in revocandis ad vitam mortuis non te latet; quare, etsi minime sum ignarus quanti hominem facis—facis enim plurimi,—velim tamen mea etiam causa eum tibi carissimum fieri.

---

<sup>a</sup> αυλά Legrand

<sup>b</sup> The scribe of Rc omits the Greek but writes *grecum est*, after *Panormitae*; then he writes prematurely and erases *animae dimidium meae si* before *Sal. d. Salve*, and writes them in their proper sequence, directly after *Salve*. N5 omits the Greek entirely.

# NOTES

1. Our text is from V.R. Giustiniani, 1980, 37–42; we have not seen the MSS, which he lists there: (1) Milan, Biblioteca Trivulziana, 873; (2) Paris, Bibl. Nationale, *Cod. Par. lat.* 4842; (3) Munich, Bayerische Staatsbibliothek, *Cod. Monac. lat.* 18801.

Bibliography: Filelfo, *Ep. Fam.*, 1502 ed., fols. 2-2v; V.R. Giustiniani 1980, 33–44, a new critical edition of the entire text of this letter, based primarily on MS Trivulzianus 873; Robin, 1991, 53, note 141 (excerpt only, from Giustiniani), 55, note 143, 75, and 155; Colin, 1981, 393–394, 2nd 475–476 (portions translated into French).

2. See Robin, 53.

3. Filelfo, *Ep. Fam.*, 1502, fol. 3v.

4. Not seen. The portion of text reproduced here is from Colin, 1981, 394.

5. Milan, Biblioteca Trivulzio, 873 (83,7), edited and translated by Legrand, 1896, no. 8, pp. 17–18. Paraphrase on p. 18.

6. Manuscripts: (1) T, fol. 164v; (2) Naples, Bibl. Nazionale V.E.64 (N5), fol. 3r.; Rome, Bibl. Casanatense, 3636 (Rc), fol. 122v. Published by Olivieri, 63, from a MS now lost.

Date: The letter is undated. The date given here is based on the supposition that Ciriaco's first encounter with Panormita, which this letter of recommendation would have preceded, was on the occasion of his visit to Milan at this time. Panormita left the Visconti court in 1434 to join the court of Alfonso V of Naples: see *Vita*, translation, note to para. 112.

# APPENDIX IV

## Letter of Antonio Leonardi to Felice Feliciano
### 5 October 1457

## Latin Text[a]

### IMM.DEO.

1.　　　Antonius Leonardi Felici Feliciano amico suo salutem dicit. Litterae tuae apud nos perlectae nobis maximam attulerunt laetitiam quia amatorem ac restauratorem oblitarum antiquitatum his nostris perditis diebus reperimus. Quum adeo rari ac perditi sint ut vix inter mortales pauci inveniantur, maxime igitur penes omnis laudandus es, quum ex infinito hominum grege quasi solus supersis.

2.　　　Multa in tuis litteris de Kiriaco nostro Anconitano scribis: qui utinam extaret, nam superioribus annis natura vitae suae finem fecit. Habeas <quod> vir ille inter antiquos antiquissimus fuisset, beneque in variis rebus eruditus, litteris praesertim Graecis atque Latinis; nam opuscula ab eo edita quae vagantur testes sunt <de eo> qui, ne longius quam statui sim, totum ferme peragravit mundum. Nam aedificia, templa deorum marmorea,[b] statuas,[c] epigrammata, antiquitates omnes hic propriis oculis conspectus est; nec huic unquam nocuit itineris asperitas, nec pelagi saevitia neque longae peregrinationis lassitudo; omnia ob virtutem, ob antiquitates inveniendas facillima, suavia, iucundaque fuerunt.

3.　　　Sed inter alia haec tibi narrare de patientia huius viri libet. Quum provintiam quandam Graeciae perscruptasset, postea sarcinullae navim impositae ac vela[d] ventis dedissent, quum per XXC milia[e] passuum abesset, ab amico suo audivit epigramma quoddam vidisse post moenia civitatis nuper

---

[a] T, fols. 198v-201r. For a translation of this letter see the Introduction.

[b] marmorae

[c] statuae

[d] vella

[e] millia

196

ab eis relictae, Kiriacus ob hoc summo affectus dolore, postquam terram applicuit, relicta trireme, redivit ut epigramma videret ac pernotaret, qui minime, ut dixi, longiorem viam metuit.

4.  Ipse etiam apud omnes ferme nationes notus carusque fuit. Nam apud Theucros plurimum claruit, unde genitor[a] huius qui Byzantium nuper delevit cheirographum[b] suo signatum nomine optumo Kiriaco donavit, qui tutus per civitates, oppida, loca, ac villas sine offensione, vectigale, et ulla laesione ire posset ac si unus ex familia suae domus esset.

5.  Quapropter haec pauca ex multis ad te scribere haud ingratum fuit, quum vestigia huius hominis te approbare videar, quae erga omnes virtuti deditos probanda amplexandaque sunt.

6.  Igitur huius Kiriaci nostri clarissimi facta lauda, inquire, dilige, ama, atque cole, nec ignobilem aut obscurum aemulaveris hominem sed clarum sanguine, postea clariorem virtute.

7.  Postremo si quid humanitatis[c] apud nos dignum fore aspicies, petas amice atque illico obtinebis. Vale, antiquitatum amator decusque. Ex Venetiis IIII° Nonas Octobris MCCCCLVII.

8.  Et quia, ut hominem eruditum decet, antiquitatis delectatione teneris, mitto ad te epigrammata Torcelli reperta nec non Muriani. Hac in re iudicium tuum expecto:

Torcelli apud Venetias.
LOGIVS. PATROCLVS
SECVTVS. PIETATEM
COL[ega]. CENT[urionum].HORTOS
CVM.AEDIFICIO
HVIC.SEPVL[ture].IVNCTO
VIVOS.DONAVIT.VT
EX.REDITV.EOR[um]
LARGIVS.ROSAE.ET
ESCE.PATRONO.SVO
ET. QVANDOQ. SIBI
PONERENTVR          [Not found in *CIL* V]

---

[a] Senitor Colucci

[b] cyrographum

[c] humanitati Colucci

Venetiis
.L. HERENNIVS
AESOPVS
CARVS. AMICIS         [*CIL* V, 2234]

Muriani apud Venetias
VIVI. FECE.
.L. PLOTIVS. GEMINIAN.
Q. MVRTIVS HERMES
ET.M.TERENTIVS
VARIANVS
AMICI.INTER.SE.REDATVR
PARTIERVNT. INFRO$^{nte}$. P$^{edes}$. LX.
RE$^{tro}$. P$^{edes}$. LX.
.D. M.         [*CIL* V, 2258]

# APPENDIX V

## Ciriaco's *'Itinerarium'*

Gathered here are the passages in the *'Itinerarium'* (Vo4, fols. 1r–21v, ed. Mehus, 1742, pp. 1–52) that are related to similar passages in the *Vita*. Where the wording of the *'Itinerarium'* coincides with that of the *Vita*, these expressions are italicized. Texts are from the unique manuscript of the *'Itinerarium'* (Vo4), corrected only where necessary, with the readings of Vo4 reported in the apparatus along with the variants (usually, corrections), in Mehus' edition. They are arranged in the order in which the parallel passages occur in the *Vita*.

1. **Egypt** (*Vita*, para. 17; Vo4, fol. 20r–v, ed. Mehus 48–50).

"<H>inc etenim[a] ego rei nostrae gratia, et magno utique et innato visendi orbis desiderio primum Italiae posthabitis urbibus Aegyptum petens et Memphiticam Babylona, navim Benvenuto Anconitano Scoctigolo *[sic]* ductitante praefecto conscendi,[b] et nostrum tandem per Adriaticum *Illyricum*que et *altum per Ionium* Ceraunia promontoria bonis Euris transfretantes Liburneis Dalmaticisque nec non Epiri Phaeacibus Laertiaque per aequora Odisseave Cephaloneis Zacinteisque visis et absconditis insulis, *Cretam magni Iovis insulam* superavimus et inde *Lybicum* per immensum *Alexandriam* denique nobilissimam *Aegypti venimus* urbem, ubi primum antiqui *Pharii praecelsi vestigia* vidimus et eximiae urbis moenia *porta*sque ingentes et *vetustatum*[c] egregia plurima extra intusque conspeximus. Sed inter potiora ad ipsa Ptholomeia regia immanem illum *Numidicum* olim ex[d] *Philadelpho* e Thebis advectum *obeliscum* vidimus et extra civitatis muros piperam prope portam vidimus maximam illam *columnam, quam* incertum *vulgus hodie Pompeianam appellat*, et nos vero[e] *Alexandricam* regis. *Dinocratem*[f] nobilem *architectum* eximiam per basim antiquo ex epigrammate novimus erexisse."

---

[a] Mehus omits etenim.

[b] consendi Vo4

[c] vetustarum Vo4

[d] Mehus corrects to *a*.

[e] verius Mehus

[f] regis, *quam* Dinocratem Mehus

199

## 2. Ancona.

(a)      (*Vita*, para. 47; Vo4, fols. 14v–15r, ed. Mehus 38):

Exinde vero concedens Anconitanam civitatem tuam, nostram et dulcem patriam revisi. Nam et tuam merito civitatem dixi, quam et a te bis denos ante annos *pro Martino Pontifice Legato* dignissima in parte restitutam cognovimus. Quod[a] et quem Traianus olim optimus et prudentissimus princeps condiderat *portum*, tu, Pater piisime, Brincio concive necessarioque nostro curante praefecto meque *ratiocinante*[b] *quaestore* ruinam magna ex parte minantem *reparasti*, ac magno studio, sollertia diligentiaque tua terra marique omni cum ornatu cultuque ad pristinam fere sui formam splendoremque restituisti.

(b)      (*Vita*, para. 54; Vo4, fol. 18r–v, ed. Mehus, 44–46).[c]

Huiusce quidem rei nobile testimonium in hodiernum extat *insignem apud* eiusdem civitatis *portum marmoreus* et mirabilis *arcus* quem desuper *inclytus olim ille .S.P.Q.R. huic optimo Principi* et eiusdem celeberrimi *portus conditori auream equestrem statuam conspicuas inter Divae Martianae sororis Plotinaeque iucundissimae coniugis imagines miro quidem architectoris opere dicarat hoc* nobilissimo suo testante aureis litteris *epigrammate* [CIL IX, 5894]:

[Between the short inscription on the left and the central, main, inscription Vo4 has the drawing of a Doric column on which the words PORTUS ANCONIS are inscribed vertically.]

|  | Imp.Caes.Divi Nervae f.Nervae Traiano |  |
|---|---|---|
| Plotinae | opt° Aug.Germanic.Dacico pont.maxo[d] | Divae |
| Aug. | tr Pot.XVIIII Imp IXI[e] Cos.VI.pp.provi | Martianae |
| Coniugi | dentiss principi S.P.Q.R.Quod acces | Aug. |
| Aug. | sum Italiae.hoc etiam addito ex pecunia | Soro |
|  | sua portu Tutiorem navigantibus | ri Aug. |
|  | Reddiderit. |  |

Ipse etiam Princeps inclytus auream eiusdem statuae atque praeclaram imaginem *huic tam egregiae civitati civibusque omne per aevum honorabile signum gestare regia liberalitate donavit. Cuiusce vero splendentem iconis*

---

[a] Mehus omits Quod.

[b] ratiotinante Vo4

[c] For a comparison of this passage with the nearly identical parallel text of Ciriaco's *Anconitana Illyricaque laus et Anconitanorum Raguseorumque foedus* see Campana, 1959, 495. Campana's argument from this passage for the dependence of the *Vita* on the *'Itinerarium'* is rejected implicitly in our Introduction.

[d] MAX. Mehus

[e] Mehus corrects to IX, but Ciriaco always (mistakenly) reads IXI.

*effigiem per publica* nostrae *civitatis loca purpureaque pretoriana vexilla* te[a] *saepe per Latium et Ausonias urbes enitescere* <vidisse>[b] non dubito.

3. **Nicosia, Cyprus** (*Vita*, para. 68; Vo4, fol. 20v, ed. Mehus 50 [from Ciriaco's description of his visit to Egypt, where he saw the captured armor of King Janus displayed]):

Equidem inde Icaream amplissimam civitatem petens amoenam per Traianam Nilei fluminis fossam barbaram geruneamque[c] cymbam amplum ad Nilum venimus et adverso quinos[d] per dies amne superato regiam illam magnam Soltanei principis venimus. Sed quisnam diceret quam ingentem domorum multitudine confertam populosam et barbarica omnigenum ope copiosissimam vidimus urbem immaniaque et lapidum perornata foedae illius et temeratae deum opinionis delubra? Sed quid memorem nostrae ob incuriam gentis dedecus in foro pendentia alto in vestibulo templi Cyprii regis pientissimi Iani spolia, insignem galeam clipeumque? Quod et forte saepius meminisse iuvabit.[e]

4. **Kardhamyla, on the island of Chios** (*Vita*, para. 74; similar language apropos of a visit to the Paduan country estate of his relative and patron, Zaccharia Contarini of Venice [Vo4, fol. 10v, ed. Mehus, 29]):

Inde vero Cenomanos[f] per campos et Euganeos colles Patavinum ad agrum Zachariam[g] Conterraneum necessarium nostrum sua rura colentem convenimus, ubi postquam homines inter agrestes inculta sylvarum una et agrorum culta lustravimus, *alii per* dumos *pictas* quaeritant[h] avibus *aves, alii quidem escatis sub unda hamis varigenos*[i] *laqueare pisces sua pro voluptate*

---

[a] Mehus omits te.

[b] supplied from *Vita*, para. 59: enitescere videntur

[c] Mehus reads geruntamque.

[d] Mehus changes to novenos.

[e] cf. Virgil, *Aen.* 1.203

[f] Zenomanos Vo4

[g] Zacheriam Vo4

[h] Mehus changes to quaeritabant.

[i] variginos Vo4

curabant. Nempe animi praestantioris alii ad altos per invia lustra colles[a] orthoceros insectari cervos aprosve setigeros plerique venabulis armis canibusque percurrunt.[b] Ego sed enim interea *ut non omnes diei horas omni ex parte vacuas amitterem*,[c] utque non me meis totum et inexpertem curis viderem, *dum graeca librorum fragmenta*, quae aliqua nuper Italiae sub insula Phaeacum advexeram, lectitarem, in eum incidi libellum, quem brevissimum de virtute conscripserat Aristoteles ille philosophorum egregius. At et cum[d] is [eum][e] tam paucis exarare[f] litteris conspectaretur ea de inclyta re, quae tam divinarum quam humanarum rerum omnium summa est ut Latiis non foret ignotus, praedigne Paulo Pergulensi viro philosophico[g] optimo transducendum, latineque transmittendum curavi . . . .

5. **Rome** (*Vita*, para. 99; Vo4, fols. 7r–8r , ed. Mehus 21–22), where there is a most striking, *verbatim* agreement between the texts of the *Vita* and the '*Itinerarium*':

Quid et magnis de principibus dicendum? Quod cum[h] Romae te pontifice *ad Sigismundum* caesarem me tui suique gratia contulissem, postquam de rebus agendis meaque de potissima rerum indagandarum cura maiestati suae quae pro re digna visa sunt detexi, *dum* saepe *tanto cum principe vetustatum reliquias undique per urbem disiectas* inspectamus, talia et sibi *Romanorum* priscorum *afflatus numine* dixi:

*N(on)*[i] *equidem parum putabam* optimi Augusti *caesarei principis animum lacessere quod qui nunc vitam agunt Romana inter moenia homines*

---

[a] colle Vo4

[b] See the parallel passage in Ciriaco's letter to Francesco and Crasso, dated *die IIII. K (alendas) Jan(uarias) 1435: Nam alii per dumos pictas quaeritant avibus aves, alii quidem sub undas hamis varigenos laqueare pisces amabant. Sed animi praestantiores* [Mehus *praestantioris*] *alii ad altos per invia lustra montes orthoceros insectare* [Mehus *insectari*] *cervos plerique venalibus* [Mehus *venabulis*] *armis canibusque cucurrunt.* (Vo4, fol. 30v, ed. Mehus, 60).

[c] admitterem Vo4

[d] Mehus changes to quum.

[e] is *eum* Vo4

[f] Mehus corrects to exarasse.

[g] philosogico V04

[h] Mehus changes to quum.

[i] N equidem Vo4

*marmorea ingentia atque ornatissima undique per urbem aedificia, statuas insignes, et columnas tantis olim sumptibus, tanta maiestate, tantaque fabrum et architectorum arte conspicuas, ita ignave, turpiter et obscoene*[a] *in dies ad albam tenuemque convertunt cinerem, ut eorum nullam*[b] *brevi tempore speciem vestigiumve posteris apparebit. Proh scelus! et ω vos inclytae Romuleae gentis manes, aspicite haec meritumque malis advertite numen.*[d]

Hic cum bonus[e] ille *princeps* tanta de hominum *incuria* rerumque calamitate indoluit, meum deinde tam dignae rei desiderium *laudavit*, et *Matheo* illo nobili *praefecto suo* curante sua me caesarea *familiaritate* decoravit.[f]

## 6. Modena (*Vita*, para. 105, 183; Vo4, fol. 10r, ed. Mehus 27):

Ac deinde *per Bononiam* ad Liguras me iterum et Cenomanas urbes converti, et primum *Togatam apud Galliam* Mutinensia egregia monumenta *Scipionis* eiusdem urbis *optimi pontificis gratia* conspectare[g] litterisque mandare malui.

## 7. Milan (*Vita*, para. 112–113, 151, 190; Vo4, fol. 8r, ed. Mehus 22–23):

Exinde vero apud *Mediolanum nobilissimam Insubrum civitatem* Philippus ille insignis Ligurum dux, cum meam epistolis curam intelligeret, ipsam haud aspernandam duxit. Sed *Urbano Iacob(o)*[h] *optimo suo* illo *intercurante secretario*, sua quaeque civitatis egregia *et extra Ticinianae arcis* copiosa *ab antiquae gentis origine* monumenta *hortosque*[i] *regios et ingentia ferarum claustra, nobile sui magnificentissimi* principis *opus*, vidimus late, nec non eo iubente Insubrum quicquid nobile reliquum vetustatis extat inspeximus, Beatissime Pater.

---

[a] Mehus corrects to obscene.

[b] ullam Vo4 Mehus also corrects to nullam.

[c] o Mehus

[d] Cf. Virgil, *Aen.* 4.611: accipite haec meritumque malis advertite numen

[e] Mehus corrects Hic cum to Heic primum, omitting bonus.

[f] Cf. *Vita*, para. 98 *ad fin.*

[g] Mehus changes to inspectare.

[h] Iacob Vo4

[i] hortusque Vo4

**8. Verona** (*Vita*, para. 165–167; Vo4, fol. 10r–v, ed. Mehus 28–29):

Et his demum exactis Veronam venimus, alteram et praeclaram Cenomanae regionis urbem, Catulli Pliniique Secundi inclytis nominibus claram et aevo utique nostro apprime Guarini rhetoris cl(arissimi)[a] perornatam, ubi et insignia vetustatum plurima vidimus et *Harenarum*[b] *Augusta* et L. Vitruvio nobilissimo architecto theatra, antiqua deinde moenia *portas*que regias, et veterem abbatiae *Sanctissimi*[c] *Zenonis* bibliothecam.

**9. Mantua** (*Vita*, no. 191, 194; Vo4, fol. 10r, ed. Mehus 27–28):

Exin magno videndi patriam mei vatis amore *Mantuam* antiquam venimus Cenomanam et fortunatam tanti nominis urbem, ubi Ioanne Francisco clarissimo principe favitante et Victorino Feltrensi natorum eius optimo praeceptore viroque apprime docto magnopere intercurante, *Pietolam* ipsius vatigenam *Maronis* villam, eiusque tuguria[d] et memorabile solum contigimus: ac ipsa in civitte marmoreum tam sanctissimi poetae simulachrum[e] suo cum dignissimo epigrammate laete iocundeque conspeximus.

**10. Genoa** (*Vita*, no. 203; Vo4, fol. 6r–v, ed. Mehus 16–18):

Sed quos alios illa de inclyta Genuensium urbe praeclaros aetate nostra viros praeteream, quos peregregie meam cognovimus exornasse curam, ut vel in primis Baptisten Cicadam[f] praestantissimum equitem Senis et ipsa in urbe apud Sigismundum Caesarem, Andream *Imperialem* Mediolani apud Philippum ducem et exinde, dum Genuam ipsam peterem, ad *Paulum* fratrem et *Iacobum Bracellum egregium publicae rei* scribam elegantissimum epistolas ad me dantem. Omittamne et ipsa in civitate nobiles illos cives *Franciscum Spinulam, Ioannem Grillum, Benedictumque Nigronem*, qui et duce Philippo mei gratia moniti me postquam humane susceperant, *omnia* mihi *civitatis* insignia ostentantes nobilem *illum*[g] *preciosissimo*[h] de *smaragdo cratera* lubentissime vidimus et praetentavimus manu.

---

[a] CL. Vo4; Mehus writes Clariss.

[b] Mehus corrects to Arenarum.

[c] SS Vo4; Mehus writes S. (= sancti).

[d] tiguria Vo4

[e] Mehus corrects to simulacrum.

[f] cicalam Vo4; Mehus also corrects to Cicadam.

[g] nobile illud Vp4; Mehus also corrects to nobilem illum.

[h] preciosissima Vo4; Mehus also corrects to preciosissimo.

11. **Southern Italy** (*Vita*. no. 206 ff.; Vo4, fols. 8r–9v, immediately after the account of the visit to Milan [expl. *Beatissime Pater*: see above, no. 7],[a] ed. Mehus 23-25). The text goes on:

(a) **Liternum, Terraccina** (*Vita*, para. 207, 206; Vo4, fol. 8v, ed. Mehus 24):

Exinde, Christophoro iuvante Caietano, *Linternea Scipionis* monumenta et *Terrecinarum*[b] *marmorea Aug(usti)* Caes(aris)[c] *templa* vidimus et *ingentia silicum strata viarum.*

(b) **Naples** (*Vita*, para. 209; Vo4, fol. 8r–v, ed. Mehus 23):

Exinde vero concedens apud Neapolim *Parthenopeam illam nobilem* Campaniae *civitatem* me quam avidissime contuli, *Ioanna* muliere illa *sereniss(ima) Karoli filia* et Ladislai sorore regis nobiliss(imi) regnante regina, quae me postquam Kiriaci Sylvatici illius egregii olim familiaris regiae maiestatis patriae nepotem cognoverat, me perbenigne suscepit, Ioanne Caraciolo[d] viro nobilissimo equite et b(ene) m(erente) praefecto suo curante favitanteque. At ibi postquam marmoreum Castoris et Pollucis vetustissimum templum Graeco cum epigrammate et alia egregia vetustatis vidimus, nostris et adiecimus commentariis.

(c) **Pozzuoli, Virgilian Sites (Sibyl's Temple, Lake Avernus, Capo Miseno, Cumae), Baiae** (*Vita*, para. 210; Vo4, fol. 8v, ed. Mehus 23–24):

Iussus ab iis[e] *Hercules Putheolanus*[f] *pr(aetore)*[g] me *Puteolos* usque comitatus est, quo duce vetusta *Sybillae templa*, *Averni lacus* et *usque Misenum* ad celebrem *montem omnia Cumarum Baiarumque monumenta* inspexi, ubi *Luculliana Neronianaque* magnifica opera[h] plurima *nostram ad diem* vestigia prospectantur.

---

[a] For the chronological problems created by this section see the Notes to the Translation, para. 206 ff. For the 'unreliable chronology' of the '*Itinerarium*' in general, see the Introduction.

[b] Mehus corrects to Tarracinarum.

[c] AVG. CAES. Vo4

[d] Mehus corrects to Caracciolo.

[e] Mehus changes to his.

[f] Mehus corrects to Puteolanus.

[g] PR. Vo4; Mehus expands to Praefectus.

[h] Mehus corrects to Lucullianorum Neronianorumque magnificorum operum.

(d) **Benevento** (*Vita*, para. 211; Vo4, fol. 8v, ed. Mehus 24):

    Et inde apud Sannites[a] ad egregiam illam *Beneventanam urbem* nobiles *vetustatum* reliquias *theatra* et *insignem divi Traiani Caesaris arcum* inspeximus.

(e) **Gaeta, Capua, Sessa** (*Vita*, para. 207, 208; Vo4, fol. 9r, ed. Mehus 24):

    Et inde pariter Caietanis Capuanis[b] Suessanisque visis munimentis,[c]

(f) **Voyage to Messina, Circumnavigation of Sicily** (*Vita*, para. 215–216 and 32; Vo4, fol. 9r–v, ed. Mehus 24–25):

    Tyrrhena demum maria Anconitana navi transfretantes una tuis cum *Daniele Parentino pontifice et Ioanne Bosculo, ad Alphonsum* inclytum Taraconensium[d] *regem oratoribus, Siciliam* venimus, Lipareis Vulcaneisque fumantibus insulis procul inspectis et *Pachino*[e] *per Scyllea*[f] *pernitiosa vada superato.* Sed et Trinacriae tria illa nobilia vidimus promontoria, Pelorum, Pachinum Lylibeumque, et egregias maritimas urbes *Messanam, Panhormum*[g] Drepanumque, et arduum *Taurominium oppidum, Aethneum*[h] *celsum fumiferumque* suspicere *montem* curavimus; et inde implacabilem per Carybdim[i] Ausonicum Leucopetrae adivimus promontorium et antiquam Rhegium civitatem; et tandem per Lucaniam e Calabris Apuliam venimus, ubi Sfortiano illo Francisco comite illustrissimo favitante sua quoque vidimus loca, Manfredoniamque inter dirutam Sipontum et Gargani montis promuntorium[j] sitam. Sed antea exitiales apud Cannas Baroletum vidimus

---

[a] Mehus corrects to Samnites.

[b] Mehus omits Capuanis.

[c] Mehus corrects to monumentis.

[d] Mehus corrects to Tarraconensium.

[e] Mehus corrects to Pachyno, here, and Pachynum, below.

[f] Syllea Vo4

[g] Mehus corrects to Panormum.

[h] Mehus corrects to Aetneumque.

[i] Mehus corrects to Charybdim.

[j] Mehus corrects to promontorium.

oppidum ac ingens in eo ex aere simulachrum,[a] quod Heraclem sanctum incertum vulgus appellare consueverat.[b]

12. **Return to Piceno** (Vita, para. 217; Vo4, fol. 9v, ed. Mehus, 25).

Inde vero me nostram ad Picenam provinciam verti et Firmianae coloniae vidimus augustam Girofulcaneamqu arcem praecelsam.

---

[a] Mehus corrects to simulacrum.

[b] For similar language describing Ciriaco's visit to Manfredonia and Barletta in 1437 see Moroni, *Epigrammata*, p. 37 (Bodnar, 1960, 45).

# APPENDIX VI

## Ciriaco's Drawings of Hagia Sophia in Constantinople.[1]

It is impossible to determine the actual date on which Ciriaco made the original drawings of Hagia Sophia (he visited Constantinople often in his travels—in 1418–1419, 1428, 1431, and several times in the years 1444–1447: for the first three visits, see the Introduction, 'Chronology.' Although the only lengthy verbal description of Constantinople's antiquities attributable to Ciriaco occurs in the *Vita* in connection with his earliest visit in 1418, it is unlikely that Ciriaco knew enough Latin at that time to be able to write either the detailed description reported in the *Vita* (para. 38–43) or the headings to the drawings of Hagia Sophia recorded here (see *Vita*, translation, note to para. 40). Nevertheless, we include the headings here on the good chance that they are contemporaneous with the description in Ciriaco's lost diary on which para. 38–43 are based, whenever that may have been written.[2]

Description of Parma MS 1191 (Pp), fols. 61–66:

fol. 61r: blank

fol. 61v:

[Introductory paragraph]:

> *Almae Sophiae sapientiaeve sacrum in Bizantio a Iustiniano Caesare Templum maximum et CIIII porfireis serpentinis ac marmoreis columnis diversorumque nobilium et conspicuum lapidum insigne, Anthemio Tralleo et Isidoro Milesio nobilibus architectorum principibus.*[3]

[Heading for drawing no. 1]:

> *Ab externa templi et occidua parte figura a qua primum vestibulum atque ingressum habuisse videtur: cuius amplitudo per lat(itudinem) cubito(rum) C et L, altitudo vero cubi(torum) CXX metita est.*[4]
>
> [The rest of the page was left blank, presumably in order to accommodate the drawing of the church's exterior from the west, showing also the front of the atrium. This is one of the two drawings reproduced by Giuliano da Sangallo in his 'sketchbook,' Vb2, fol. 28r.][5]

fol. 62r:

> [Heading for drawing no. 2]:
>
> *Pronaon Pentapilon Bizantiani maximi Sophiae sapientiaeve delubri nobile. Longitudo cubi(torum) XC, la(titudo) X, alt(itudo) p(edum?) XX.*[6]
>
> [The rest of the page is blank, to leave room for a drawing, presumably of the first narthex, or vestibule.]

fol. 62v:

> [Heading for drawing no. 3]:
> *Propylea templi IX portarum diversorumque conspicuum lapidum et aurea testudine insigne. Lon(gitudo) cu(bitorum) XC, lat(itudo) XV, altitudo cub(itorum) XXV.* [7]
> [The rest of the page is left blank for a drawing, presumably of the second narthex, whose measurements are about the same as those of the first.]

fol. 63r:

> [Drawing no. 4]
> *Opus inimitabile* [Ms: *in imitabile*] *tempus minatur destruere. Prohibetur autem nostram per curam. Sed, o rex excelse, aperi nobis domum quam tempus non tangit.* [8]
> [Not a caption, but "Ciriaco's Latin version of an inscription once in the north tympanum of Hagia Sophia."[9] The rest of the page is left blank for a drawing, probably not of the north wall, as the inscription might lead us to expect, but "a general, perspective view of the interior looking toward the apse."][10]

fol. 63v:

> [Heading for drawing no. 5]:
> *Ad alta templi ab interiori parte deambulatoria quae catacumina vocitant in medio primariae partis pavimento.* [11]
> [The rest of this page is left blank for a drawing of the interior of the west facade, i.e., the whole front third of the church viewed from under the dome looking west, including the two western piers that support the dome, which in the drawing—also copied by Sangallo in Vb2, fol. 28r—are made to appear as if they were on the same plane with the two piers on either side of the entrance.[12] The drawing also shows the "high ambulatories, called galleries" (κατηχούμενα) mentioned in this heading and, in the galleries, the "porphyry and serpentine marble columns" of the introductory paragraph (and the *Vita*, para. 40), which either Ciriaco or Sangallo misinterpreted as "twisted porphyry and marble columns."][13]

fol. 64r:

> [Heading for drawing no. 6]
> *Pavimentum media testudine templi DC marmoreis expolitis tabulis insigne et suacte natura.* [14]
> [The rest of the page is left blank for a drawing, perhaps of a detail of the pavement under the dome, perhaps as seen from the gallery, though more likely it accompanied "the groundplan reproduced on fol. 44r of the Barberini Codex."][15]

fol. 64v:

> [Space for drawing no. 7]:
> Blank, except at the bottom.

[The whole page is left blank, probably for a drawing showing the elevation from the top of the dome to the floor, i.e., a longitudinal section through the building, including the nave arcade and the dome,[16] with the following subscript at the bottom:]

*A summo testudinis culmine ad pavimentum cubitorum C, lat(itudo) p(edum?) LX, diametrum p(edum) IIII.*[17]

fol. 65r: blank

fol. 65v:

[Headings for two inscriptions, side by side]:[18]

*Ad magnam de marmore basim ad marmoream columnam*[19]

*Latinis litteris inscriptio: in Neronem Caesarem epigramma*[20]

[The rest of page is left blank, presumably for two Greek inscriptions, written side-by-side, in columns.]

fol. 66r:

[Heading for drawing no. 8?]:[21]

*Latitudo cubitorum C et similiter ad summum testudinis culmen altitudo cubi(torum) C. Ab interiore parte.*[22]

[This looks like the heading for an eighth drawing of Hagia Sophia showing, perhaps, a view up into the dome from floor level; or possibly, the half-dome over the apse. This latter interpretation would supply the one element missing from the description: the eastern interior wall with its apse and altar-table. Otherwise, we may have to say that he considered the east interior wall too much like the western one, which he did represent, to repeat.]

## NOTES

1. The Manuscripts: (1) Parma, Biblioteca Palatina, 1191 (Pp). Paper, third quarter of the fifteenth century: headings for eight separate drawings of the church of Hagia Sophia in Constantinople occur on fols. 61–66. Space is left on each page for the drawings, which were never executed. (2) Vatican City, Biblioteca Vaticana, *Vat Barb. Lat.* 4424 (Vb2): 'sketchbook' of Giuliano da Sangallo, which includes, on fols 28r and 44v, two drawings of Hagia Sophia, with the same headings as two of the eight headings in Pp.

Bibliography: Bodnar, 1960, 106–114, 227 (with bibliography prior to 1958); Brown and Kleiner, 1983 (on Giuliano da Sangallo's use of Ciriaco's drawings); Huelsen, 1910, I (fasimile of the Sangallo 'sketchbook' [Vb2]); Mitchell, 1974 (for Sangallo's copy of Ciriaco's drawing of the Parthenon); C. Smith, 1987 (interpretation of the headings).

2. Smith, 27, dates it in the late 1440s, after Ciriaco has seen Brunelleschi's dome in Florence and after he has become acquainted with Alberti's *De Re Aedificatoria*, which was composed during the 1440s. This dating is dependent on her interpretations of these headings, which we have followed here, namely that this manner of describing a building, i.e., a walk-through of the building, with detailed architectural plans, showing, not the most important elements first (the medieval, hierarchical approach), but the parts of the building as the spectator experiences it, is very early in the history of modern architectural description. Literarily, this "new conception of the task of architectural drawing" was inspired, Smith thinks, by Alberti's book, although its formulation starts with Manuel Chrysoloras' *Compendium of Old and New Rome*, written in Rome *ca.* 1410/11 and mediated to Italian humanists by Guarino, who had a copy. It is thought

that Alberti also owned a copy. Smith's translations are included in these Notes.

3. "The great temple dedicated to Hagia Sophia, i.e., wisdom, in Byzantium [founded] by Caesar Justinian. Notable for 104 Porphyry, sepentine, and marble columns of various noble and remarkable stones. Anthemius of Tralles and Isidore of Miletus, noble princes among architects." Smith, 17.

4. "A figure from the exterior and western part of the temple, from which it is seen to have first had a vestibule and entrance: the dimension is 150 cubits wide and 110 or 120 cubits high." Smith, 18.

5. See Smith's lengthy discussion of this drawing, pp. 18–21. Her conclusion is that Ciriaco attempts here to render, not the fifteenth-century west façade of the church, but its original, Justinianic façade, "excising the corruptions and additions inflicted by time and reconstituting it in its original purity" in a way analogous to the humanists' attempt to reconstitute texts in their original forms.

6. "The noble five-doored vestibule of the greatest Byzantine temple of divine Sophia, or wisdom. Length 90 cubits, breadth 10, height 20 p." Smith, 21.

7. "The narthex [literally, monumental entrance], of the temple, of nine doorways and diverse, noteworthy stones and remarkable for its golden ceiling. Length 90 cubits, breadth 15, height 25 cubits." Smith, 21–22.

8. "Time threatens to destroy the inimitable work. This we prevent through our efforts. But, O most-high king, open to us a mansion which time does not touch." Smith, 22.

9. Smith, 22, who gives the text of the Greek inscription and comments that "of the many inscriptions in Hagia Sophia Cyriacus chose the one that aptly expressed his own concerns as an antiquarian, and heightened its relevance by changing the tense from past to present in his translation."

10. Smith, 23.

11. "Towards the high ambulatories, called catacumina, from the interior of the temple in the middle of the pavement of the most important part." Smith, 23.

12. This 'flattening out' (Smith calls it a 'non-perspectival drawing') of the view west from under the dome was pointed out to us by Robert Van Nice, director of the Haghia Sophia project of the Dumbarton Oaks Center for Byzantine Studies.

13. Smith, 23, thinks it was Sangallo who misunderstood *serpentinis* (a kind of marble) to mean 'twisted,' "thinking of the late Gothic forms of Florence Cathedral."

14. "The pavement [beneath] the temple's central dome [literally, ceiling]: noteworthy for its dressed marble slabs and its singular character." Smith, 23.

15. Smith, 23, was the first to recognize this groundplan as derived "from the same Cyriacan source."

16. Smith, 24.

17. "From the very top of the dome to the pavement 100 cubits, breadth 60 p., diameter 4 p." Smith, 24.

18. Not included by Smith.

19. "On a large marble base by a marble column."

20. "A Latin inscription in honor of Nero Caesar."

21. Not included by Smith.

22. "Width, 100 cubits. Similarly, the height to the top of the dome is 100 cubits. Interior view."

# BIBLIOGRAPHY[a]

Agostini, Giovanni degli. *Notizie istorico–critiche intorno la vita, e le opere degli scrittori Viniziani*. Venice, ?1754 ?1752.

Alighieri, Dante. *Divina Commedia*. Ed. and tr. by Charles S. Singleton. Bollingen Series 80. 3 vols. in 6. Princeton, 1970–1975.

Alsop, Joseph. *The Rare Art Traditions*. Bollingen Series XXXV, 27. New York, 1982.

Apianus, Petrus, and Bartholomaeus Amantius. *Inscriptiones sacrosanctae vetustatis, non illae quidem Romanae, sed totius fere orbis, summo studio ac maximis impensis terra marique conuisitae* ....Ingolstadt, 1534.

Argenti, Philip. *The Occupation of Chios by the Genoese and their Administration of the Island 1346–1566*. 3 Vols. Cambridge, 1958.

Ashmole, Bernard.
1956 = "Cyriac of Ancona and the Temple of Hadrian at Cyzicus." *Journal of the Warburg and Courtauld Institutes* 19 (1956) 179–191.
1959 = "Cyriac of Ancona." *Proceedings of the British Academy* 45 (1959): 25–41 (Italian Lecture, delivered 1957).

Ashtor, Eliyahu. *Levant Trade in the Later Middle Ages*. Princeton, N.J., 1983.

Babinger, Franz (works listed here in chronological order):
1950 = "Von Amurath zu Amurath, Vor– und Nachspiel der Schlacht bei Varna <1444>." *Oriens* 3 (1950): 229–265.
1951 = "Mehemmed II, der Eroberer, und Italien." *Byzantion* 21 (1951): 127–170. Translated, with some corrections and additions, as "Maometto II, il Conquistatore, e l'Italia." *Rivista storica italiana* 63 (1951): 469–505.
1961 = *Johannes Darius (1414–1494), Sachwalter Venedigs im Morgenland und sein griechischer Umkreis*. Bayerische Akademie der Wissenschaften, Philosophisch–Historische Klasse. Sitzungsberichte 1961, 5. Published as a monograph. Munich, 1961.
1962 = "Notes on Cyriac of Ancona and Some of his Friends." *Journal of the Warburg and Courtauld Institutes* 25 (1962): 321–324.
1964 = "Veneto–kretische Geistesstrebungen um die Mitte des XV.Jahrhunderts." *Byzantinische Zeitschrift* 57 (1964): 62–77.
1966 = "Maometto il Conquistatore e gli umanisti d'Italia." In *Venezia e l'Oriente fra tardo Medioevo e Rinascimento*. Ed. A. Pertusi. Florence, 1966. 433–449.

---

[a] Works are listed alphabetically according to author. Multiple works by a single author are listed in chronological order.

1978 = *Mehmed the Conqueror and his Time*. Ed. by William C. Hickman. Tr. by Ralph Manheim. Bollingen Series XCV. Princeton, N.J., 1978. "Translated from *Mehmed der Eroberer und seine Zeit: Weltenstürmer einer Zeitenwende* ... Munich; 1953; second edition, 1959; with further revisions by the author and editors."

Baedeker's *Southern Italy and Sicily*. Leipzig and London, 1896.

Bandini, A.M. *Catalogus Codicum Latinorum Bibliothecae Mediceae Laurentianae*. Vol. 3. Florence, 1776.

Banti, L. "Inscrizioni di Filippi copiate da Ciriaco Anconitano nel codice vaticano latino 10672." *Annuario della R. Scuola Archaeologica di Atene e delle missioni italiane in Oriente* n.s. 102 (1939–1940): 213–220.

Baron, H. *Leonardo Bruni Aretino, humanistisch-philosophische Schriften mit einer Chronologie seiner Werke und Briefe*. Berlin, 1928.

Bean, G.E. *Aegean Turkey*. London, 1966.

Becatti, G. *La colonna coclide istoriata*. Rome, 1960.

Belgrano, T.
   1877–1884 = "Documenti reguardanti la colonia di Pera." *Atti della Società Ligure di Storia Patria* 13 (1877–1884): 979–986 (365–392 in the separate publication).

Berra, L. "Per la biografia di Ciriaco d'Ancona." *Giornale storico della letteratura italiana* 63 (1914): 461–462.

Bertalot, Ludwig, and Augusto Campana. "Gli scritti di Iacopo Zeno e il suo elogio di Ciriaco d'Ancona." *La Bibliofilia* 41 (1939): 356–376 [= Bertalot. *Studien zum italienischen und deutschen Humanismus*. Ed. Paul Oskar Kristeller. Rome, 1975. II, 311–332].

Bertalot, L. (with A. Wilmanns). "Lauri Quirini 'Dialogus in Gymnasiis Florentinis,' ein Nachklang zum 'Certame Coronario' (1442)." *Archivum Romanicum* 7 (1923): 478–509 (=*Studien zum italienischen und deutschen Humanismus* I, 339–372).

Billanovich, Myriam. "Intorno alla 'Jubilatio' di Felice Feliciano." *Italia Medioevale e Umanistica* 32 (1989): 351–358.

Bisticci, Vespasiano da. See below, s.v. 'Vespasiano.'

Bodnar, Edward W.
   1960=*Cyriacus of Ancona and Athens*. Collection Latomus 43. Brussels–Berchem, 1960.
   1972 = "A Visit to Delos in April, 1445." *Archaeology* 25 (1972): 210–215.

1988 = "Ciriaco d'Ancona and the Crusade of Varna: A Closer Look." *Mediaevalia* 14 (1988): 253–280. A revision, with full documentation, of: "Ciriaco d'Ancona e la crociata di Varna. Nuove Prospettive." *Il Veltro* 27 (1983): 235–251.
— and Charles Mitchell, ed. *Cyriacus of Ancona's Journeys in the Propontis and the Northern Aegean 1444–1445.* Memoirs of the American Philosophical Society 112. Philadelphia, Pa.: The American Philosophical Society, 1976.

Böckh, August. See below, s.v. *Corpus Inscriptionum Graecarum (CIG)*.

Bracciolini, Poggio,
1964 = *Opera omnia* (Monumenta Politica et Philosophica Rariora ex optimis editionibus phototyptice expressa curante Luigi Firpo, Series II, Numerus 4). Torino, 1964. Vol. I = *Scripta in editione Basilensi anno MCXXXVIII collata.* Vol. III = *Poggii Epistolae,* ed. Thomas de Tonellis, vols. 1 and 2. Florence, 1832 and 1859.
1984 = *Lettere,* ed. Helene Harth. Vol. II. *Epistolarum Familarium Libri.* Firenze, 1984.

Branca, Vittore, ed. *Lauro Quirini umanista.* Studi e Testi a cura di Konrad Krautter, Paul Oskar Kristeller, Agostino Pertusi, Giorgio Ravegnani, Helmut Roob, Carlo Seno, Raccolti e presentati da Vittore Branca. Firenze, 1977. Civiltà Veneziana Saggi, 23. Firenze, 1977.

Brinton, Selwyn. *The Gonzaga—Lords of Mantua.* New York, [1927].

Brown, Beverly Louise, and Diana E.E. Kleiner. "Giuliano da Sangall's Drawings after Ciriaco d'Ancona: Transformations of Greek and Roman Antiquities in Athens." *Journal of the Society of Architectural Historians* 42 (1983): 321–335.

Brown, Virginia. "Portraits of Julius Caesar in Latin Manuscripts of the Commentaries." *Viator* 12 (1981): 319–353.

Bruni, Leonardo. *Historiarum Florentini Populi.* Florence, 1857.
---. Letters. See below, s.v. 'Mehus.'

Buondelmonti, Cristoforo. *Chr. Bondelmontii Florentini Librum Insularum Archipelagi.* Ed. G.R.L. De Sinner. Leipzig and Berlin, 1824.

Campana, Augusto.
1950 = "Scritture di umanisti." *Rinascimento* 1 (1950): 239, 255–256.
1959 = "Giannozzo Manetti, Ciriaco e l'arco di Traiano ad Ancona." *Italia medioevale e umanistica* 2 (1959): 483–504.
1973–1974 = "Ciriaco d'Ancona e Lorenzo Valla sull'iscrizione greca del tempio dei Dioscuri a Napoli." *Archeologia classica* 25–26 (1973–1974, publ. 1976): 84–102.

Cancellieri, F. *De Secretariis Basilicae Vaticanae Veteris ac Novae* . . . . I, Part 2 (of 4 vols.). Rome, 1786.

Casson, S. "The excavations." *Preliminary Report upon the Excavations carried out in the Hippodrome of Constantinople in 1927 on behalf of the British Academy.* London, 1928.

Cognasso, Francesco et al. *Storia di Milano* VI. *Il Ducato Visconteo e la Repubblica Ambrosiana (1292–1450).* Milan, 1955.

Colin, Jean. *Cyriaque d'Ancône. Le voyageur, le marchand, l'humaniste.* Paris, 1981.

Colucci, Giuseppe. *Antichità Picene.* Vol. 15. Fermo, 1792. ('Colucci, 1792' designates works of Ciriaco other than the *Vita* of Scalamonti that occur in Colucci's treatment of the Treviso MS. '*Vita,* ed. Colucci' designates vol. 15, pp. 50–100 of this work only).

*Corpus Inscriptionum Graecarum (CIG).* Ed. August Böckh et al. 5 vols. Berlin, 1828–1877.

*Corpus Inscriptionum Latinarum (CIL).* Ed. Theodor Mommsen et al. Berlin, 1873–. Vol. 3, 1873. Vol. 5, 1, 1872. Vol. 9–10, 1883.

Cortesi, Mariarosa, and Enrico V. Maltese. "Ciriaco d'Ancona e il 'De virtutibus' pseudoaristotelico." *Studi medievali* 33 (1992): 133–164.

Dabrowski, Ian. "L'année 1444." *Bulletin international de l'académie polonaise des sciences et des lettres (Polska Akademia Nauk), classe de philologie–classe d'histoire et de philosophie.* N°. supplémentaire 6 (1951). Cracow, 1952.

Decembrio, Pier Candido. *Vita Philippi Mariae.* In *Rerum Italicarum Scriptores,* ed. L. Muratori XX, p. 1014, no. 63. Città di Castello, 1900. German transl. by Philip Frank, *Leben des Filippo Maria Visconti und Taten des Francesco Sforza.* Jena, E. Diederichs, 1913.

Dennis, Holmes Van Mater. "The Garrett Manuscript of Marcanova." *Memoirs of the American Academy in Rome* 6 (1927): 113–126.

Dessau, *CIL.* XIV, *Latium.*

Dini–Traversari. *Ambrogio Traversari e suoi tempi.* Florence, 1912.

Edson, C., ed. *Inscriptiones Graecae (IG)* X, 2, 1. *Inscriptiones Macedoniae.* Berlin, 1972.

Eubel, Conrad, et al. *Hierarchia Catholica Medii et Recentioris Aevi.* 6 vols. Second Edition. Monasterii, 1913–1935.

Faraglia, M.F. *Storia della lotta fra Alfonso V d'Aragone e Renato d'Angio.* Lanciano, 1908.

Fava, Domenico. "La scrittura libraria di Ciriaco d'Ancona." In *Scritti di paleografia e diplomatica in onore di Vincenzo Federici*. Florence, 1944. 295–305. Separate publication: Florence, 1945, 1–13.

Filelfo, Francesco. *Francisci Philelphi . . . epistolarum familiarium libri XXXVII*. Venice, 1502.

—. *Cent–dix lettres grecques de François Filelfo . . . d'apres le codex Trivulzianus 873 avec traduction, notes e commentaire*. Publications de l'école des langues orientales vivantes, IIIᵉ, vol. XII. Ed. E.L. Legrand. Paris, 1896.

Filippini, F. *Il cardinale Egidio Albornoz*. Bologna, 1933.

Finlay, G. *A History of Greece from its Conquest by the Romans to the Present time, 146 B.C. to A.D. 1864*. 7 vols. London, 1877.

Fois, Mario, *Il pensiero cristiano di Lorenzo Valla nel quadra storico–culturale del suo ambiente*. Analecta Gregoriana, 174, Series Facultatis Historiae Ecclesiasticae: sectio A, no. 10. Rome, Libreria Editrice del'Università Gregoriana, 1969.

Fraser, P. *Ptolemaic Alexandria*. 3 vols. Oxford, 1972.

Gams, Pius Bonifacius. *Series Episcoporum Ecclesiae Catholicae . . . .* Ratisbon, 1873.

Gentile, Sebastiano. "Crisolora e Tolomeo." In *Dotti bizantini e libri greci nell'Italia del secolo XV*. Atti del Convegno internationale Trento 22–23 ottobre 1990. Ed. Mariarosa Cortesi and Enrico V. Maltese. Naples, 1992.

Giannone, P. *Istoria civile del regno di Napoli*. Haya, 1753.

Gill, Joseph.
    1959 = *The Council of Florence*. Cambridge, 1959.
    1961 = *Eugenius IV, Pope of Christian Union*. Westminster, Md., 1961.

Giustiniani, Vito R. "l Filelfo, l'interpretazione allegorica di Virgilio e la tripartizione platonica dell'anima." In *Umanesimo e rinascimento. Studi offerti a Paul Oskar Kristeller* da V. Branca, A. Frugoni, E. Garin, V.R. Giustiniani, S. Mariotti, A. Perosa, C. Vasoli. Florence, 1980. 33–44.

Gorni, G. "Storia del Certame Coronario." *Rinascimento*, ser. 2, 12 (1972): 135–186.

Graesse, Johann Georg Theodor, Friedrich Benedict, and Helmut Plechl. *Orbis Latinus*. Fourth edition. Braunschweig, 1971.

Gregorovius, F.
    1881 = *Siciliana⁵*. Leipzig, 1881.

1898 = *History of the City of Rome in the Middle Ages*. Fourth edition, translated by A. Hamilton. London, 1898.

Grendler, Paul F. *Schooling in Renaissance Italy: Literacy and Learning, 1300–1600*. Johns Hopkins University Studies in Historical and Political Science: 107th ser., no. 1. Baltimore, Md., 1989.

Guerrini, L. "'Las Incantadas' di Salonicco." *Archeologia classica* 13 (1961): 40–70.

Gutkind, Kurt S. *Cosimo de' Medici, Pater Patriae, 1389–1464*. Oxford, 1938.

Halecki, O. *The Crusade of Varna: A Discussion of Controversial Problems*. Polish Institute Series, 3. New York City, 1943.

Hammond, N.G.L. *Epirus: The Geography, the Ancient Remains, the History and the Topography of Epirus and Adjacent Areas*. Oxford, 1967.

Harlfinger, Dieter. "Ptolemaios–Karten des Cyriacus von Ancona." *In ΦΙΛΟΦΡΟΝΗΜΑ, Festschrift für Martin Sicherl zum 75. Geburtstag. Von Textkritic bis Humanismusforschung*. Herausgegeben von Dieter Harlfinger (Studien zur Geschichte und Kultur des Altertums 1. Reihe, 4. Band) Paderborn–München–Wien–Zürich, 1990. Pp. 225–236. 6 Tafeln.

Harth, Helene. See above, s.v. 'Bracciolini.'

Hill, G.F. *History of Cyprus*. 2 vols. Cambridge, England, 1940–1952.

Hobson, Anthony. *Humanists and Bookbinders, the Origins and Diffusion of the Humanistic Bookbinding 1455–1559 with a Census of Historiated Plaquette and Medallion Bindings of the Renaissance*. New York: Cambridge University Press, 1989.

Huelsen, Christian.
    1907 = *La Roma antica di Ciriaco d'Ancona*. Rome, 1907.
    1910 = *Il libro di Giuliano da Sangallo, Vaticano Barberiniano 4424*. 2 vols. Leipzig, 1910.

*Inscriptiones Graecae (IG)*. Berlin, 1873–. See above, s.v. Edson.

Isidore of Seville. *Etymologiae*. Ed. W.M. Lindsay. 2 vols. Oxford, 1911.

Jacks, Philip. *The Antiquarian and the Myth of Antiquity: the Origins of Rome in Renaissance Thought*. Cambridge, 1993.

Jacobs, E. "Cyriacus von Ancona und Mehmed II." *Byzantinische Zeitschrift* 30 (1929–1930): 197–202.

Janin, R. *Constantinople byzantine, développement urbain et répertoire topographique*. Paris. First edition 1950. Second edition 1964.

Kaibel, G. "Cyriaci Anconitani Inscriptionum Lesbiacarum Sylloge Inedita." *Ephemeris Epigraphica* 2 (1875): 1–24.

Kitzinger, E. "The Mosaics of the Cappella Palatina in Palermo, An Essay on the Choice and Arrangement of Subjects." *Art Bulletin* 31 (1949): 269–292.

Krautheimer, R. and T.
1970 = *Lorenzo Ghiberti*. 2 vols. Princeton Monographs in Art and Archaeology, 31. Princeton, N.J., 1970.
1971 = *Ghiberti's Bronze Doors*. Princeton, N.J., 1971.

Kretschmayr, Heinrich. *Geschichte von Venedig*. 3 vols. in 2. Gotha, etc., 1905–1934.

Krischen, F. *Die Landmauern von Konstantinopel*. Berlin, 1938.

Kristeller, Paul. *Andrea Mantegna*. London, 1901.

Kristeller, Paul Oskar. *Iter Italicum: A Finding List of Uncatalogued or Incompletely Catalogued Humanistic Manuscripts of the Renaissance in Italian and Other Libraries*. 6 Vols. London, 1963. Vol. 1. *Italy: Agrigento–Novara* [With a Preface to the Whole Work]. 3rd impression 1977. Vol. 2. *Italy: Orvieto–Volterra; Vatican City; Addenda and Corrigenda to Volumes 1 and 2*. 2nd impression 1977. Vol. 3. *Alia Itinera: Australia to Germany*. 1983. *Index to vol. 3 (Alia Itinera 1)*. Compiled by B.D. Kent and R. Raine in Collaboration with the Author. 1987. Vol. 4. *Alia Itinera 2: Great Britain to Spain*. 1989. Vol. 5. *Alia Itinera 3: Sweden to Yugoslavia, Utopia. Italy 2: Supplement to Italy*. 1990. Vol. 6. *Italy 3 and Alia Itinera 4: Supplement to Italy (G–V), Supplement to Vatican and Austria to Spain*. 1992. Index to volume 5. Index to volume 6 is in preparation.

Labalme, Patricia H. *Bernardo Giustiniani, A Venetian of the Quattrocento*. Rome, 1969.

Lancellotti. *Dizionario d'uomini illustri Anconitani*. In Colucci, *Antichità Picene*. Vol. 27. Ferno, 1792.

Lane, F. *Venice, a Maritime Republic*. Baltimore, 1973.

Lawrence, Elizabeth Bailey. "The Illustrations of the Garrett and Modena Manuscripts of Marcanova." *Memoirs of the American Academy in Rome* 6 (1927): 127–131.

Legrand, E.L. See above s.v. Filelfo.

Lehmann, Phyllis Williams.

1959 = "Theodosius or Justinian? A Renaissance Drawing of a Byzantine Rider." *Art Bulletin* 41 (1959):39–57, with a response by Cyril Mango, ibid., 351–356; and a reply to Mango by P.W. Lehmann, ibid., 356–358.

1977 = *Cyriacus of Ancona's Egyptian Visit and its Reflections in Gentile Bellini and Hieronymus Bosch.* Mary Flexner Lecture, Bryn Mawr College. Locust Valley, N.Y., 1977.


Leoni, A. *Ancona Illustrata.* Ancona, 1832.


Lightbown, Ronald. *Mantegna. With a Complete Catalogue of the Paintings, Drawings and Prints.* Berkeley, Los Angeles, 1986.


Litta. *Famiglie celebri italiane.* Milan 1820/1856–1885.


Luiso, F.P. *Riordinamento dell' epistolario di A. Traversari con lettere inedite e note storico-cronologiche.* Florence, 1898–1903.


Luttrell, Anthony.

1978 = *The Hospitallers in Cyprus, Rhodes, Greece, and the West, 1291–1440.* Collected Studies. Variorum Reprints, London, 1978.

1986 = "The Later History of the Maussolleion and its Utilization in the Hospitaller Castle at Bodrum." In *The Maussolleion at Halikarnassos, Reports of the Danish Archaeological Expedition to Bodrum.* Vol. 2, Pt. 2. Aarhus, 1986. 114–214.

1989 = "The Latins and Life on the Smaller Aegean Islands: 1204–1453." In *Latins and Greeks in the Eastern Mediterranean after 1204*, ed. Benjamin Arbel, Bernard Hamilton, David Jacoby. London, 1989. 146–157.


Lyttleton, M. *Baroque Architecture in Classical Antiquity.* London, 1974.


Maas, Paul. "Ein Notizbuch des Cyriacus von Ancona aus dem Jahre 1436." *Beiträge zur Forschung. Studien und Mitteilungen aus dem Antiquariat Jacques Rosenthal, München.* I Folge, Heft I (1915 [article dated 1913]): 5–15. Reviewed by G. Sabbadini (see below s.v. 'Sabbadini').


MacKendrick, Paul. "A Renaissance Odyssey, the Life of Cyriac of Ancona." *Classica et Medievalia* 13 (1952): 131–145.


Macrobius, Ambrosius Aurelius Theodosius. *Opera.* London, 1694.


Mamboury, E. and Th. Wiegand. *Die Kaiserpalaste von Konstantinopel.* Berlin, 1934.


Mancini, A. "Macrobio Parmense." *Archivio storico per le provincie Parmensi* n.s. 28 (1928): 2–5.


Mancini, Girolamo. *Vita di Leon Battista Alberti.* 2nd ed. Florence, 1911, repr. Rome, 1971.

Mardersteig, G., ed. *Felice Feliciano Veronese: Alphabetum Romanum.* Verona, 1960. Reviewed by C. Mitchell (see below, s.v. Mitchell).

Martène, Edmond, and Ursinus Durand. *Veterum Scriptorum et Monumentorum Historicorum, Dogmaticorum, Moralium Amplissima Collectio.* VIII, Paris, 1733.

Mehus, Lorenzo, ed.
1741 = *Leonardi Bruni Arretini Epistolarum Libri VIII.* Ed. Laurentius Mehus. Florence, 1741.
1742 = *Kyriaci Anconitani Itinerarium Nunc Primum ex Ms. Cod. in Lucem Erutum ex Bibl. Illus. Clarissimique Baronis Philippi Stosch, Editionem Recensuit, Animadversionibus ac Praefatione Illustravit, Nonnullisque Eiusdem Kyriaci Epistolis Partim Editis, Partim Ineditis, Locupletavit Laurentius Mehus.* Florence, 1742. Reprinted Bologna, 1969.
1759 = ed. *Ambrosii Traversari Generalis Camaldalensium Aliorumque ad Ipsum et ad Alios de Eodem Ambrosio Latinae Epistolae a Domino Petro Canneto Abbate Camaldulensi in Libros XXV Tributae, Variorum Opera Distinctae, et Observationes Illustratae. Accedit Eiusdem Ambrosii Vita in Qua Historia Literaria Florentina ab Anno MCXCII usque ad Annum MCCCCXL ex Monumentis Potissimum Nondum Editis Deducta Est a Laurentio Mehus.* 2 vols. Florence, 1759. Reprinted Bologna, 1968.

Meiggs, R. *Roman Ostia.*[2] Oxford, 1973.

Mercati, Giovanni. "Una lettera inedita di Ciriaco. Section VIII of "Miscellanea di note storico–critiche." *Studi e documenti di storia e diritto* 15 (1894): 303–347 (= *Opere minori* I. Città del Vaticano, 1937. 93–135).

Mercati, Silvio G. "Lettera inedita di Giovanni Argiropulo ad Andreolo Giustiniani." *École Française de Rome, Mélanges d'Archéologie et d'Histoire* 39–40 (1922–1923): 154–163.

Miller, William.
1908 = *The Latins in the Levant. A History of Frankish Greece, 1204–1566.* London, 1908, repr. New York, 1964.
1913 = "The Gattilusi of Lesbos (1355–1462)." *Byzantinische Zeitschrift* 22 (1913): 406–447.
1921 = "The Genoese in Chios." In *Essays on the Latin Orient.* Cambridge, 1921, repr. New York, 1983. 298–312.

Mitchell, Charles.
1960 = "Archaeology and Romance in Renaissance Italy." In *Italian Renaissance Studies,* ed. E.F. Jacob. London, 1960. 455–483.
1961 = "Felice Feliciano Antiquarius." Italian Lecture, British Academy, Read 28 June 1961. *Proceedings of the British Academy* 47 (1961): 197–221.
1962 = "Ex libris Kiriaci Anconitani." *Italia medioevale e umanistica* 5 (1962): 283–299.

1963 ▪ "The First Alphabet Book." Review of Giovanni Mardersteig, ed. *Alphabetum Romanum* (see above). *The Times Literary Supplement*. Friday April 26, 1963. 312.

1974 ▪ "Ciriaco d'Ancona: Fifteenth–Century Drawings and Descriptions of the Parthenon." In *The Parthenon*. Ed. Vincent J. Bruno. New York, 1974. 111–123.

Momigliano, Arnaldo. "Ancient History and the Antiquarian." *Journal of the Warburg and Courtauld Institutes* 13 (1950): 285–315. Reprinted in *Studies in Historiography*. London, 1966. 1–39.

Mommsen, Theodor.
    See above, s.v. *Corpus Inscriptionum Latinarum*.
    1883 ▪ "Über die berliner Excerptenhandschrift des Petrus Donatus." *Jahrbuch der königlich preussischen Kunstssammlungen* 4 (1883): 73–89.
    1895 ▪ Ed. *Collectanea Rerum Memorabilium*. Berlin, 1895.

Mommsen, Theodor E. "Petrarch and the Decoration of the Sala Virorum Illustrium in Padua." *Art Bulletin* 34 (1952): 95–111.

Montevecchi, L. "Lettera inedita di Ciriaco d'Ancona." *Epigraphica* 1 (1939): 80–82.

Morici, Medardo.
    1896 ▪ *Lettere inedite di Ciriaco d'Ancona* (1438–1440). Pistoia, 1896. Reviewed by G. Mercati, *Rivista bibliografica italiana* (1896): 65–69 (▪ *Opere Minori*, vol. 1, 394–397).
    1897 ▪ *Per gli epistolari di due discepoli e di un amico di Guarino Guarini*. Pistoia, 1897. 10–24.
    1898 ▪ "Sulla cronologia dei viaggi di Ciriaco d'Ancona." *Archivio storico italiano*. Serie 5.22 (1898): 101–104.
    1899 ▪ "Dante e Ciriaco di Ancona." *Giornale Dantesco* 7 (1899): 70–77.

[Moroni, Carlo, ed.]. *Epigrammata reperta . . . a Cyriaco Anconitano*. [n.p., n.d., but: Rome. ca. 1660].

Morozzo della Rocca, Raimondo, and Maria Francesca Tiepolo. "Cronologia veneziana del Quattrocento." In *La civiltà veneziana del Quattrocento*. Guido Piovene, ed. Centro di Cultura e Civiltà della Fondazione Giorgio Cini. Conferences held in the Spring of 1956. Venice, 1957. 186–241.

Nardi, B. "Letteratura e cultura veneziana del quattrocento." In *La civiltà veneziana del quattrocento*. Venice, 1957: 137–138.

Natalucci, Mario. *La vita millenaria di Ancona*. 2 vols. Ancona, 1975.

Neuhausen, Karl August. "Die Reisen des Cyriacus von Ancona im Spiegel seiner Gebete an Merkur (1444–1447)." In *Diesseits–und Jenseitsreisen im Mittelalter / Voyages dans l'ici–bas et dans l'au–delà au moyen âge*. Ed. Wolf–Dieter Lange. Bonn, Berlin, 1992. 147–174.

Neuhausen, K.A., and Erich Trapp. "Sprachliche und Sachliche Bemerkungen zu einer neuen Ausgabe des Cyriacus von Ancona." *Humanistica Lovaniensia – Journal of Neo–Latin Studies*. Part I, 32 (1983): 45–74; Part II, 33 (1984): 22–70.

Nicol, Donald M.
  1972 = *The Last Centuries of Byzantium, 1261–1453*. New York. 1972.
  1986 = *Studies in Late Byzantine History and Prosopography*. Variorum Reprints. London, 1986.
  1988 = *Byzantinum and Venice: A Study in Diplomatic and Cultural Relations*. Cambridge, 1988.
  1991 = *A Biographical Dictionary of the Byzantine Empire*. London, 1991.

Olivieri degli Abati, Annibale, ed. *Commentariorum Cyriaci Anconitani Nova Fragmenta Notis Illustrata*. Pesaro, 1763.

Paatz, Walter und Elizabeth. *Die Kirchen von Florenz, ein kunstgeschichtliches Handbuch*. Vols. 2 and 3. Frankfurt a/M., 1952.

Pall, Francesco. *Ciriaco d'Ancona e la crociata contro i Turchi*. Valenii–e–Munte, 1937 (= *Académie Roumaine, Bulletin de la section historique* 20 [1938]: 9–68).

Panofsky, E., and F. Saxl, "Classical Mythology in Medieval Art," *Metropolitan Museum Studies* 4 (1933): 228–280.

Papias. *De Linguae Latinae Vocabulis*. 1476.

Pastor, Ludwig. *The History of the Popes from the Close of the Middle Ages*. Vol. I, ed. F.I. Antrobus. St. Louis, Mo., 1923.

Patitucci, Stella. "Per la storia della topografia nel VI centenario della nascita di Ciriaco. Italia, Grecia e Levante, L'eredità topografica di Ciriaco d'Ancona." *Journal of Ancient Topography/Rivista di Topografia Antica* 1 (1991): 147–162.

Patrinelis, Ch. G. "Κυριακὸς ὁ Ἀγκωνίτης: ἡ δῆθεν ὑπηρεσία του εἰς τὴν αυλὴν τοῦ σουλτάνου Μωάμεθ τοῦ Πορθητοῦ καὶ ὁ χρόνος τοῦ θανάτου του (Ciriaco d'Ancona: His Service in the Court of the Sultan Mehmed the Conqueror and the Date of His Death)." *Ἐπέτηρις τῆς Ἐταιρείας Βυζαντινῶν Σπουδῶν* 36 (1968): 152–162. In Greek with a summary in English.

Peruzzi, A.
  1818 = *Dissertationi anconitane*. Two vols. Bologna, 1818.
  1835 = *Storia d'Ancona dalla sua fondazione* II. Pesaro, 1835.

Pesce, Ambrogio. "Il bacile d'oro della repubblica di Genova al re di Napoli nel 1455." *Bolletino storico–bibliografico subalpino* 22 (1920): 1–2.

Petrarca, Francesco. *Le familiari*. Ed. V. Rossi. 4 vols. Florence, 1933.

Petrucci, F. "Caracciolo, Gianni (Sergiann)." *Dizionario biografico degli italiani (DBI)* 19 (1976): 370–375.

Pizzicolli, Ciriaco de'. *Commentariorum Cyriaci Anconitani Nova Fragmenta.* See above, s.v. 'Olivieri.'

—. *Epigrammata Reperta . . . a Cyriaco Anconitano.* See above, s.v. 'Moroni.'

—. *Journeys in the Propontis and the Northern Aegean 1444–1445.* See above, s.v. 'Bodnar and Mitchell.'

Poggio Bracciolini. See above, s.v. 'Bracciolini.'

Ponte, G. "Precedenti classici del Certame Coronario." *Miscellanea di studi albertiani.* Genoa, 1975, 133–136.

Pontieri, Ernesto. *Alfonso il Magnanimo re di Napoli (1435–1458).* Naples, 1975 = *Storia di Napoli* IV, I. Naples, 1974.

Porro-Lambertenghi, Giulio, ed. *Relazione dell'attacco e difesa di Scio nel 1431 di Andreolo Giustiniani.* [n.p., n.d. ?1865]

Praga, G. "Indagini e studi sull'umanesimo in Dalmatia. Ciriaco de'Pizzicolli e Marino de Resti." *Archivio storico per la Dalmazia* 13 (1932–1933): 262–280.

*Prosopographisches Lexikon der Palaiologenzeit (PLP).* Ed. Erich Trapp, H.–V. Beyer, et al. Österreichische Akademie der Wissenschaften, Komm. für Byzantinistik. Faszikeln 1–11, Wien, 1976–1991 (down to Ταυ–). Beihefte: *Abkürzungsverzeichnis und Register zum PLP 1–6 Faszikeln und Addenda* (1983). *Beiheft zu Faszikeln 7–10 u. Addenda und Corrigenda zu Faszikeln 1–8* (1990). [The Register in each Beiheft lists (1) Greek names (*Verweise*), (2) Non–Greek names, (3) *Berufe.*]

Raby, Julian. "Cyriacus of Ancona and the Ottoman Sultan Mehmed II." *Journal of the Warburg and Courtauld Institutes* 43 (1980): 242–246.

Reinach, T. "Temple d'Hadrien à Cyzique," *BCH* 14 (1890): 517–545.

Resta, G. "Beccadelli, Antonio." *Dizionario biografico degli italiani (DBI)* 7 (1965): 400–406.

Rhodokanakis, Demetrios. *Ἰουστινιαναί–Χίος.* Syros, 1900. In Greek.

Richardson, L.A., Jr. *A New Topographical Dictionary of Ancient Rome.* Baltimore and London, 1992.

Rinaldi. *Annales Ecclesiasticae.* Ad annum 1404, n. 1.

Robert, L. *Revue des études grecques* 74 (1961): 123–124.

Robin, Diana. *Filelfo in Milan: Writings 1451–1477*. Princeton, 1991.

de Rossi, G.B. *Inscriptiones Christianae Urbis Romae Septimo Saeculo Antiquiores*. Vol. 2. Rome, 1888.

Rossi, V. See above, s.v. Petrarca.

Rubinstein, Nicolai. *The Government of Florence under the Medici, 1434–1494*. Oxford, 1968.

Ryder, Alan.
1976 = *The Kingdom of Naples under Alfonso the Magnanimous: The Making of a Modern State*. Oxford, 1976.
1990 = *Alfonso the Magnanimous, King of Aragon, Naples, and Sicily 1396–1458*. Oxford, 1990.

Saalman, Howard. *Filippo Brunelleschi: The Cupola of Santa Maria del Fiore*. Studies in Architecture, ed. A. Blunt and John Harris, vol. 20. London, 1980.

Sabbadini, R.
1910 = "Ciriaco d'Ancona e la sua descrizione autografa del Peloponneso trasmessa da Leonardo Botta." In *Miscellanea Ceriani*. Milan, 1910. 183–247. Republished without the illustrations in *Classici e umanisti da codici ambrosiani*. Fontes Ambrosiani, 2. Florence, 1933. 1–52.
1931 = "Ciriaco d'Ancona." *Enciclopedia italiana*. Vol. 10. 438–439.

Sabia, Liliana Monti. "La Naumachia Regia di Ciriaco d'Ancona." *Annali della Facoltà di Lettere e Filosofia dell'Università di Napoli*. 20, n.s. 8 (1977–1978): 129–186.

Sandys, J.E. *A History of Classical Scholarship* I. Cambridge, 1903, repr. 1958.

Saracini, G. *Notizie historiche delle città d'Ancona*. Rome, 1675. Repr. Bologna, 1958.

Sarayna, Torellus. *De Origine et Amplitudine Civitatis Veronae*. Verona, 1540.

Saxl, Fritz. "The Classical Inscription in Renaissance Art and Politics." *Journal of the Warburg and Cortauld Institutes* 4 (1940–1941): 19–46.

Scalamonti, Francesco. *Vita Kiriaci Anconitani*. In *Antichità Picene*, ed. Giuseppe Colucci. Vol. 15, 50–100. Fermo, 1792.

von Schlosser, Julius. "Giusti's Fresken in Padua und die Vorläufer der Stanza della Segnatura." *Jahrgang der Kunsthistorischen Sammlungen der allerhöchsten Kaiserhauses au Wien* 17 (1896): 13 ff.

Schwarz, H.M. *Sizilien, Kunst, Cultur, Landschaft*, Vienna, 1945.

Segarizzi, Arnaldo. "Lauro Quirini, umanista del sec. XV." *Memorie della R. Academia delle Scienze di Torino* 2 serie, 54 (1904): 28 ff.

Seno, Carlo, and Giorgio Ravegnani. "Cronologia della vita e delle opere di Lauro Quirini." In *Lauro Quirini Umanista*, ed. Vittore Branca. Florence, 1977.

Shepherd, William. *The Life of Poggio Bracciolini*. London, 1837.

de Sinner, G.R.L., ed. *Chr. Bondelmontii Florentini Librum Insularum Archipelagi*. Leipzig and Berlin, 1824.

Smith, Christine.
1987 = "Cyriacus of Ancona's Seven Drawings of Hagia Sophia." *Art Bulletin* 69 (1987): 16–32.
1992 = *Architecture in the Culture of Early Humanism 1400–1470*. Oxford, 1992.

Spadolini, Ernesto.
1901 = "Il biografo di Ciriaco Pizzecolli." *Le Marche*, dispensa 5, a.1 (1901): 70–72.
1901[2] = "Il romanzo d'arguto." *Le Marche*, dispensa 8 and 9 (1901): 120–121.
1902 = "Un' opera inedita di Ciriaco d'Ancona." *Le Marche* 3, nos. 3–4 (1902): 179–185.

Sphrantzes, George. *Annales. Corpus Scriptorum Historiae Byzantinae (CSHB)*. Bonn, 1838.

Spreti, V. Ed., *Enciclopedia storico-nobiliare italiana*. Vol 4. Milan, 1931.

Stinger, Charles L. *Humanism and the Church Fathers. Ambrogio Traversari (1386–1439) and Christian Antiquity in the Italian Renaissance*. Albany, 1976.

*Storia di Milano* VI. See above, s.v. Cognasso.

Summonte. *Historia di regno di Napoli*. Vol. 3. 1749.

Targioni Tozzetti, G. *Relazioni d'alcuni viaggi fatti in diverse parti della Toscana*. Vol. 5. Florence, 1773.

Tenenti, Alberto. "Venezia e la pirateria nel Levante 1300c.–1460." In *Venezia e il Levante fina al secolo XV*. Convegno internazionale di storia della civiltà veneziana, 1968. Ed. Agostino Pertusi. Vol. I, parte seconda, 705–771. Florence, 1973.

Tiraboschi, Girolamo. *Storia della letteratura italiana*. Vol. 6. Rome. 1783. Second edition, Florence, 1807.

Trachtenberg, Marvin. *The Campanile of Florence Cathedral: "Giotto's Tower."* New York, 1971.

Traversari, Ambrogio. See above, s.v. 'Mehus.'

Ughelli. *Italia sacra*. Venice, 1717.

Ullman, B. "Leonardo Bruni and Humanistic Historiography." In his *Studies in the Italian Renaissance*.[2] Rome, 1973.

van Essen, C.C. "Cyriaque d'Ancône en Egypte." *Mededelingen der koninklijke Nederlandse Akademie van Wetenschappen, afd. Letterkunde*. n.r. 21,12 (1958): 293–306.

Vespasiano da Bisticci. *Vite di uomini illustri del secolo XV*. Edizione critica con introduzione e commento di Aulo Greco. 2 vols. Florence: Istituto nazionale di studi sul Rinascimento. Florence, 1970–1976.

Vickers, Michael.
    1976[1] = "Mantegna and Constantinople." *The Burlington Magazine* 118 (1976): 680–687. Letters in 119 (1977): 41, 506.
    1976[2] = "Cyriac of Ancona at Thessaloniki." *Byzantine and Modern Greek Studies* 2 (1976): 75–82.
    1976[3] = "Theodosius, Justinian, or Heraclius?" *Art Bulletin* 58 (1976): 281.
    1977 = Review of H.P. Laubscher, *Der Reliefschmuck des Galeriusbogens in Thessaloniki* (Berlin 1975). In *Journal of Roman Studies* 67 (1977): 224–230.

Voigt, Georg. *Die Wiederbelebung des classischen Alterthums oder das erste Jahrhundert des Humanismus*. Second edition, Berlin, 1880–1881. Vol. I, 271–288. Third edition, besorgt vom Max Lehnerdt, 1893 (contains all the author's corrections embodied in the Italian translation).

Weiss, Roberto.
    1964 = "Un umanista antiquario: Cristoforo Buondelmonti." *Lettere italiane* 16 (1964): 105–116.
    1965 = "L'arco di Augusto a Fano nel rinascimento." *Italia medioevale e umanistica* 1(1965): 351–358.
    1969 = *The Renaissance Discovery of Classical Antiquity*.[2] Oxford, 1988.
    1972 = "Buondelmonti, Cristoforo." *Dizionario biografico degli italiani (DBI)*. 15 (1972): 198–200.

White, John. *Art and Architecture in Italy 1250–1400*. The Pelican History of Art, ed. Nikolaus Pevsner. Vol. 28. Baltimore, Md., 1966.

Wind, E. *Pagan Mysteries in the Renaissance*. Second Edition. New York, 1958.

Woods–Marsden, Joanna. *The Gonzaga of Mantua and Pisanello's Arthurian Frescoes*. Princeton, 1988.

Ziebarth, Erich.

1901 = "Cyriaci Anconitani epistula inedita." *Rheinisches Museum* 56 (1901): 157–159.

1902 = "Cyriacus von Ancona als Begründer der Inschriftenforschung." *Neue Jahrbücher für das klassische Altertum, Geschichte und deutsche Litteratur* 9 (1902): 214–226.

1903 = "Nachfolger des Cyriacus von Ancona." *Neue Jahrbücher für das klassische Altertum* 11 (1903): 480–493.

1926 = "Κυριακὸς ὁ ἐξ ᾿Αγκῶνος ἐν ᾿Ηπείρῳ" *᾿Ηπειρωτικὰ Χρονικά* 2 (1926): 110–119.

## Recent Work on Ciriaco

I.  Papers read at the international conference, "Ciriaco d'Ancona e la Cultura Antiquaria dell'Umanesimo in Occasione del VI Centenario della Nascità, Ancona," Ancona, 5–7 February 1992.:[a]

Beschi, Luigi. "I disegni ateniesi di Ciriaco: analisi di una tradizione."

Bodnar, Edward. "Ciriaco d'Ancona: the Cycladic Diary."

Bossi, Patrizia. "Vicende editoriali della 'Vita Cyriaci' di F. Scalamonti."

Campana, Augusto. "Ciriaco d'Ancona e l'elefante malatestiano."

Cappelletto, Rita. "Ciriaco nel ricordo di Pietro Ransano."

Catani, Enzo. "Ciriaco e l'iscrizione fermana (*CIL* IX 540\*)."

Di Benedetto, Filippo. "Il punto su alcune questioni riguardanti Ciriaco."

Landolfi, Maurizio. "Ciriaco e il collezionismo di antichità greche nel Piceno."

Luni, Mario. "Ciriaco e la riscoperta dell'antico nel Ducato di Urbino."

Marchi, Gian Paolo. "Ciriaco negli studi epigrafici di Scipione Maffei."

Mayer, Marc. "Ciriaco de Ancona y Anio de Viterbo y la historigrafía hispánica."

Neuhausen, Karl August. "Dominicus quidam Cyllenius Graecus quo loco quatenus Cyriacum Anconitanum sit imitatus insignem Mercurii dei cultorem."

Parroni, Piergiorio. "Il latino di Ciriaco."

Pascual, Helena Jimeno. "El despertar de la ciencia epigráfica en España: Ciriaco de Ancona ¿Un modelo para los primeros compiladores españoles?"

Pontani, Anna. "Il greco di Ciriaco: lingua e scrittura."

Quaquarelli, Leonardo. "Felice Feliciano e Francesco Scalamonti `iunior.'"

Sabia, Liliana Monti. "Due nuovi codici della 'Naumachia Regia' di Ciriaco."

Sconocchia, Sergio. "Ciriaco e i prosatori latini."

Vagenheim, Ginette. "Gli studi di G.B. De Rossi su Ciriaco nel carteggio con Th. Mommsen."

---

[a] The publication of the conference's *Atti* is in press (as of February 1996).

II. Relevant papers read at the international conference, "L''Antiquario' Felice Feliciano Veronese tra Epigrafia Antica, Letteratura e Arti del Libro," Verona, 3–4 June 1993.

Avesani, Rino. "Felice Felicano tra mito e realtà."

Campana, Augusto. "Il codice epigrafico di Faenza, Bibl. Com. 7."

Di Benedetto, Filippo. "Precisazioni sul codice I,138 della Capitolare di Treviso."

Fattori, Daniela. "Per la biografia del Feliciano."

Marcon, Susy. "Aspetti decorativi dei manoscriti del Feliciano."

Montecchi, Giorgio. "Lo spazio del testo scritto nella pagina del Feliciano."

# INDEXES[1]

## I. Index of Personal Names

*A. Mythological, Ancient, and Early Medieval Names*

Abdon, judge of Israel 193

Abimelech, judge of Israel 193

Abraham, birth date of 193; contemporary of Janus 199

Achilles 9, 39

'Aemilius Paulus,' arch of, in Salonica 77

Aeneas 58

Alexander the Great of Macedon 17, 76, 89

Amphion 29

Ananias, house of, in Damascus 65

Anchises 21, App. I, 4, 8

Antoninus, emperor 44, 58

Apollo 26, 29, 30, 37, 49, 70; Rhodian coin depicting the head of the colossal Apollo at Naxos 165n

Arcadians, App. I, 9

Arcadius, emperor, spiral column of, in Constantinople 42n

'Aristotle,' *De Virtute*, translated by Ciriaco 74n, App. V,4

Augustine, St., memorial of, in Pavia 112; *City of God*, on the date of Abraham's birth 193; cited Virgil in writings, App. I, 10

Augustus 166; temple of, in Alexandria 17n; Augusteion in Constantinople 40n; gold coin of, given by Petrarch to Charles IV of Bohemia 97n; temple of, in Terracina 206, App. V, 11a; and Rome, App. V,5

Bacchus, lost drawing of 64n

Bede, the Venerable, his date for the founding of Genoa 201

Bellovas[i]us, leader of Gauls, as founder of Genoa 201

Bianor = Ocnus (Ocius, Obnus), son of Tiberis and Manto 192

Blessed Virgin, image of, set up in Varano as thanks for salvation from the plague 46n; cathedral church of, in Orvieto 60; cathedral church of, in Parma 111

Boethius, Severinus, memorial of, in Pavia 112

Bucephalus, Alexander's horse, 'manger' of, near Philippi 76

Caesar: see Julius

Caliope, muse, App. I.5

Castor and Pollux, temple of, in Naples App. V, 11b

Catullus and Verona, App. V,8

Cicero, *Epistolae ad Familiares* 3n

Claudius Gothicus, emperor, gate of, in Nicaea 84n

Constantine, emperor, and the Plataea monument 41n

Constantius, emperor, and the tetrastyle arch at Mitylene 86

Constantius and Sebastian, Sts., images of, set up in Varano 46n

Daphne 26, 49

Demetrius, St., church of, in Salonica 77

Diana 49; 'temple' of, in Salonica 77; temple of, in Brescia 155n

---

1. Reference numbers are to the numbered paragraphs of the text and translation, not to pages. A number followed by 'n' (e.g. '49n') indicates that the term is found *only* in one of the notes attached to the paragraph of that number. If a term occurs in both the paragraph and one of its notes, only the number of the paragraph is given.

## B. Late Medieval and Renaissance Names[2]

2. The term *patronus* can mean either the owner of a ship or its captain or its owner who is also its captain.

## II. Index of Geographical Names and Locations

# III. Index of Ancient, Medieval, and Renaissance Monuments and Artifacts

**Amphitheaters:** in Pola 44; in Verona 166, App. V,8; in Cyzicus 83; in Liternum 207; of Capua 208; of Benevento 211

**Aqueducts:** of Valens in Constantinople 42n; (unspecified) in Rome 55; on Lesbos 87; of Germanicus Caesar near Tivoli 95

**Arches:** of Trajan in Ancona 54, App. V,2b; of Augustus in Fano 54n, App. I, App. V, 12; (unspecified) in Rome 55; of Septimius Severus and Antoninus in Rome 57; of 'Aemilius Paulus' (= Galerius) in Salonica 77; tetrastyle, of Constantius, Diocletian, and Maximianus in Mytilene 86; of Trajan in Benevento 211, App. V, 11d

**Armor:** 'arms of Achilles' at the Golden Gate in Constantinople 39

**Baths:** (unspecified) seen in Rome 55

**Bridges:** (unspecified) in Rome 55; 'Salernian' (=Aurelian? 57n) in Rome 57; of Lucanus at Tivoli 93; Cimbrian/Salarian at Tivoli 95; of Florence 101

**Caged Animals:** lions, in Florence 101; menagerie, in the castle of Pavia 151, App. V,7

**Castle** of Pavia, built by Giangaleazzo Visconti 112n, 151

**Churches:** of the Annunciata in Trapani 21; of the Martorana (= S. Maria dell' Ammiraglio) in Palermo 32n; Palatine Chapel of St. Peter in Palermo, 32n; cathedral of the Blessed Virgin in Monreale 33; Hagia Sophia in Constantinople 40, App. VI; of Galata 43; San Lorenzo in Damaso in Rome 55; cathedral of the Blessed Virgin in Orvieto 60; of St. Demetrius in Salonica 77; basilica of Hagia Sophia in Nicaea 84; St. Peter's in Rome 92, 97n; cathedral and *Campo Santo* of Pisa 100; of St. Reparata, campanile, and baptistery of St. John the Baptist (= 'temple of Mars') in Florence 101; cathedral of the Blessed Virgin in Parma 111; of San Lorenzo in Genoa 203n; see also below s.v. 'Inscriptions located by churches.'

**Coins:** gold, of Philip, Alexander, and Lysimachus, seen in Foglia Nuova 89; gold, of Trajan presented by Ciriaco to emperor-elect Sigismund in Siena 97; gold and silver, of Augustus, presented by Petrarch to emperor-elect Charles IV of Bohemia in Mantua 97n; silver, of Vespasian, presented by Ciriaco to Raffaelle Castiglione 97n; Rhodian, depicting head of the colossal Apollo of Delos 165n

**Columns, monumental:** of 'Pompey' (= of Diocletian) in Alexandria 17, App. V,1; spiral, of Theodosius and Arcadius in Constantinople 42; other marble and porphyry columns in Constantinople 42; of Trajan in Rome 42n; others (unspecified) in Rome 55; spiral, in Smyrna 88

**Columns of ruined buildings:** on Rhodes 73; of temple of 'Jupiter' in Cyzicus 83; in Mytilene 86; in Rome App. V,5

**Domestic buildings:** house of Ananias